Words of Comfort & Cheer

Books by Mrs. Cowman—

Words of Comfort & Cheer

Mrs. Charles Cowman

B. McCALL BARBOUR
28 GEORGE IV BRIDGE
EDINBURGH EH1 1ES, SCOTLAND

Zondervan Publishing House
Grand Rapids, Michigan

WORDS OF COMFORT AND CHEER
Copyright © 1944, 1972 by Mrs. Charles E. Cowman

Daybreak Books are published by the
Zondervan Publishing House
1415 Lake Drive, S.E.,
Grand Rapids, Michigan 49506

Library of Congress Cataloging-in-Publication Data

Cowman, Charles E., Mrs., 1870–1960.
    Words of comfort and cheer.

    "Daybreak Books."
    1. Consolation. 2. Devotional calendars.   I. Title.
BV4905.C692   1988   242'.4   88-20855
ISBN 0-310-35400-5

The twentieth printing of *Consolation* was the first to appear as *Words
of Comfort and Cheer*.

The thirty-seventh printing was the first to appear as *Streams in the
Desert—5*.

This thirty-ninth printing appears as *Words of Comfort and Cheer*.

Printed in the United States of America

88 89 90 91 92 93 / AK / 44 43 42 41 40

I dedicate this volume
to the largest household of the world,
THE HOUSEHOLD OF THE SORROWING

FOREWORD

It was when my heart seemed breaking under the anguish of a terrible bereavement that Jesus was revealed to me as the *"God of all comfort."* Between the shadows of Gethsemane and Calvary, He made Himself to me a "living, bright reality." I longed to call out to my fellow-Christians who were treading the vales of sorrow and tell them that HE went with me through the Garden, that He heard me when my prayer was but a cry, that He kept me and bore me up where the very air was still, that He whispered peace, that He gave courage, that His grace was all-sufficient.

The various messages and poems contained in this volume, sent by friends from all over the world, came to me with a peculiar power. I was conscious of the gentle and refined touch that can only come to those who have suffered. They contributed largely in healing the broken heart and binding up its wounds.

"Consolation" is intended as a companion to *"Streams in the Desert,"* though purposely its pages are addressed to those whose hearts have been storm-swept. In the first awful days of heart-loneliness after a bereavement, the mind is not able or disposed to follow pages of continuous thought—hence this volume is in the form of a reading for every day.

There is a touching tradition regarding the Jewish Temple of old, that it had a gateway reserved exclusively for mourners. Such is the present volume. It opens up a pathway to God's sanctuary trodden by the footsteps of pilgrims of the night. It addresses no hearts but broken ones. Though it is not in our power to make sorrow no sorrow, yet it is in our power to take off the edge of it by a steady view of those divine joys prepared for us in the beautiful Summerland yonder.

May the messages herein bring comfort to the loneliest pilgrims to eternity! They may not drive off all the dark; but they are glints of light in the dark that may make the night more tolerable, or show you where to place your feet in the next step of the journey and perchance to you may be given a *song* in your Desert of Sorrow, a note of praise from Him who "giveth songs in the night."

Death, a sad fact, yet remains. It is still mysterious and we comprehend not. But the word of promise still echoes *"What I do thou knowest not now, but thou shalt know hereafter."* Staying ourselves on this as on a staff, let us journey bravely on toward the sunrising.   *Lettie B. Cowman.*

As one who walks through solemn woods at night,
When every star is blotted out with cloud,
And storm winds moan with rising passion loud,
Holds high abouve his head a torch to light
The path he takes, not knowing how to fight
The cursed blackness back except endued
With radiance from his torch of pine—else bowed
In darkness and defeat his manly might—
So I above the grave of my sweet dead
Hold high this torch of God, to light the gloom
And pour in sunshine, while with praising breath
I track the footsteps of my loved one fled
To God's dear land and fair beyond the tomb:
And this my torch, "There shall be no more death!"

Bishop Quayle.

Jesus Himself drew near and went with them (Luke 24:15).

They two went on (2 Kings 2:6).

How can we face a Happy New Year when all its mirth and happiness of life are covered by a pall of grief? The holiday season is an ordeal—an almost insupportable one—to many suffering hearts. Who shall roll away the stone from the door of their sorrow? It is the old question, forever new. And the old answer is forever true—the answer of eternity to time. It is the angels that roll away the stone. Never is heaven nearer to us than when we celebrate the day that is associated with the coming of Christ—the incarnation of the Eternal in our clay—and close upon it, the passing of the old year according to the calendar of earth.

Those who have left us for heaven are very near—and theirs is a Happy New Year, the immortal year, whose joys cannot fade or fail. The sense of loss abides with us. *That* we cannot change or cease to feel. But the sense of the love of God, at this holy day time, can be felt, too, that the thought of the little child taken up in His arms, the gentle saint gone home to Him, the strong souls whom He has called up higher, will lift our spirits into the joy in which those loved ones stand transfigured, safe from all the chances and changes of the years.

Love is the immortal thing against which time and death can not prevail; and God is love. To look from the earthly years upward to the heavenly is to rejoice, even through tears.

> Farewell, Old Year, the rustle of whose garment,
>   Fragrant with memory, I still can hear;
> For all thy tender kindness and thy bounty,
>   I drop my thankful tribute on thy bier.
>
> What is in store for me, brave New Year, hidden
>   Beneath thy glistening robe of ice and snows?
> Are there sweet songs of birds, and breath of lilacs,
>   And blushing blooms of June's scent-laden rose?
>
> As silent art thou of the unknown future
>   As if thy days were numbered with the dead;
> Yet, as I enter thy wide-open portal,
>   I cross thy threshold with glad hope, not dread.

11

To me no pain or fear or crushing sorrow
   Hast thou the power without His will to bring;
And so I fear thee not, O untried morrow!
   For well I know my Father is thy King.

If joy thou bringest, straight to God, the giver,
   My gratitude shall rise, for 'tis His gift;
If sorrow, still, 'mid waves of grief's deep river,
   My trembling heart I'll to my Father lift.

So, hope-lit New Year, with thy joys uncertain,
   Whose unsolved mystery none may foretell,
I calmly trust my God to lift thy curtain;
   Safe in His love, for me 'twill all be well.   *Selected*

JANUARY 2

Hitherto hath the Lord helped us (1 Samuel 7:12).

SAIL ON!

So now into another year we sail, O Time Mariner! And something of what we may expect as we continue our voyage we may infer from the past. Without doubt storms will come as they came in the bygone days. But we will give them firm and courageous welcome, for we have already weathered so many storms that we are unafraid of the wind and the tide, the lightning and the snow.

And some calm days will come! Sunny days when the winds are still as sleeping flowers, and when the slumberous clouds floating in mid-heaven will be reflected in the unrippled sea below and those days will be rare days, unusual days! For our rigging is doomed to be rudely tested by the shrieking blast, and with many hard blows will the sea savagely smite us, but we will care not for all that. For in no land-locked harbour would we abide; but out where the sky dome meets the horizon all around us, and where the hurricane has its unimpeded sway, there would we be. And the raging storm shall but reveal how sturdy is the ship in which we sail. And though head winds prevail, and rolling hills or water seek to hinder our progress, yet ever will we cry, Sail on! Sail on!

And we shall make the Voyage, dear heart, of that we are sure. And no blustering blast can say us Nay, and no heaving billow swerve our helm, for we are bound for the happy Isles, and

12

towards them we ever steadfastly steer though the Egyptian darkness drops about us, and all hell be let loose. Yes, we shall make the Harbour. Sails torn of course as they should be, spars and masts all strained and creaking without doubt, and many a mark of the tempest upon us, but still master of the waves and winds we shall be. And so we shall—when the Voyage is completed drop anchor where no storms come, but where the green swell is at last in the haven dumb, and we are forever out of the swing of the Sea.   *Dr. Hinson.*

HITHERTO

We have come very safely—hitherto;
And sometimes seas were calm, and skies were blue;
Sometimes the wild waves rose—the tempests roared;
But never barque went down with Christ on board.

And so it shall be to the very end—
Through ebb or flow, the one unchanging Friend,
Ruling the waves which sink at His command,
Holding them in the hollow of His hand.

A lonely track perchance, a darkened sky,
A mist of tears, and only God knows why—
Is He not worth our trust the voyage through,
He who has never failed us—hitherto?

Here all things pass, but Heaven keeps them fair;
The partings here—the joyous meetings there—
God's waves and winds drive onward to that rest;
Tossed home, as children to a Father's breast.

There comes an hour, when, every tempest o'er,
The harbour lights are reached, the golden shore:
Never, oh nevermore to fret or fear—
Christ, give us faith to praise Thee even here!

Mary Gorges

JANUARY 3 —————————————————————————————

As thou goest, step by step, I will open up the way before thee (Prov. 4:12) (Heb. Trans.).

L et us go forward. God leads us. Though blind, shall we be afraid to follow? I do not see my way: I do not care to: but I know that He sees His way, and that I see Him.   *Charles Kingsley.*

Child of My love, fear not the unknown morrow,
   Dread not the new demand life makes of thee;
Thy ignorance doth hold no cause for sorrow
   Since what thou knowest not is known to Me.

Thou canst not see today the hidden meaning
Of My command, but thou the light shalt gain;
   Walk on in faith, upon My promise leaning,
And as thou goest all shall be made plain.

One step thou seest—then go forward boldly,
   One step is far enough for faith to see;
Take that, and thy next duty shall be told thee,
   For step by step thy Lord is leading thee.

Stand not in fear, thy adversaries counting,
   Dare every peril, save to disobey;
Thou shalt march on, all obstacles surmounting,
   For I, the Strong, will open up the way.

Wherefore go gladly to the task assigned thee,
   Having My promise, needing nothing more
Than just to know, where'er the future find thee,
   In all thy journeying I go before.   *Frank J. Exeley, D.D.*

JANUARY 4 ─────────────────────────────

He shall give you another Comforter, that he may abide with you forever (John 14:16).

D ear Heart, thou are not forsaken. Solitude and peace are 'round about thee, and God is over all. Like a pure white dove with folded wings His sweet messenger—Peace—is waiting near thee. Thou hearest a Voice speaking tenderly to thy soul. It is the whisper of the Eternal, bidding thee cast all thy cares upon Him. Through the long winter days may His peace abide with thee and thine!

GOD'S COMFORTING

The world grows lonely, and, with many a tear,
  I stretch out longing hands in vain, to clasp
The treasures of my life, and hold them here;
  But "all dear things seem slipping from my grasp."

Oh, say not so, my heart! One stands beside
  Whose love, in all its fulness, is thine own;
That love is changeless, and, whate'er betide,
  He will not leave thee—thou art not alone!

God keeps my treasures, and some glad, bright day,
  He'll give them to my longing sight again;
So Faith and Hope shall cheer me all the way,
  And Love, their sweetest sister, soothe my pain.

Thus, taking God's full cup of comforting,
  Let me give thanks! and, pouring out most free
My life in loyal service, let me bring
  To other lives the joy God giveth me.

JANUARY 5

How excellent is Thy loving kindness, O God! therefore the children of men put their trust under the shadow of thy wings (Psalm 36:7).

A PRAYER

Thou who livest and wast dead, we bless Thee. We believe Thou art the Resurrection and the Life, and that, gone from among us these many, many years, Thou hast been making ready a place for us, so that when we come all things may be in good readiness and in waiting like a mansion for its expected lord long absent on a dangerous journey. Thou knowest my name long since, and hast never forgotten it; even Thy hands are writ with it. Thou art making ready for me. This is too good for truth, yet also too good not to be all truth. Thou hast promised, and Thou keepest faith with the puniest of Thy children; wherefore I take great, sure encouragement. Heaven is my home. I am tried betimes and almost spent with the stress of battle and of climbing the rugged way; but Thou dost promise a rest for the people of God, among whom I humbly hope God may have counted me.

The soul's everlasting rest! How high the word and topless! I shall meet Thee in the morning, and my dear ones,

"Loved long since and lost awhile."

How sweet the meeting! I shall be faint with the long march, and with blood spilt in the long war; but one look on Thee (for we shall see Him as He is) will refresh me more than a plunge in the fountain of life.

If I have broken faith with Thee, my Lord, forgive me. If I have been coward when the fight was on, forget that in Thy courtesy of love. If I have shamed Thee by my dim perceptions of Thyself and Thy service, as I have, forget this also. Thou knowest that I love Thee. Be near me while I stay yet a little longer where clouds gather and tempests storm. Be near me when I grope in the valley of the shadow of death; sow it with glory. Meet me on the threshold of the land which is very far off. Let me walk into heaven with Thee, and let me keep Thee before my eyes while eternity sings its endless psalm. There I will love Thee, and worship for ever and ever. Amen! *Bishop Quayle.*

JANUARY 6 ────────────────────────────

Wait on the Lord, be of good courage and He shall strengthen thine heart (Psalm 27:14).

R obert Louis Stevenson closes one of his prayers with these words: "Help us with the grace of courage that we be none of us cast down when we sit lamenting over the ruins of our happiness. Touch us with the fire of Thine altar, that we may be up and doing, to rebuild our city.

"We can rebuild our houses instead of grieving over their destruction, like the birds, their nests."

> Have courage, soul of mine,
> The path that you must keep
> Is long and lone and steep;
> But many thousand feet
> Have passed this way before;
> All through the vanished years
> These stones were wet with tears.
> If others knew this road,
> And bore their heavy load;

If others went this way,
You, too, can bear the heat
And burden of the day;
You, too, can bear dark night
Until the morning light.
If others passed this way
Have courage, soul of mine!   *Mary E. Rock.*

Somehow strength lasted through the day,
Hope joined with courage in the way;
The feet kept the uphill road,
The shoulders did not drop the load,
And unseen power sustained the heart
When flesh and will failed in their part;
  While God gave light
  By day and night,
And also grace to bear the smart—
  For this give thanks.

JANUARY 7

A heart broken and crushed, O God, Thou wilt not despise (Psalm 51:17).

It is when we feel all broken up and wasted, and can only bring the bits to God, that He says "Come," and He will take us and mend us and make us whole again.

BROKEN TO BE MENDED

(Suggested by the remark of a bereaved friend: "We cannot be mended unless we are broken.")

Jesus, our tears with blessed smiles are blending,
  For thou who knowest how our hearts to break,
Knowest the happy secret of their mending,
  And we rejoice in sorrow for Thy sake.

Yes, break us all to pieces, at Thy pleasure,
  For the poor fragments can be joined by Thee;
Snatch from us, if Thou wilt, our every treasure!
  Possessing Thee we never poor can be.

There is a sweetness in a spirit broken,
  That lofty souls attain not—cannot know;

To such a heart Thy promises are spoken,
  Thou hast a solace for its silent woe.

And when our weary days on earth are ended,
  And from its agitations we are free,
We shall rejoice that we were broken, mended,
  By Thine own skilful hand, dear Lord, by Thee!

JANUARY 8

Jesus wept (John 11:35).

Do not chide yourself for feeling strongly. Tears are natural. Jesus wept. A thunderstorm without rain is fraught with peril; the pattering rain-drops cool the air, and relieve the overcharged atmosphere. The swollen brooks indicate that the snows are melting on the hills and spring is near. To bear sorrow with dry eyes and stolid heart may befit a stoic, but not a Christian. We have no need to rebuke fond nature crying for its mate, its lost joy, the touch of the vanished hand, the sound of the voice that is still, provided that our will is resigned. This is the one consideration for those who suffer—*is the will right?* If it is, then the path will inevitably lead from the valley of the shadow of death to the banqueting table and the overflowing cup.

May I not cry, then? Yes, just as the night does, and in the morning it is dew. There is not a flower that does not look sweeter for it. True tears make souls beautiful. True sorrows are, after all, but the seeds out of which come fairer joys.

Steps into the Blessed Life.

While the storm was fiercely blowing,
While the sea was wildly flowing,
Angry wind and angry billow
Only rocked the Saviour's pillow;
  Jesus SLEPT.

But when sudden grief was rending
Human hearts, in sorrow bending:
When He saw the sisters weeping
Where the brother's form was sleeping,
  Jesus WEPT.

Tears may soothe the wounds they cannot heal.

18

On Jesus' bosom (John 13:23).

I am trying to trust," said one to me, who had heard the earth falling on the casket which held the cold form of the dearest human friend. "I am trying to trust"; just so I have seen a bird with a broken wing trying to fly. When the heart is broken, all our *trying to trust* will only increase our pain and unrest. But if, instead of trying to trust, we will press closer to the Comforter, and lean our weary heads upon His sufficient grace, trust will come without our trying, and the promised "perfect peace" will calm every troubled wave of sorrow.   *A.E. Kittridge.*

> On Jesus' bosom—nowhere else is found
>   Balm for all wounds, and solace for all tears;
>   Calm mid the clouds which gather thickly round,
>   Peace from the pain which lingers through life's years.
>
> On Jesus' bosom! Broken, weary, yet
>   Finding His welcome—loving, tender, sure:
>   Soothed by His kiss; some sorrows helped forget;
>   Strengthened for those the heart must still endure.
>
> On Jesus' bosom! Truly welcomed there!
>   Warmed by His love—His tender, sweet embrace:
>   Made strong, once more, life's overweight to bear;
>   Lightened again by radiance from His face.
>
> On Jesus' bosom! This my refuge be
>   Till shadowed days for evermore are past;
>   Till, in the home Christ now prepares for me,
>   I find my everlasting place at last.   *J. Danson Smith.*

Behold, I have refined thee but not with silver; I have chosen thee in the furnace of affliction (Isa. 48:10).

This world is not abandoned, and it is not lawless; and pain does not run riot as it pleases. Suffering is God's appointed minister. And by and by, when it has cleared off, it will be about suffering just as it is in the factories, where, when they paint vases with beautiful flowers and running vines, they swear them with black and put them into the furnace. They are black on coming out, until they are brushed, when the black disappears, and naught but these beautiful flowers and vines remains. Behind the groans and the anguish of men in this world God has been writing, and in the light of the eternal world, results will be seen of which we have no conception here. It does not yet appear what we shall be. We are sons of God. We come through tears. There have been many in every age of the world who have been saved by the washing of their garments in the blood. A strange bath! A strange white that comes from crimson! But so it is.

If all my years were summer, could I know
What my Lord means by His "Made white as snow"?

If all my days were sunny, could I say,
"In His fair land He wipes all tears away"?

If I were never weary, could I keep
Close to my heart, "He gives His loved ones sleep"?

Were no graves mine, might I not come to deem
The life eternal but a baseless dream?

My winter, and my tears, and weariness,
Even my graves, may be His way to bless!

I call them ills, yet that can surely be
Nothing but love that shows my Lord to me!

JANUARY 11

I must be about my Father's business (Luke 2:49).

One of the most serious dangers of inconsolable sorrow is that it may lead us to neglect our duty to the living in our mourning for the dead. This we should never do. God does not desire us to give up our work because our heart is broken. We may not even pause long with our sorrows; we may not sit down beside the graves of our dead and linger there, cherishing our grief.

A distinguished General related this pathetic incident of his own experience in time of war. The General's son was a lieutenant of battery. An assault was in progress. The father was leading his division in a charge; as he pressed on in the field, suddenly he caught sight of a dead battery-officer lying just before him. One glance showed him it was his own son. His fatherly impulse was to stop beside the loved form and give vent to his grief, but the duty of the moment demanded that he should press on in the charge; so, quickly snatching one hot kiss from the dead lips, he hastened away, leading his command in the assault.

Ordinarily the pressure is not so intense, and we can pause longer to weep and do honor to the memory of our dead. Yet in all sorrow the principle is the same. God does not desire us to waste our life in tears. We are to put our grief into new energy of service. God's work must never be allowed to suffer while we weep. The fires must be kept burning on the altar. The work in the household, in the school, in the store, in the field, must be taken up again—the sooner, the better. Our bereavement is a call, not to sad weeping, but to new duty.   *Dr. J. R. Miller.*

OUR LEGACIES

If some hand is quite still
    That we have loved, and kept in ours until
        It grew so cold;
If all it held hath fallen from its hold,
        And it can do
    No more: perhaps there are a few
    Small threads that it held fast
        Until the last,
That we can gather up and weave along,
        With patience strong
    In love. If we can take
But some wee, single thread, for love's sweet sake,
        And keep it beaten on the wheel
            A trifle longer; feel
The same thread in our hands to add unto and hold,
        Until our own grow cold,
We may take heart above the wheel and spin
        With weak hands that begin
    Where those left off, and going on
        Grow strong.
If we bend close to see
    Just what the threads may be
    Which filled the quiet hands,
        Perhaps some strands
So golden, or so strong may lie there still,
    That we our empty hands may fill.

And even yet
Smile though our eyes be wet.

Selected.

JANUARY 12 _____

I know not how (1 Kings 3:7).

The Lord knoweth how (2 Peter 2:9).

How can I face the future without my loved one? You have asked a hundred times already. I do not know, and it is better for you not to ask what no one can answer. Today's burden is enough; do not add to it tomorrow's. You will never need God's help and comfort more than now. Tomorrow's burden will come and soon enough, but today's burden will have been lifted before the new one is fastened upon your shoulders.

You have been thinking that you could bear today's if it were not for the dread tomorrow, and you are right. Then bear today's burden faithfully, and if tomorrow's load is to crush you, let it do it tomorrow, and not today.

It is the piling up of future sorrow upon the sorrow of the present that makes the breaking load. The burden is heavy, but God's grace is sufficient.

> Lie still, be strong, today! "But Lord, tomorrow—
> What of tomorrow, Lord!
> Shall there be rest from toil, be truce from sorrow,
> Be living green upon the sword
> Nor but a barren grave to me,
> Be joy for sorrow?"
> "Did I not die for thee?
> Do I not live for thee? Leave me tomorrow."
> *Christina G. Rossetti.*

JANUARY 13 _____

Thou hast enlarged me when I was in distress (Psalm 4:1).

There are some natures that only a tempest can bring out. I recollect being strongly impressed on reading the account of an old castle in Germany with two towers that stood upright and far apart, between which an old baron stretched large wires, thus making a huge Aeolian harp. There were the wires suspended, and the summer breezes played through them, but there was no vibration. Common winds, not having power enough to move them, split, and went through them without a whistle. But when there came along great tempest-winds, and the heaven was black, and the air resounded, then these winds, with giant touch, swept through the wires, which began to sing and roar, and pour out sublime melodies. So God stretches the chords in the human soul which under ordinary influences do not vibrate; but now and then great tempests sweep them through, and men are conscious that tones are produced in them which could not have been produced except by some such storm-handling. *Life-Thoughts.*

THE STORM'S MESSAGE

All day fierce heat had held the quivering earth
In iron grip. The sky from red to pale
Had turned with fear; and white and still
The clouds had crept away in masses, to the north.
The meadow hazels, 'neath their clustered load
Of satin and green-ruffled nuts, had dropped.
Sweet ferns had knelt to die; and choked and mute
Since morn had lain the cricket, hid below
The fallen spear of water-flags. In dumb
Amaze the patient cattle to their bars
Had crowded, waiting help. All nature gasped;
All life seemed sinking into death!

Then rose,
In distant sunset depths, a solemn sound—
The wheels of God's great chariot, rolling slow!
An instant more, and, with sharp blaze and boom,
His signal-guns lit up and shook the sky,
With word and succor on the way! and then
The still, small voice of rain, in which He was,
And cooled and lulled His fainting world to sleep.
. . . O iron-handed grief, which holds my soul
In searing grasp, and leaves my stifled days
No voice, no life! Will there a sound of help
Arise in sunset depths for me? Does God
Remember? Will His chariot-wheels draw near?
Will He command this cloud to break in rain
Of healing tears? And will He give to me
At last, as unto His beloved, sleep?   *Selected.*

_____

I would not have you to be ignorant, brethren, concerning them which are asleep, that ye sorrow not, even as others which have no hope (1 Thess. 4:13).

H ope of what? What possible *hope* can bring comfort at such a time?—in *"The first dark day of nothingness"*—or the still darker days which follow? Listen, and thank God with all your heart for every word: *"For if we believe that Jesus died and rose again, even so them also which sleep in Jesus will God bring with Him."*—*(1 Thess. 4:14).*

The faces, for the sight of which we hunger, shall look on us again; the voices that have left this world so tuneless shall once more bless our ears; we shall see our loved ones again, and be with them forevermore!

> So long Thy Power hath blest me, sure it still
>   Will lead me on
> O'er moor and fen, o'er crag and torrent, till
>   The night is gone.
> And with the morn those angel faces smile
> Which I have loved long since, and lost awhile.

_____

Perfect through sufferings (Heb. 2:10).

T here is much, very much, in Christianity that I cannot and do not pretend to understand, but I can understand enough to make me very loving and very trustful.

The only mystery which still sometimes troubles me is that most terrible of all mysteries—the mystery of human suffering. But even that I am content to leave, for is not our God Himself a suffering God? And who that witnessed the sufferings of Jesus Christ (and what sufferings were ever like His?) could have foreseen that the cruel Cross whereon He hung should hereafter be the finger-post to point the way to heaven—or that beneath His cry of agony in the Garden, God heard the triumph-song of a ransomed world?

Christ's heart was wrung for me; if mine is sore,
And if my feet are weary, His have bled;
He had no place wherein to lay His head;
If I am burdened, He was burdened more;
The cup I drink, He drank of long before;
He felt the unuttered anguish which I dread;
He hungered, who the world's refreshment bore.
If grief be such a looking-glass as shows
Christ's face and man's in some sort made alike
Then grief is pleasure with a subtle taste;
Wherefore should any fret or faint or haste?
Grief is not grievous to a soul that knows
Christ comes—and listens for that hour to strike.

Christina Rossetti.

JANUARY 16

Within the veil (Heb. 6:19).

The stars that go out when the morning begins to dawn do not sink into night: they only cease to shine on us, and begin to shine on some one else; and what is to us the evening star is the herald of dawn to some other eyes.

There are two sides to dying—the earth side and the heaven side.

Here the hushed lips that shall never speak again, *there* the first burst of song that shall never cease; *here* the quiet feet that have ceased walking, *there* the starting-out upon immortal pathways; *here* the unclasping of hands and tears of farewells, *there* the greetings and gratulations and fresh-linked unions, and the lighting-up of recognitions that play over deathless features.

I question sometimes whether we may not be selfish in our grief. It often happens in our day that a family becomes divided, a part of it remaining in one country, while another removes to a far country. The day for sailing arrives. Farewells are said, tears fall, hearts are heavy as lead while the ship swings off, and gradually lessens to a speck on the horizon. But on the other side there is glad expectation and impatient waiting. As the vessel heaves in sight, there is a shout; and it hardly touches the wharf before the expectant ones are over the side, clasping in long-waiting arms the glad welcome of blessed re-unions. What say you? Ought not

25

those left behind to subtract from the gross amount of their sorrow something of the gladness of those who in the new country greet their arrival?

I know a family divided: half is on earth, and half in heaven. The white-sailed boat, whose oarsman none can see, pushes off for another voyage. A fair-haired boy is passenger now. Cruel and hard it seems. Could not the children stay? Why is sorrow added to sorrow? The home was shadowed before: why this additional gloom? So strange and mysterious are the ways of God. This is the earth-side view. On the other shore the father stands waiting for the time to go by when the rest shall be gathered into the new home. And perhaps he says, "There are two: cannot she spare me one?" And while there is weeping here, there is joy of meeting again up there. The boat shall hardly scrape its keel on the golden marge of the immortal land, when the boy shall leap out in his undying beauty into the arms of his father.

O this earth-side is only a small part of life! Let us offset the events and happenings of this by what these earthly things mean in the spiritual country.

> As voyagers, by fierce winds beaten and broken,
>   Come into port beneath a calmer sky,
> So we, still bearing on our brows the token
>   Of tempest past, draw to our haven nigh.
> A sweet air cometh from the shore immortal,
>   Inviting homeward at the day's decline;
> Almost we see where from the open portal,
>   Fair forms stand beckoning with their smiles divine.

JANUARY 17

Behold, I have created the smith that bloweth the coals in the fire, and that bringeth forth an instrument for His work (Isa. 54:16).

A LOST SORROW

I once heard a man speak of a lost sorrow. A first I did not know what he meant. But his thought quickly emerged and I saw it all. A lost sorrow was a sorrow out of which a man failed to get the blessing which God meant to come out of it for him. Out of every sorrow God means there should come submission; a drawing nearer to His own great heart of love; a new vision of the shallowness of worldly streams and the depths of Divine ones; a closer devotion to Jesus Christ than ever before known; a loosening of the grasp on time, and its tightening upon eternity. It is a solemn fact which some of us know all too well that sorrow leaves us either closer to God or farther away. It is a double-edged tool. It either scars or beautifies. By our resistance we make it a head-wind baffling and driving our tiny craft back from its destined haven of rest. But by our submission God will make it to be a favoring one to waft us onward into the safety and tranquil rest of His perfect will. *James H. McConkey.*

> Let sorrow do its work,
>   Send grief and pain;
> Sweet are thy messengers,
>   Sweet their refrain,
> When they can sing to me—
>   More love, O Christ to Thee!

Blessed are they that mourn—and *mend!*

JANUARY 18 ———————————————————————————

The God of all comfort (2 Cor. 1:3).

A mong all the names that reveal God, this, the *"God of all comfort,"* seems to me one of the most lovely and the most absolutely comforting. The words *"all comfort"* admit of no limitations and no deductions. The Apostle tells us that whatsoever things are written in the Scriptures are for our learning, in order that we "through patience and comfort of the Scriptures may have hope."

If we want to be comforted, we must make up our minds to believe every single solitary word of comfort God has ever spoken; and we must refuse utterly to listen to any words of discomfort spoken by our own hearts, or by our circumstances. We must set our faces like a flint to believe, under each and every sorrow and trial, in the Divine Comforter, and to accept and rejoice in His all-embracing comfort. I say, "set our faces like a flint," because when everything around us seems out of sorts, it is not always easy to believe God's words of comfort.

We must put our wills into this matter of being comforted, just as we have to put our wills into all other matters in our spiritual life. We must choose to be comforted. We MUST believe it. We must say to ourselves, "God says it, and it is true, and I am going to believe it, no matter how it looks."

And then we must never suffer ourselves to doubt or question again.   *Hannah Whitall Smith.*

JANUARY 19 —————————————————————————

He knoweth the way that I take. When He hath tried me, I shall come forth as gold (Job 23:10).

A number of years ago I knew a woman who found God to be a very wonderful Friend. She had a rich Christian experience. But there came into her life a very great trial: her home was broken up; the crash was unspeakable; in the midst of it all it seemed that the Father forsook her.

One evening at prayer-meeting she arose and gave this testimony. We all knew how precious God was to her. Her face was pale and thin. She had suffered much. "God and I have been such wonderful friends, but He seems very far away. He seems to have withdrawn Himself from me. I seem to be left utterly alone." Then looking off in the distance, and with tears, she continued, "But if I never see His face again, I will keep looking at the spot where I saw His face last."

I have never seen nor heard of anything finer than that. That is mighty, sublime, glorious faith that keeps going on. There is a wonderful outcome to the trials in a life of victorious faith like this. This was Job's greatest triumph. "He knoweth the way that I take. The Lord gave and the Lord hath taken away. Blessed be the Name of the Lord."   *Dean Dutton, D.D.*

ENDURANCE

If some great angel came to me to-night,
　Bearing two fatal cups, and bade me sip
The sweet contentment or the bitter fight,
　I know full well which draught would kiss my lip.
Give me the suffering. Let me taste the dregs
　Of life's full cup of bitterness, and share
The tortured hour of silent night that begs
　Oblivion from the pale eyes of Despair.

Then, and then only, shall my love be free
  From earth-born shackles. Gladness never clears
The heart of selfish dross, or yields the key
  Which opens the flood-gates of enhallowed tears.
Give me the suffering! But I would be strong,
  To meet the hours bravely, with a song!

"THE HEART HAS REASONS THAT REASON DOES NOT
UNDERSTAND."

JANUARY 20

Yet a little while (John 14:19).

ETERNITY AND LONELINESS

When you are feeling lonely, think of the hosts of friends you will make during the endless ages you are to live in the spirit world. Think of the great men and women you will meet there, the beautiful ones with whose lives your life will be entwined, the joys of unbroken friendship and exalted communion. Can we not endure a little loneliness, if necessary, during these brief years of preparation? Let us turn to the Father. He knows. In the lonely hour, let us, like Christ, commune with God and find comfort and fellowship.

Come unto Me thou child distressed,
Come find a refuge on My breast,
Lay down thy burden and be blest.

A little while, wait patiently;
A little while, and thou shalt be
With thy beloved, and with Me.   *Henry J. Van Dyke.*

Be the day weary, be the day long,
At length it ringeth to evensong.

JANUARY 21

Fret not (Psalm 37:1).

Trouble not thyself regarding an unknown and veiled future; but cast *all* thy cares on God. "Our sandals," says a saint now in glory, "are proof against the roughest path." He whose name is "the God of *all* grace," is better than His word. He will be found equal to all the emergencies of His people—enough for each moment and each hour as it comes. He never takes us to the bitter Marah streams but He reveals also the hidden branch. Paul was hurled down from the third heaven to endure the smarting of his "thorn," but he rises like a giant from his fall, exulting in the sustaining *grace* of an "all-sufficient God." The beautiful peculiarity in this promise is that God proportions His grace to the nature and the season of trial. He does not forestall or advance a supply of grace, but when the needed season and exigency comes, then the appropriate strength and support are imparted. He does not send the bow *before* the cloud, but when the cloud appears, the bow is seen in it!

> Look not through the sheltering bars
>   Upon to-morrow,
> God will help thee bear what comes,
>   Of joy and sorrow.

God never permits any of His children to come upon a steep hill along life's pathway without having provided at the foot of the hill a cooling spring from which the traveler may drink in refreshment and strength ere he begins to climb.

He climbs beside you; lean upon Him!

JANUARY 22 _____

Blessed are they that have not seen, and yet have believed (John 20:29).

B lessed are they—heroes and heroines of God—who, in the midst of baffling providences, and the crossing and severing of yearning affection, are able to sing the song of faith in the night.

Undoubtedly one of the severest appointments and tests is the protracted burden one has to bear; the baffled prayers; the delay in a gracious answer.

"I shall never believe in prayer again," said a broken-hearted girl. "If ever any one prayed in faith, I prayed that my mother might recover. But she died! Oh, how could God be so cruel?"

Wisely her friend answered: "There are few deaths, thank God, where no one present prays that the dear one may live. Do you suppose that the gift of prayer was given us in order that no one may ever die? If God gave us all we ask for—gave it to all men— we should never dare to pray. Prayer is a blessing because God knows best how to answer. God knows when to say no.

"You prayed. Thank God that you could pray. You prayed in hope, and even now you would not have it otherwise. Pray still, but pray in trust. Pray that God will give you strength for the present burdens, and light enough to follow in the path of duty, one day at a time. You said that you could never pray again, but you will.

"There are no unanswered prayers. Pray that you may know your duty; pray for rest and hope and trust. With those will come peace and new courage, but not absence for sorrow. The peace and courage will enable you to bear the sorrow. That will be the answer to your prayer."

So, with calmness of spirit, the sad young woman faced the world again, and daily prayer gave her daily strength. In the deepening of her life and the strengthening of her character her friends discovered the answer to her prayers, even those that had seemed unanswered.

> If thou wilt keep the incense burning there,
> His glory thou shalt see, sometime, somewhere."

JANUARY 23

Whether we be afficted, it is for your consolation . . . or whether we be comforted, it is for your consolation and salvation (2 Cor. 1:6).

THE FELLOWSHIP OF PAIN

It is a tremendous moment when first one is called upon to join the great army of those who suffer.

That vast world of love and pain opens suddenly to admit us one by one within its fortress.

We are afraid to enter into the land, yet you will, I know, feel how high is the call. It is a trumpet speaking to us, that cries aloud, "It is your turn—endure!" Play your part. As they endured before you, so now, close up the ranks—be patient and strong as they were. Since Christ, this world of pain is no accident, untoward or sinister, but a lawful department of life, with experiences, interests, adventures, hopes, delights, secrets of its own. These are all thrown open to us as we pass within the gates—things that we could never learn or know or see, so long as we were unacquainted with trouble.

God help you to walk through this world now opened to you as through a kingdom, regal, royal and wide and glorious.

Canon Scott-Holland

If Himself He come to thee, and stand
Beside thee, gazing down on thee with eyes
That smile and suffer; that will smite thy heart
With their own pity, to a passionate peace;
And reach to thee Himself the Holy Cup;
Palid and royal, saying "Drink with Me!"
Wilt thou refuse? Nay, not for Paradise!
The pale Brow will compel thee, the pure Hands
Will minister unto thee; thou shalt take
Of this Communion through the solemn depths
Of the dark waters of thine agony,
With heart that praises Him, that yearns to Him
The closer for that hour. Hold fast His Hand
Though the nails pierce thine too! Take only care
Lest one drop of the sacramental wine
Be spilled, of that which ever shall unite
Thee, soul and body, to thy living Lord!

Ugo Bassi.

JANUARY 24

I stretch forth my hands unto Thee: my soul thirsteth after Thee, as a thirsty land (Psalm 143:6).

The way is steep, the path is narrow, the conflict of life is severe. And how tired our feet are! How weary our eyes become! We need that rest which Thou hast in Thyself. Thou art at eternal labor and eternal ease. Thou sittest rejoicing, Thyself calm, sending forth the storm, and rebuking and laying it low. Thou hast in Thyself all that we need in the conflicts of life; and we desire to rise into Thy presence with our thoughts, and with all the needs and inward and unspeakable wants of our soul. We desire to feel the atmosphere in which Thou dost dwell, and to go away as those that have walked in the garden, and borne the very perfume of all that grows and is beautiful. O Thou, who dost command the morning to come forth from the night, shine upon our dark and troubled souls—and grant us Thy joy and peace. Amen!

Henry Ward Beecher.

There's a sweet little lane with the wild roses growing,
There's a steep uphill road where the rough winds are
    blowing,
And I turn wistful eyes to the lane in its beauty,
While I shrink from the hill with its stern call of duty.

Yet I look once again, and behold One awaits me!
One who stands on the hill—while the rose lane is empty
And I'd rather, with Him, walk where rough winds are
    blowing,
Than alone in the lane with the wild roses growing.

Oh, the presence of Jesus! worth all of earth's roses;
Oh, the rest of a heart that in His heart reposes!
My eyes see the beauty, the lane calls me still;
But my heart finds its rest with the One on the hill.

JANUARY 25

The will of the Lord be done (Acts 21:14).

Dr. J. R. Miller tells the following beautiful incident: "I sat one evening with a father and mother beside the bedside of their little child, who seemed about to leave them. We talked of the will and love of God, and before offering prayer I asked the parents, 'What shall we ask God to do?' There was a moment of silence, and then the father with deep emotion said, 'We would not dare decide. Leave it to Him.' Only God knows what will be best—to live in this world, enduring its wintry weather, or to be taken to the summerland of heaven, to grow up there, getting the crown without the conflict. We are not wise enough to decide what will be best; we would rather leave it to our Father."

I wonder, oh, I wonder, where the little faces go,
That come and smile and stay awhile, and pass like
    flakes of snow—
The dear, wee, baby faces that the world has never
    known,
But mothers hide, so tender-eyed, deep in their hearts
    alone.

I love to think that somewhere, in the country we call
    Heaven,
The land most fair of everywhere, will unto them be given,
A land of little faces—very little, very fair—
And everyone shall know his own, and cleave unto it
    there.

"Oh, grant it, loving Father, to the broken hearts that
    plead!
Thy way is best—yet, oh, to rest in perfect faith indeed!
To know that we shall find them, even them, the wee,
    white dead,
At Thy right hand, in Thy bright land, by the living waters
    led!"

JANUARY 26 ⎯⎯⎯⎯⎯⎯⎯⎯⎯⎯⎯⎯⎯⎯⎯⎯⎯

For we which live are always delivered unto death for Jesus' sake, that the life also of Jesus might be made manifest in our mortal flesh (2 Cor. 4:11).

Every phase of nature about us is a wonder. Beauty from ugliness, good out of evil, everywhere. The rose sucks its life from some festering death beneath the sod. The white pond-lily climbs up out of the muddy waters, and lifts its pure petals above slime and corruption. The fleece-cloud of the upper heaven is the evaporation of stagnant pools and swamps.

And in the human sphere, the most beautiful lives are the outcome of anguish and tears. Then may we not say, "We glory in tribulations; knowing that tribulation worketh patience; and patience, experience; and experience, hope." The roses of life, as well as of the garden, the sweet-scented flowers of character, whose savor is precious incense before God—these, though they climb up to such a height as to overrun the jasper walls, and bloom fairest among the plants in the garden of God, do yet start from the root of some death or loss, and grow strong as they are shaken by the sharp winds of sorrow.

The elevating and perfecting of character come largely through sorrow. This is the "mystery of the Cross." All process is by crucifixion. Experiences sad and dark, seemingly cruel, press upon us. The past is tear-worn and furrowed, and the future glooms with shapes of trial. Like Paul, we "know not what shall befall us there." Only the Holy Spirit witnessed to him, and experience witnesses to us, that "afflictions abide" us. I murmured at this, until I saw the crosses and stakes and racks and scaffolds of all ages, and the white feet of those who made these the stairways up which they climbed to light, to truth, to God. Light breaks when I see Jesus, scarred with whipping, thorn-crowned, staggering up Calvary beneath His Cross. I falter sometimes when I try to say, "It is good for me that I have been afflicted." But I can now and then catch a glimpse of the truth of it, when the light of some suffering and conquering hero breaks through the blinding mist of my tears. I can sometimes see the grandeur of the truth so clearly, that, looking back over the pathway of my life, I can say, "Let every sunny spot of the past be darkened, rather than memory should lose one of the tear-hallowed places where I knelt and prayed. Gethsemanes have deeper and grander meanings than Canas."

The richer natures are the suffering natures. Give me for a friend one who, "with strong crying and tears," has battled with trial and midnight, and in thicker darkness of soul has prayed in agony, for light. Shallow and loose-rooted is the tree that has only known sunshine, and never felt the wrench of the gale. God, who loves us like a father, though He pities, would rather that we patiently bear our crosses than be free from them.

THE SORROW TUGS

It seems as you look back over things, that all that you
treasure dear
Is somehow blent in a wondrous way with a heart pang
and a tear.
Though many a day is a joyous one when viewed by itself
apart,
The golden threads in the warp of life are the sorrows
that tug at your heart.   *Edgar Guest.*

JANUARY 27 _____

I will never, never let go thy hand (Isa. 41:13, Weymouth).

Which of you, clasping the hand of the child that you love, leading it home in the eventide darkness, or across some stony way, would let go that feeble hand, so that the little thing came to harm in unaided loneliness?

It may be that to you life's path is rough and hard just now; the skies may be darkened, the track perplexing. Yet never dream the hand of your God and Father has ceased to guide you. He holds you all the more closely because the road is dark.

THE CLASP OF THE FATHER'S HAND

I am a child in the darkness—
  A little frightened child;
The winds are moaning about me,
  And the storm in my heart is wild;
My fear would increase to terror,
  Only, wherever I stand,
It is mine to feel, for my comfort,
  The clasp of my Father's hand.

Duty has ordered me forward,
  But I am afraid to go;
The work is too great for my doing,
  So little I see and know;
And yet I can find my courage,
  And obey my Lord's command,
For I feel the force of a guidance
  In the clasp of my Father's hand.

I am as weak as the children,
  But my Father is wise and strong;
I trust in Him when in danger,
  And He helps me to raise a song;
For every night has a morning,
  And HOME IS IN EVERY LAND;
I am not afraid to go onward
  With the clasp of my Father's hand.

It is true that the end is coming,
  And mystery, like a shroud,
Hangs over the parting waters:
  I should fear to enter the cloud,
But that is my happy secret,
  As I wait awhile on the strand,
Closer, and yet more tender,
  Grows the clasp of my Father's hand.
Marianne Farningham

Don't try to hold God's hand; let Him hold yours. Let Him do the *holding* and you do the *trusting*.   *H. W. Webb-Peploe.*

For the Lamb which is in the midst of the throne shall feed them, and shall lead them unto living fountains of waters: and God shall wipe away all tears from their eyes (Rev. 7:17).

C onsider the kindness and helpfulness of Time. We speak of him as the destroyer, and picture him with his scythe sweeping away all that man would preserve. But, on the other hand, what a healer and restorer is Time! As we grow older, we see nothing more plainly than that wounds of the spirit, which to youthful eyes appear incurable, are most gently soothed and made whole by the passing years. Under the old scars flows again the calm, healthful tide of life. Nowhere more plainly than here is it seen how much better God's ways are than man's thoughts. Under a great loss the heart impetuously cries that it can never be happy again, and perhaps in its desperation says that it wishes never to be comforted. But, though angels do not fly down to open the grave and restore the lost, the days and months come as angels with healing in their wings. Under their touch, aching regret passes into tender memory; into hands that were empty new joys are softly pressed; and the heart, that was like the tree stripped of its leaves and beaten by winter's tempests, is clothed again with the green of spring.

WAIT A BIT

Some glorious morn—but, when?—ah, who shall say?
The steepest mountain path shall become a plain,
And the parched land be satisfied with rain.
The gates of brass, all broken; iron bars,
Transfigured, form a ladder to the stars.
Rough places smooth, and crooked ways all straight,
For him who with a patient heart can wait.
These things shall be on God's appointed day:
It may not be tomorrow—yet it may!

Now we see through a glass, darkly; but then face to face: now I know in part but then . . . (1 Cor. 13:12).

"But then shall I know!" All enigma and difficulty will then vanish—all will be made plain to ennobled, refined, and purified powers. Here a passing breath from a carnal world dims my glass, and obscures my spiritual vision. *There,* there will be no taint of sin to mar or blight my lofty contemplations. *Here,* amid the twilight shadows of an imperfect state there is much to cause doubt, and, alas! disagreement among God's children. *There,* all shall see "eye to eye," they will only wonder that trifles should have been suffered so sadly to divide and estrange. *Here,* we are in the gloomy crypt, walking amid the humiliating wrecks of sin and death, reading the mysterious records of mortality. *There,* it will be in the "cathedral aisles" of light and love, harmony and peace—the noon-day splendour of eternity. Glorious prospect! All made bright before that Sapphire Throne. That mysterious providence, that desolating bereavement, which, like a sweeping avalanche, tore up by the roots the fibres of affection, *then* I shall know, and *see,* and acknowledge it to have been all for good. Then I shall understand (what my aching heart cannot know), that the child I wept over—the parent I laid prematurely in the grave— the friend, early severed from my side—were all thereby taken from much evil to come, and invested with an earlier bliss. I shall wonder how I could ever have sorrowed on their behalf.

J. R. Macduff.

I sometimes think that God must surely smile,
    While looking on His world so tenderly;
And whisper softly to His angels there:
    "Could they but see."

His fretted world perplexed and worn and sad,
    Distrustful of His watching thought the while;
Unmindful of the strength of love which shines
    Behind God's smile—

The kindest smile a weary world could know—
    A smile that pities, loves, forgives and plans;
That knows earth's strivings, failings, hopes and fears,
    And understands.

Could they but see how near His angels are,
    And know the grandeur of the ways they tread,
Or glimpse the land of happiness untold
    Which lies ahead.

I sometimes think that God must surely smile,
    When looking on His troubled world below,
And whisper softly, tenderly, His thought:
    "Could they but know."

JANUARY 30

I would hasten my escape from the windy storm and tempest (Psalm 55:8).

HIGHER THAN STORMS

Henry Ward Beecher tells us that he has stood upon Mount Holyoke while the thunder rolled below; people hurried up the side, anxious to escape the storm, and at last upon the top they were secure. "Many storms there are," said the great preacher, now beyond the reach of tempest, "that lie below and hug the ground. The way to escape them is to go up the mountain-side and get higher than they are."

Perhaps today we are tempest-tossed, distressesd by cloud and blast of sorrow, or dreading some threatening storm; let us haste to seek the heights, "the mount of God;" the calm, pure air of spiritual health and strength that is breathed by those who forsake the gloomy flats of doubt and despondency. Physically, we are braced by the mountain air; have you not climbed, ere this, some grand, flower-girt peak, and forgotten weariness in the fresh atmosphere of the ascent, the scene wherein there is inspiration and joy at every opening prospect?

"Ah! but our mountain-climbing days are over now," you sigh in your present sorrow. Whether it be so or not as regards the *visible* heights, it is certain you can at this moment ascend higher than storms and tumult, for on the wings of faith and prayer the humble soul can reach the Shining Mountains, and commune with the eternal God, its refuge and its strength.

Tomorrow you need *not* survey; on the heights of communion with the Lord, you learn to leave with Him the next step, the coming way.

We must get to the place of real solitude with Christ. He is our mountain height and our sea-calm. He is the re-creating power.

We are more than conquerors through Him that loved us (Rom. 8:37).

I t is better that we should not sing of sadness. There are sad
notes enough already in the world's air. We should sing of
cheer, of joy, of hope. We do not need to be defeated in our
battles, to sink under our loads, to be crushed beneath our
sorrows. We may be victorious. Sorrow comes into every life; we
cannot shut it away, but we can be conquerors in it. When the
snow melts away in the springtime, I have often seen under it
sweet flowers in bloom. The very drifts are like warm blankets to
keep them safe. So it is with sorrow: under the cold snows of grief
the flowers of the Christian graces grow unhurt. We can overcome
in sorrow. This does not mean that we should not shed tears. The
love of Christ does not harden the heart; it really makes it more
sensitive. The grace of Christ does not save us from suffering in
bereavement; yet we are to be conquerors. Our sorrow must not
crush us: we must go through it victoriously, with sweet submission, and joyous confidence. Let us keep in mind that it is
"through Him that loved us."

> Then nestle your hand in your Father's,
>   And sing if you can as you go;
> Your song may cheer some one behind you
>   Whose courage is sinking low;
> And if your lips do quiver—
>   God will love you the better so.

It is the Lord. Let Him do what seemeth Him good (1 Sam. 3:18).

T he glory glistens in our view, but we are not always ready to
consider its cost. The only path to glory is that which lies
through the tangled thorn-brake of sorrow. The corn of wheat
must fall into the ground and die, lying alone and forsaken
through the winter with its pitiless blasts and frost.

I see not but that my road to heaven lieth through this very
valley.   *John Bunyan.*

From vintages of sorrow are deepest joys distilled,
And the cup outstretched for healing is oft at Marah filled;
God leads to joy through weeping, to quietness through
    strife;
Through yielding unto conquest, through death to endless
    life.
Be still! He hath enrolled thee for the Kingdom and the
    Crown.
Be silent! Let him mould thee, who calleth thee His own!

FEBRUARY 2

*Yet the Lord will command his loving-kindness in the daytime, and in the
night His song shall be with me (Psalm 42:8).*

THE MINISTRY OF NIGHT

Let us not forget what the sorrow has done for us while it lasted;
and what the night has been, though dark and sad. It has
been a night of grief, yet a night of blessing; a night in which there
may have been many things which we could wish to be
remembered forever. Often, during its gloom, we called it
"wearisome," and said, "When shall I arise, and the night be
gone?" (Job 7:4). Yet how much was there to reconcile us to it;
nay, to fill us with praise because of it! It was then that the Lord
drew near, the world was displaced, self was smitten, our will
conquered, faith grew apace, hope became brighter and more
eager, and the things that are unseen were felt to be the real and
the true: Jerusalem that is above was seen by us as our proper
home.   *Horatius Bonar.*

And do not fear to hope. Can poet's brain
More than the Father's heart rich good invent?
Each time we smell the autumn's dying scent
We know the primrose time will come again;
Not more we hope, nor less would soothe our pain.
Be bounteous in thy faith, for not misspent
Is confidence unto the Father lent;
THY NEED IS SOWN AND ROOTED FOR HIS RAIN;
His thoughts are as thine own; nor are His ways
Other than thine, but by their loftier sense
Of beauty infinite and love intense.
Work on. One day beyond all thoughts of praise,

A sunny joy will crown thee with its rays;
Nor other than thy need, thy recompense.

George MacDonald.

He Careth (1 Peter 5:7).

What can it mean? Is it aught to Him
That the nights are long, and the days are dim?
Can He be touched by the griefs I bear,
Which sadden the heart, and whiten the hair?
Around His throne are eternal calms,
And glad, strong music of happy psalms,
And bliss unruffled by any strife,
How can He care for my little life?

And yet I want Him to care for me
While I live in the world where the sorrows be;
When the lights are down from the path I take;
When strength is feeble, and friends forsake;
When love and music that once did bless
Have left me to silence and loneliness;
And my life-song changes to sobbing prayers,
When my heart cries out for a God who cares.

When shadows hang o'er me the whole day long,
And my spirit is bowed 'neath shame and wrong;
When I am not good, and the deepening shade
Of conscious sin makes my heart afraid;
And the busy world has too much to do
To stay in its course to help me through;
And I long for a Saviour—Can it be
That the God of the universe cares for me.

Oh, the wonderful story of deathless love!
Each child is dear to that heart above;
He fights for me when I cannot fight,
He comforts me in the gloom of night,
He lifts the burden for He is strong,
He stills the sigh, and awakens the song;
The burdens that bow me down He bears,
And loves and pities because He cares.

Oh, all that are sad, take heart again!
You are not alone in your hour of pain;

The Father stoops from His throne above
To soothe and comfort us with His love.
He leaves us not when the storm beats high,
And we have safety, for He is nigh.
Can it be trouble when He doth share?
Oh, rest in peace, for your Lord does care!   *Selected.*

FEBRUARY 4 _____

O death, where is thy sting? (1 Cor. 15:55).

When I look back and read of the early Christians, I am charmed to find how they always felt about dying. They had such a sense of dying in Jesus, such a sense of the reality of the Heavenly Home, such a sense of the glory of the future state, that they could take their children, and put them, as it were, into the hand of God, and rejoice, and sing hymns of gratulation that they were about to go; and they could meet together over their dead as men meet to celebrate a great victory. This feeling is lost out of the Church; it is largely lost out of men's apprehension; and it seems to me that it will be one of the beneficent features in the development of Christianity in our age, and in the future ages, to bring back again in the experience of men the beauty of death, the triumph of death, and the overhanging light and glory that ought to destroy that darkness which to us, for the most part, envelops the door of the grave.

When we comprehend the fullness of what death will do for us, in all our outlook and in all our forelook, dying is triumphing. Not any bower of roses is so festooned in June. Not where the jessamine and honeysuckle twine, and lovers sit, is there so fair a sight, so sweet a prospect, as where a soul in its early years is flying away, out of life and out of time, through the gate of death—the rosy gate of death, the royal gate of death, the golden gate of death, the pearly gate of death.

STEPPING ASHORE

Oh! think to step ashore,
  And find it Heaven;
To clasp a hand outstretched,
  And find it God's hand!
To breathe new air,

And that celestial air;
   To feel refreshed,
      And find it immortality;
Ah, think to step from storm and stress
   To one unbroken calm;
To awake and find it Home.   *Robert E. Selle.*

*Dying! What is it? To shut out the black night, and join the
fireside of your Father's Home.*

FEBRUARY 5

Peace from God our Father (Rom. 1:7).

Peace, perfect peace!" What music there is in these words! The
very mention of them fills the heart with longings, which cry
out for satisfaction, and will not be comforted. Sometimes, indeed,
we may succeed in hushing them for a little, as a mother does a
fretful child; but soon they will break out again with bitter
insatiable desire. Our natures sigh for rest, as the ocean shell,
when placed to the ear, seems to sigh for the untroubled depths of
its native home.

There is peace in those silent depths of space—blue for very
distance—which bend with such gentle tenderness, over the
fevered, troubled lives. There is peace in the repose of the
unruffled waters of the mountain lake, sheltered from the winds by
the giant cliffs around. There is peace at the heart of the whirlwind,
which sweeps across the desert waste in whirling fury. The peace
of the woodland dell, of a highland glen, of a summer landscape—all touch us. And is there none for us whose nature is so
vast, so composite, so wonderful?

There is! Weary generations passed by until at length there
stood among men One, whose outward life was full of sorrow and
toil; but whose calm face mirrored unbroken peace that reigned
within His breast. He had peace in Himself; for He said, "My
peace." He had the power of passing on that peace to others; for
He said, "My peace I *give* unto you."

His peace is *perfect,* unbroken by storms, unreached by the
highest surges of sorrow. His peace is *as a river:* it is there in the
scorching noon; it is there when the stars shine, hushing one to
sleep with the melody of the waves. His peace is *great:* its music is

louder than the tumult of the storm. Learn the lesson of the Lake of Galilee—that the peace which is in the heart of Jesus, and which He gives to His own, can quell the greatest hurricane that ever swept down the mountain ravine and spent itself on the writhing waters beneath. For when the Master arose and rebuked the wind, and said unto the sea, "Peace, be still," the winds ceased, and there was a great calm.

On the evening of His resurrection, our Lord entered through the unopened doors into the chamber where His disciples were cowering with fear—His benediction, *"Peace be unto you,"* fell on their ears like the chime of bells. But He did not rest satisfied with this. Indeed, His words alone would have been in vain. But when He had showed unto them His hands and His side, fresh from the Cross, with the marks of the spears and the nails, do you wonder that they were glad? The heart must always be glad when it learns the sure basis of Peace in the Blood shed on the Cross. Rest on that precious Blood; make much of it; remember that God sees it, even if you do not; be sure that it pleads through the ages, with undiminished efficacy; and be at peace.   *Selected.*

FEBRUARY 6

In a moment (1 Cor. 15:52).

> Quite suddenly—it may be at the turning of a lane,
>   Where I stand to watch a skylark soar from out the
>   swelling grain,
> That the trump of God shall thrill me, with its call so
>   loud and clear,
>   And I'm called away to meet Him, Whom of all I hold
>   most dear.
> Quite suddenly—it may be in His house I bend my knee,
>   When the kingly Voice, long hoped for, comes at last
>   to summon me,
> And the fellowship of earth-life that has seemed so
>   passing sweet,
>   Proves nothing but the shadow of our meeting round
>   His feet.
> Quite suddenly—it may be as I tread the busy street,
>   Strong to endure life's stress and strain, its every call
>   to meet,
> That through the roar of traffic, a trumpet, silvery clear,

Shall stir my startled senses and proclaim His coming
near.
Quite suddenly—it may be as I lie in dreamless sleep,
God's gift to many a sorrowing heart, with no more tears
to weep
That a call shall break my slumber and a Voice sound
in my ear;
"Rise up, my love, and come away, behold the
bridegroom's here."

So shall we ever be with the Lord (1 Thess. 4:17).

FEBRUARY 7 _____

Raised in glory (1 Cor. 15:43).

From the pen of a missionary writer comes this beautiful story.
A faithful missionary in distant Korea sat by the bedside of
his dying wife. For fifteen years they had toiled together in the
Gospel of Jesus Christ. And now her summons had come. The
heart-broken husband sat waiting for the end. She knew what the
parting meant to him. She realized the keeness of his suffering. So,
with her last thought an unselfish one for him, she left him this last
message of eternal comfort, "Do not grieve for me, my dear.
You'll get me back; you'll get me back." A month passed and the
grief-stricken husband sat by the same bedside watching the spirit
of their only child, a little four-year-old boy, take its flight to the
same Lord to whom his darling mother had gone. Again the
father's heart was crushed. Again he faced a parting which meant
untold anguish to him. But the little fellow had the same message
as his mother for the sorrowing father. "Don't cry, daddy," said
he. "Don't cry. Daddy, I see a great shining light. It's coming
nearer, daddy, it's coming nearer. And daddy, it's mudder; it's
mudder! And I want to go, I want to go. But don't cry, daddy,
don't cry. You'll get me back; you'll get me back!" A few days
later the stricken father was riding in the funeral train behind the
body of his dead boy. From behind the curtains of the chair in
which he was being borne by the natives he heard the voice of a
woman weeping. Presently the voice of another Korean woman
spoke up and said, "Why are you weeping?" The sorrowing
woman answered, "I am weeping for the foreigner who has lost

46

his little boy." "Don't weep for the foreigner; weep for yourself, woman," came the answer. "You have lost a little girl, and you will never get her back. I have lost a little boy, and I shall never get him back. But let me tell you something. These foreigners have a strange way of getting back their dead!" And then as the stricken father laid the white lily upon the coffin of his little one, he bowed his head before his Lord and gave himself anew to Him to preach to these heathen people that blessed Gospel of Jesus Christ which would give back their dead to all who believed in Him as Saviour and Lord of the glory that is one day to come with Him. For he knew that if death came he would go to them, but if resurrection first, they would come to him.

THE TWO GREAT CREEDS OF CHRISTENDOM—"I BE-LIEVE . . . IN THE RESURRECTION OF THE BODY AND LIFE EVERLASTING."

These bodies were the bodies of the sons of God, yet they went down into the dust like the beasts of the field. These bodies, laid away in the darkness and night of the tomb shall some day "swarm up the steeps of light." These bodies, now crumbling to dust and ashes, shall some day, changed, sit down with Him on His throne. These bodies, the prey of corruption and decay, shall live on, changed, through all the ages of eternity in deathlessness and incorruption. These bodies, now chained to the narrow limits of a grave, shall some day, changed, sweep in an instant of time through the boundless spaces of the universe. Sown in dishonor indeed! But we will get them back. For they shall be "raised in glory." Like the glory of the sun blazing the mid-day heavens: like the glory of the planets in their pathway through the midnight skies; like the glory of the seven times heated furnace which fills the skies with the red glare of its presence so shall be the glory of these resurrected bodies. Sown in dishonor, forsooth, but we will get them back in glory. For we, His children, are "in Christ Jesus" and "the dead in Christ shall rise" in the stupendous glory of that resurrection instant.   *James McConkey.*

FEBRUARY 8 ─────────────────────────────

And fill up that which is behind of the afflictions of Christ . . . for His body's sake, which is the church (Col. 1:24).

Perhaps sorrows have overwhelmed you. You have followed to the grave your best beloved. You have entered into the experience of Job and known in succession poverty, the anguish of a stricken affection, and the pains of an incurable disease. Still you can have happiness. Your sorrow is meant to be a strength-giver to you, and to equip you for giving strength to others. You are called by your Gethsemane to render the highest service which one can ever render in the kingdom of God: the service of filling up that which is lacking of the afflictions of Christ in the world's redemption. Christ called His three favorite disciples to watch outside while He wrestled in agony within the garden. He calls you to share with Him in that wrestling; could He give you greater honor? Could He bring you into closer fellowship?

I think that God is proud of those who bear
    A sorrow bravely. Proud indeed of them
Who walk straight through the dark to find Him there,
    And kneel in faith to touch His garment's hem.
Oh, proud of them who lift their heads and shake
    The tear away from eyes that have grown dim;
Who tighten quivering lips, and turn to take
    The only road that leads to Him.

How proud He must be of them. He who knows
    All sorrow, and how hard grief is to bear.
I think He sees them coming, and He goes
    With outstretched arms and hands to meet them there,
And with a look—a touch, on hand or heart—
    Each finds his hurt heart strangely comforted.

FEBRUARY 9 ⎯⎯⎯⎯⎯⎯⎯⎯⎯⎯⎯⎯⎯⎯⎯⎯⎯⎯⎯⎯⎯

Blessed is the man whose strength is in thee . . . who passing through the valley of Baca (weeping) make it a well (Psalm 84:5, 6).

THE VALLEY OF WEEPING

I have been through the valley of weeping,
    The valley of sorrow and pain;
But the "God of all comfort" was with me,
    At hand to uphold and sustain.

As the earth needs the clouds and the sunshine,
    Our souls need both sorrow and joy;

So He places us oft in the furnace,
  The dross from the gold to destroy.

When He leads thro' some valley of trouble,
  His omnipotent hand we trace;
For the trials and sorrows He sends us,
  Are part of His lessons in grace.

Oft we shrink from the purging and pruning,
  Forgetting the Husbandman knows
That the deeper the cutting and paring,
  The richer the cluster that grows.

Well He knows that affliction is needed;
  He has a wise purpose in view,
And in the dark valley He whispers,
  "Hereafter Thou'lt know what I do."

As we travel thro' life's shadow'd valley,
  Fresh springs of His love ever rise;
And we learn that our sorrows and losses,
  Are blessing just sent in disguise.

So we'll follow wherever He leadeth,
  Let the path be dreary or bright;
For we've proved that our God can give comfort,
  Our God can give songs in the night.   *Selected.*

After a season of tears, a sober and softened joy may return to us.   *Amiel's Journal.*

FEBRUARY 10 _____

I will not leave you comfortless: I will come to you (John 14:18).

The beloved and honored HEAD of some home is suddenly stricken down. All the needs of that little community were met by the hand of this one provider. His life was the fountain from which flowed all the copious streams of supply. So steady and satisfying were the streams that the sense of dependence was scarce expressed or felt. The ministries of comfort were almost like the laws of nature—regular, constant, abundant. Suddenly the streams have failed, and the fountain is dry. The clinging fingers, torn from their hold—upon *whom* or *what* shall they fasten? The empty hands—who shall fill them?

Is there nothing written for Faith and Hope against such an hour of gloom? "A Father of the fatherless and a judge of the widows is God in His holy habitation." "Leave thy fatherless children, I will preserve them alive; and let the widows trust in Me." These desolate ones are not left unprovided for or uncomforted. The very ties that seem to have withered offer still their sweet utterance to their lips—"Husband!" "Father!" And casting all their care upon Him, they can never again be widowed or orphaned.

The valley may be dark, the shadows deep,
But O, the Shepherd guards His lonely sheep;
And through the gloom, He'll lead me Home,
My Heavenly Father watches over me.

FEBRUARY 11 —————————————————————————

And truly our fellowship is with the Father and with His Son Jesus Christ (1 John 1:3).

When the Lord Jesus went to the Cross, it was He and the Father—both of them together—who went. And when you come to your cross, and carefully and prayerfully consider the question as to whether you will take it up or not, remember this for your encouragement, that you do not go to it alone. The Lord Jesus, who knows what crucifixion means, goes with you, and you can humbly and trustfully say, "We went together."

Some of us have turned back from new and heavier crosses. Now the Lord leads us back to that place where we have failed, and He says, "We will go together," and as we go, He will help and lead. *J. Russell Howden.*

I cannot do it alone;
    The waves run fast and high,
And the fogs close chill around,
    And the light goes out in the sky;
But I know that We Two shall win—in the end,
        —Jesus and I.

I cannot row it myself—
    The boat on the raging sea—
But beside me sits Another,
    Who pulls or steers—with me;

50

And I know that We Two shall come safe into port,
    —His child and He.

Strong and tender and true,
    Crucified once for me;
Ne'er will He change, I know,
    Whatever I may be.
But all He says I must do,
    Ever from sin to keep free;
We shall finish our course, and reach Home at last!
    —His child and He.   *Selected.*

FEBRUARY 12

And He said unto her, "Weep not." (Luke 7:13).

No grief is deeper than that of a mother bereft. No cry is more disconsolate than that of Rachel weeping for her children. But the innocence and joyousness from which the mother is cruelly parted here, await her in the hereafter. To her this thought is more than a comfort; it becomes an abiding motive.

Oh, say not that your little son is dead;
    The word too harsh and much too hopeless seems,
Believe, instead,
That he has left his little trundle bed
To climb the hills
Of morning, and to share the joy that fills
    God's pleasant land of dreams.

Nay, say not that your little son is dead.
    It is not right, because it is not true.
Believe, instead,
He has but gone the way that you must tread,
And, smiling, waits
In loving ambush by those pearly gates,
    To laugh and leap at you.

No knight that does you service can be dead;
    Nor idle is the young knight gone before.
Believe, instead,
Upon an envoy's mission he hath sped
That doth import
Your greatest good; for he at heaven's court
    Is your ambassador.   *T. A. Daly.*

Perhaps God does with *His heavenly garden* as we do with our own. He may chiefly stock it from nurseries, and select for transplanting what is yet in its young and tender age—flowers before they have bloomed, and trees ere they begin to bear.

Dr. Guthrie.

FEBRUARY 13

The eternal God is thy refuge and underneath are the everlasting arms (Deut. 33:27).

If we are held in the clasp of the everlasting Arms, we need not fear that we shall ever be separated from the enfolding. "Underneath." They are always underneath us. No matter how low we sink in weakness, in fainting, in pain, in sorrow, we never can sink below these everlasting Arms. We can never drop out of their clasp. God's love is deeper than human sorrow. Sorrow is very deep, but still and forever, in the greatest grief, these arms of love are underneath the sufferer.

God's love is deeper than death. When every earthly support is gone from beneath us, when every human arm unclasps and every face fades from before our eyes, and we sink away into what seems darkness and the shadow of death, we shall only sink into the everlasting arms.

Upon my meeting a friend whom I had not seen in some time, he said, "Since we last met, I have dug a deep grave." But the grave-digger's spade cannot get beneath our Father's love. God's love is deeper than that deepest grave you ever dug, and you can never dig into any dreary dwelling of death that is beyond the reach of the white-robed messengers of eternal love.

Drop your plummet into the deepest sea of sorrow, and at the end of your soundings, "Underneath are the everlasting arms." What abiding consolation! What all-embracing, never-failing strength!

Leaning on Thee, no fear alarms; . . .
I feel the "everlasting Arms," I cannot sink.

52

Shut up unto the faith (Gal. 3:23).

SOME TIME

Some time, when all life's lessons have been learned,
　And sun and stars for evermore have set,
The things which our weak judgment here has spurned,
　The things o'er which we grieved with lashes wet,
Will flash before us out of life's dark night,
　As stars shine most in deeper tints of blue;
And we shall see how all God's plans were right
　And how what seemed reproof was love most true.

And we shall see that while we frown and sigh,
　God's plans go on as best for you and me:
How, when we called, He heeded not our cry,
　Because His wisdom to the end could see.
And e'en as prudent parents disallow
　Too much of sweet to craving babyhood,
So God, perhaps, is keeping from us now
　Life's sweetest things because it seemeth good.

And if, sometimes, comingled with life's wine,
　We find the wormwood, and rebel and shrink,
Be sure a wiser hand than yours or mine
　Pours out this portion for our lips to drink.
And if some friend we love is lying low,
　Where human kisses cannot reach his face,
Oh, do not blame the loving Father so,
　But bear your sorrow with obedient grace.

And you shall shortly know that lengthened breath
　Is not the sweetest gift God sends his friends;
And that, sometimes, the sable pall of death
　Conceals the fairest boon His love can send.
If we could push ajar the gates of life,
　And stand within, and all God's working see,
We might interpret all this doubt and strife,
　And for each mystery find a key.

But not today. Then be content, poor heart;
　God's plans, like lilies pure and white, unfold.
We must not tear the close-shut leaves apart—
　Time will reveal the calyxes of gold.
And if, through patient toil, we reach the land

Where tired feet, with sandals loose, may rest—
When we shall clearly know and understand—
I think that we will say that "God know best."

May Riley Smith.

FEBRUARY 15

Jesus Christ . . . hath brought life and immortality to light through the gospel (2 Tim. 1:10).

The sorrow, the loneliness of homes from which loved ones have passed into the skies, is hard to bear; our human hearts hunger for the "touch of the vanished hand, and the sound of a voice that is still." If to this be added the feeling that they are lost to us, never to be restored, we are crushed by the weight of woe; but it is a weight our tender Father never meant us to bear. Christ came to bring life and immortality to light; to make us *know* —that there is everlasting life. Let no tear-dimmed eyes be shut against this blessed truth, let no heart sorrow as without hope of blessed reunions in our Father's house from which we shall go no more out forever. *Mary Lowe Dickinson.*

Still on the lips of all we question,
    The finger of God's silence lies;
Will the lost hands in ours be folded?
    Will the shut eyelids ever rise?
O friend, no proof beyond this yearning,
    This outreach of our hearts, we need;
God will not mock the hope He giveth,
    No love He prompts shall vainly plead.
Then let us stretch our hands in darkness,
    And call our loved ones o'er and o'er;
Some day their arms will close about us,
    And the old voices speak once more.   *J. G. Whittier.*

FEBRUARY 16

The Lord gave, and the Lord hath taken away; blessed be the name of the Lord (Job 1:21).

Our blessed Jesus walks among the roses and lilies in the garden of His church; and when He sees a wintry storm coming upon some tender plants of righteousness, He hides them in the earth to preserve life in them, that they may bloom with new glories when they shall be raised from that bed. The blessed God acts like a tender Father, and consults the safety and the honor of His children when the hand of His mercy snatches them away before that powerful temptation comes which He foresees would have defiled and distressed and almost destroyed them.

They are not lost, but they are gone to rest a little sooner than we are. Peace be that bed of dust where they are hidden, by the hand of their God, from unknown dangers! Blessed be our Lord Jesus, who has the keys of the grave, and never opens it for His favorites but in the wisest season. *Isaac Watts.*

When the dusk of evening had come on, and not a sound disturbed the sacred stillness of the place—when the bright moon poured in her light on tomb and monument, on pillar, wall and arch, and most of all (it seemed to them) upon the quiet grave—in that calm time, when all outward things and inward thoughts teem with assurances of immortality, and worldly hopes and fears are humbled in the dust before them—then, with tranquil and submissive hearts they turned away, and left the child with God.
Dickens.

> The paths that lead us to God's throne
> Are worn by children's feet.

FEBRUARY 17 ─────────────────────────────

Who is among you . . . that walketh in darkness and hath no light? Let him trust in the name of the Lord, and stay upon his God (Isa. 50:10).

Your relations to God are not to be shaken by the fact that you do not understand His providence. On the contrary, when the path is rugged and the night is dark—and very dark indeed it is sometimes—cling all the closer to your faith, for it is the only thing under the stars that can give you help. *George H. Hepworth.*

> One dark night there came a voice
> Saying, "Despair not, but rejoice!
> Lift up thy soul in song,
> For the day will break ere long."

But I answered, "Why should I believe this cunning lie?
Through the watches of the night
Have I not sought for light,
Yet discerned not even a spark
In the starless, ebon dark?

Now that my quest has ceased
Shall the morning flood the east?
Nay, thou canst not cheat my sight;
There is no such thing as light."

But, even as I spoke,
Over the hills the bright dawn broke!   *Selected.*

FEBRUARY 18

As the sufferings of Christ abound in us, so our consolation also aboundeth by Christ (2 Cor. 1:5).

Here is a blessed proportion. God always keeps a pair of scales: in this side He puts His people's trials, and in that He puts their consolation. When the scale of trial is nearly empty, you will always find the scale of consolation in nearly the same condition; and when the scale of trial is full, you will find the scale of consolation just as heavy; for as the sufferings of Christ abound in us, even so shall consolation abound by Christ. This is a matter of pure experience. Oh, it is mysterious that, when the black clouds gather most, the light within us is always the brightest! When the night lowers and the tempest is coming on, the heavenly captain is always closest to his crew. It is a blessed thing, when we are most cast down, then it is that we are most lifted up by the consolations of Christ.

There is nothing that makes a man have a big heart like a great trial. Great hearts can only be made by great troubles. The spade of trouble digs the reservoir of comfort deeper, and makes more room for consolation.

God puts consolation only where He first put pain.

Perfect through sufferings (Heb. 2:10).

GRAY DAYS

That was a *gray day* in the life of George Matheson, one of Scotland's promising young preachers, who, when he was twenty years old, went to have an operation performed on his eyes and was told by the surgeon, "You had better see your friends quickly for soon the darkness will settle on you forever, and all chance of seeing them will be gone."

That was a *gray day* in the life of the young lad, Joseph, when with love and tenderness, as he went to carry needed things to his shepherd brothers far from home, he was taken by them and sold as a slave.

That was a *gray day* in Paul's experience when, suffering from the thorn in the flesh, he besought the Lord unavailingly three times for its removal. None of us would say that the gray days never come. We know them—the day of disappointment; the day of financial crash; the day when that loved one was borne to the grave. Yes, the gray is very real.

But there is glory in the gray, and one glory is that thereby we learn endurance, steadfastness, and patience. It was through tribulation that George Matheson learned to endure after the blindness came. His biographer tells us that when the darkness finally descended upon him, he shut himself up and gave an entire day to communion with God. Then he came forth sweet in his spirit, courageous in his soul, happy in his heart, with his suffering turned to song. It was out of a furnace like that he could so endure as to sing:

> Oh light, that followest all my way,
>   I yield my flickering torch to thee;
> My heart restored its borrowed ray,
> That in thy sunshine's blaze its day
>   May brighter, fairer be.

A noble character wrought through suffering is another glory in the gray. A by-product of suffering is hope. Pain inspires to our best, and we thereby hope for the passing of the gray and the coming of the glory.

I know that an omniscient Artist planned,
With skill divinely grand,
The painting of my life's short, winding road.
I think He wrought and gazed with tender glance
Upon the scene; and as it grew
In beauty, with a cloud-fleeced heaven embowed,
He rose, as if to disentrance
Himself, and stepped aback and scanned
The product of His Master-hand.
Quick grasped His brush! His visage glowed!
Just one more touch of grey in somber hue
Must rest upon that placid sky of blue,
Before its arching depth could best enhance
The glory of the little winding road.   *Sadie Louise Miller.*

FEBRUARY 20

He knoweth thy walking through this great wilderness (Deut. 2:7).

I would not, if I could, stand at the open window and peer into the unknown beyond. I am sure that He whose mercies are new every morning and fresh every evening, who brings into every epoch of my life a new surprise, and makes in every experience a new disclosure of His love, who sweetens gladness with gratitude, and sorrow with comfort, who gives the lark for the morning and the nightingale for the twilight, who makes every year better than the year preceding, and every new experience an experience of His marvelous skill in gift-giving, has for me some future of glad surprise which I would not forecast if I could.

BEFORE me is a future all unknown,
  A path untrod;
BESIDE me is a FRIEND well-loved and known,
  That FRIEND is God.

BEFORE me lies a new and untried way.
  Midst shadows dim;
BESIDE me is my GUIDE, and day by day,
  I walk with HIM.   *Ruth Thomas.*

58

FEBRUARY 21 _____

I will give thee the treasures of darkness (Isa. 45:3).

Your Lord is constantly taking us into the dark, that He may tell us things—into the dark of the shadowed home, where bereavement has drawn the blinds; into the dark of the lonely, desolate life, where some infirmity closes us in from the light and stir of life; into the dark of some crushing sorrow and disappointment.

Then He tells us His secrets, great and wonderful, eternal and infinite; He causes the eye which has become dazzled by the glare of earth to behold the heavenly constellations; and the ear to detect the undertones of His voice, which are often drowned amid the tumult of earth's strident cries. *F. B. Meyer.*

> Storm-tossed, alone, in the starless night
>   I'm not afraid.
> With lost hope drifting from my sight,
>   I'm not afraid.
>
> Through sorrow and through mystery
> My Pilot calls o'er life's dark sea;
>   I'll follow on—
>   I'm not afraid.
>
> Somewhere the dawn shall rise for me,
>   I'm not afraid.
> Sometime in God's light, I shall see;
>   I'm not afraid. *From Flood-Tides.*

FEBRUARY 22 _____

The glory of God did lighten it (Rev. 21:23).

Who has not marked even here the glory of God as seen in the great sunset. Rivers of glory wind through meadows of gold. Lakes of glory lie embedded in the evening sky. Seas of glory lap eternal shores with their shimmering waves. Mountains of glory rear themselves to the heavens with cloud-capped summits tipped with the splendor of the dying day. Earth too is flooded with the glory. It falls in the dim aisles of great forests and illumines them with its splendor. It dances among the wind-tossed leaves. It splotches the trunks of giant trees. It bathes in light the upturned faces of those who watch and worship as the climaxing splendor of earth, sea, and sky turns the heart to God our Father who is Himself the glory of all creation and who deigns to give us, in the lavish, golden glory of the sunset the faint forth-shadowing of the glory of the Father's House.

But if the earthly glory is such, what must be the glory of the heavenly city? It needs no sun, for the glory of God doth lighten it. The nations of the earth walk in the glory of it. Its foundations can only be likened to the glory of the diamond, the sapphire, the amethyst, the topaz, and like precious stones of earthly glory. Its gates are pearls—each wondrous gate a single pearl. The city and its street are gold. But it is gold which the earth knows not. For it is called "gold like unto clear glass" (Rev. 21:18), and "transparent glass" (Rev. 21:21). That is—it is the glory-gold. It is gold through which the glory of God can shine forth in crystal splendor. God uses this earthly imagery as the nearest symbolism by which He can give us any glint of the glory of His House prepared for us. But when all has been said it is as nought to that glory of which He says—

Eye hath not seen nor ear heard, neither have entered into the heart of man, the things which God hath prepared for them that love Him. *James McConkey.*

FEBRUARY 23 ─────────────────────────────

And sorrow and sighing shall flee away (Isa. 35:10).

A pestilence broods over a great city with its dark wings, and every night the husband goes to his cottage home wondering whether he may not find that the fatal destroyer has entered there, and the wife that he left blooming in the morning he may find stricken at night.

One evening he comes, and the house is closed, and the windows dark; he knocks, and there is no answer; he rings, and he gets no response. His heart sinks within him as he thinks that she is stricken and is gone. But, as he looks and watches, suddenly he discerns on the door, in the darkening twilight, a little paper pinned. He plucks it off, opens it, and reads its, and it brings him a message from his wife: "Someone has come for me, and taken me up into the mountains, where there is no malaria, where there is no disease, where there is no danger; I am safe there, and the means are here for you to follow me." How the heart and the life spring again to his cheek, and the bitter sorrow turns into an exhilaration, an ecstasy, a joy!

So we come to the house that held our beloved. It is dark; and out of the windows that shone with the light of love, no light is shining. We are heart-broken until we turn and find here this word brought to us: "That loved one has gone to the mountains, where there is no pain, or sorrow, or temptation, or disease, but the eternal flowers and the everlasting sunlight: follow thou on." Oh! it is not strange that in the heart of man, where before there was only the throb of anguish, and into the lips of men, where before there was only the long, long wail of sorrow, this message of the everlasting Christ has put the throb of exhilaration and the song of triumph. It is not strange that we have learned to hang upon our doors, not crepe, but flowers!

> A kindly nurse shall come some day
> To us with solemn mien and say,
> "'Tis time to go to bed and sleep."
> And we, mayhap, shall sigh and weep
> To leave our playthings and our play,
> And pray a little longer while to stay.
> But she, unheeding our alarms,
> Shall fold us close within her arms,
> Until upon her mother-breast
> We sink at last to sleep and rest,
> And wake to read in angel eyes,
> Our welcome sweet to Paradise.
>
> *Zitella Cocke.*

FEBRUARY 24

And He said unto me, My grace is sufficient for thee (2 Cor. 12:9).

Strangely do some people talk of "getting over" a great sorrow. Not so. No one ever does that; at least, no nature which has been touched with the feeling of grief at all. The only way is to pass through the ocean of affliction, solemnly, slowly, with humility and faith, as the Israelites passed through the Red Sea. Then its very waves of misery will divide and become to us a wall on the right side and the left, until the gulf narrows and narrows before our eyes, and we land safe on the opposite shore.

D. M. Craik.

> Do not cheat thy Heart and tell her,
>   "Grief will pass away.
> Hope for fairer times in future,
>   And forget to-day."
> Tell her, if you will, that sorrow
>   Need not come in vain;
> Tell her that the lesson taught her
>   Far outweighs the pain.
>
> Cheat her not with the old comfort
>   Soon she will forget—
> Bitter truth, alas!—but matter
>   Rather for regret;
> Bid her not, "Seek other pleasures,
>   Turn to other things";—
> Rather nurse her caged sorrow
>   Till the captive sings.
>
> Rather bid her go forth bravely,
>   And the stranger greet—
> Not as foe, with spear and buckler,
>   But as dear friends meet;
> Bid her with a strong clasp hold her,
>   By her dusky wings—
> Listening for the murmured blessing
>   Sorrow always brings.   *Adelaide Anne Proctor.*

Not somehow, but triumphantly!

FEBRUARY 25

No night there (Rev. 22:5).

I had dropped in upon an old friend of my boyhood days. She was one of God's own saints. Rich in experience, she was ripe for the coming glory. She had gone so far in life's pilgrimage that her mind was slightly beclouded, and her memory affected. As I rose to go home she arose also and said, "I want to go home." "But mother," said her daughter, "you are home now." At that she looked a bit dazed. Then looking at me with a tender smile she said with a profound touch of pathos in her voice, *"I want to go home before it gets dark."*

I opened the door and started homeward. The twilight sky was still aglow with the vanishing glory of the sunset. Beyond it lay the glory of the Father's House. My soul was tingling with the spiritual message my dear friend's words had brought me. What an unspeakable blessing for God's children to reach home before it gets dark! Before the darkness of broken body and failing health; of dimmed senses and clouded faculties; of physical suffering and infirmities; of vanished faces, voices, and fellowships—before all these come, how blessed it is to reach home before it gets dark.

Sometimes we deplore the passing of those of God's own who die young. The young girl in the bloom of her sweet maidenhood; the lad in the flush of his strong youth—how premature it seems, and what a grievous mistake. But, is it not we who are mistaken in this? They have only reached home before it got dark. They have entered the Homeland; they have found "a place to stay;" they are "forever with the Lord;" they see His face and walk in the unfailing splendor of His glory. It is only because we look through tear-blinded eyes, "see through a glass darkly," and so fail to measure eternal values as God measures them, that we ever lament as premature the passing of the young into the Homeland. The Father's House is thronged with children. And we may be sure He made no mistake in taking them there. After all when we enter into a Homeland whose time-units are centuries and ages, instead of seconds and minutes, then the mere human distinctions of age and years shall count as nought. *James McConkey.*

FEBRUARY 26 _____

I was dumb, I opened not my mouth, because Thou didst it (Psalm 39:9).

That is not an easy thing to say. It needs a strong faith to say it: and yet what else can the heart of faith say than that? Get nearer to God yourself, crushed heart; think of this sore grief as meant to draw you at least nearer to Him. Leave it to Him to explain His own righteousness at last, as He assuredly will.

> "I will be still," my bruised heart faintly murmured,
>   As o'er me rolled a crushing load of woe;

The cry, the call, e'en the low moan was stifled;
  I pressed my lips; I barred the teardrop's flow.

I will be still, although I cannot see it,
  The love that bares a soul and fans pain's fire;
That takes away the last sweet drop of solace,
  Breaks the lone harp string, hides Thy precious lyre.

"But God is love, so I will 'bide me, 'bide me—
  We'll doubt not, Soul, we will be very still;
We'll wait till after while, when He shall lift us—
  Yes, after while, when it shall be His will."

And I did listen to my heart's brave promise;
  And I did quiver, struggling to be still;
And I did lift my tearless eyes to Heaven,
  Repeating ever, "Yea, Christ, have Thy will."

But soon my heart upspake from 'neath our burden,
  Reproved my tight-drawn lips, my visage sad;
"We can do more than this, O Soul," it whispered.
  "We can be more than still, we can be glad!"

And now my heart and I are sweetly singing—
  Singing without the sound of tuneful strings;
Drinking abundant waters in the desert;
  Crushed, and yet soaring as on eagle's wings. *S. P. W.*

The Infinite Hand behind the cloud, gives only the sorrow we can bear.

FEBRUARY 27 —————————————————————

God Himself shall be with them, and be their God. And God shall wipe away all tears from their eyes (Rev. 21:3, 4).

Burdened one, traveling onwards night-watch after night-watch, the ground you tread saturated with "dewy tears,"—keep your eyes fixed on these letters of flame, God's own hieroglyphics inscribed on the glory-symbol, telling you that there is a day coming when affliction and pain and death will have nothing left behind them but a memory. Yes, a memory—waking from a troubled dream—no more.

The seals of the roll of Providence will be broken. The

confession will be made, no longer with reserve or stammering tongue—

> And aye the dews of sorrow
> Were lustred with His love!

Specially will this be true regarding your beloved dead, and the mystery of their departure. You will meet them on the heavenly shore. There is weeping *here* spoken of in our verse, but *there* it will be glad re-unions with the loved ones, never to be lost again. You can think of that *now*. "God washes the eyes by tears," says a noted writer, "until they can behold the invisible land where tears shall come no more. O love! O affliction! Ye are the guides which show us the way through the great airy spaces where our loved ones walked; and as hounds easily follow the scent before the dew be risen, so God teaches us, while yet our sorrow is wet, to follow on and find our dear ones in Heaven."

No tears in Thy land, O Immanuel!

FEBRUARY 28 ─────────────────────────

Suffer little children to come unto Me . . . for of such is the kingdom of God (Luke 18:16).

BABY'S GRAVE

Amid all the whirl and dizziness of life's tragedy, in which creation seems to be but one great cloud, I find myself suddenly brought to a sweet baby's grave. A gray old church, a gurgling stream, a far-spreading thorn tree on a green hillock, and a grave on the sunny southerly side. That is it. Thither I hasten night and day, and in patting the soft grass I feel as if conveying some sense of love to the little sleeper far down. Do not reason with me about it; let the wild heart, in its sweet delirium of love, have all its own way.

Baby was but two years old when, like a dewdrop, he went up to the warm sun, yet he left my heart as I have seen ground left out of which a storm had torn a great tree. We talk about the influence of great thinkers, great speakers, and great writers; but what about the little infant's power? Oh, child of my heart, no poet has been so poetical, no soldier so victorious, no benefactor so kind, as thy tiny, unconscious self. I feel thy soft kiss on my withered lips just now, and would give all I have for one look of thy dreamy eyes. But I cannot have it.

Yet God is love. Not dark doubt, not staggering argument, not subtle sophism, but child-death, especially where there is but one, make me wonder and make me cry in pain. Baby! baby! I could begin the world again without a loaf or a friend if I had but thee; such a beginning, with all its hardships, would be welcome misery. I do not wonder that the grass is green and soft that covers that little grave, and that the summer birds sing their tenderest notes as they sit on the branches of that old hawthorn tree.

My God! Father of mine, in the blue heavens, is not this the heaviest cross that can crush the weakness of man? Yet that green grave, not three feet long, is to me a great estate, making me rich, with wealth untold. I can pray there. There I meet the infant angels; there I see all the mothers whose spirits are above; and there my heart says strange things in strange words—Baby, I am coming, coming soon! Do you know me? Do you see me? Do you look from sunny places down to this cold land of weariness? Oh, baby, sweet, sweet baby, I will try for your sake to be a better man; I will be kind to other little babies, and tell them your name, and sometimes let them play with your toys; but, oh, baby, baby, my old heart sobs and breaks.   *Dr. Joseph H. Parker.*

Only a baby's grave—
A foot or two at the most
  Of tear-dewed sod;
  But a loving God
Knows what the little grave cost.

Only a baby's life—
Brief as a perfumed kiss,
  So fleet it goes;
  But our Father knows
We are nearer to Him for this

Let us praise God for the brief loan.

FEBRUARY 29 ─────────────────────────

Thou hast enlarged me when I was in distress (Psalm 4:1).

There are in this world blessed souls whose sorrows spring up into joy for others; whose earthly hopes, laid in the grave with many tears, form the seed whence spring healing flowers and balm for the desolate and the lonely.

"Thou hast enlarged me"—e'en when in distress!
  "Thou hast enlarged me"—made me more like Thee,
Sorrows which came, and things of painfulness,
  Thou hast employed me—yea, but to develop me.

"Thou hast enlarged me!"—Thou dost most behold
  Need for enlargement, deep within the soul:
And Thou doest use, not always things of gold—
  Things ofttimes dark—when sorrows billows roll.

"Thou hast enlarged me!" using things of pain—
  Things I would fain have had Thee take away;
Things which, to me, betokened naught of gain—
  Thou hast used these, enlargement to convey.

"Thou hast enlarged me!" Yea, 'tis all clear now!
  "Thou hast enlarged me," e'en when sore distress'd:
"Thou hast enlarged!" I worshipfully bow,
  And gladly sing the discipline which blest."

J. Danson Smith.

MARCH 1

Jesus said unto him, follow Me; and let the dead bury their dead (Matt. 8:22).

Thou canst not cure thine own sorrow by nursing it; the longer it is nursed, the more inveterate it grows. It will be harder for thee to go out to-morrow than it is to-day; it will be harder *still* the day after. Thou canst not cure thy sorrow by nursing it; but thou canst cure it by nursing another's sorrow. Thinkest thou that Jesus wanted this young man to be a stoic! Was it from the ties of the heart He called him when He said, "Follow Me?" No, it was to the ties of the heart—*other* ties of *other* hearts. It was no foreign scene to which Jesus called him—no scene foreign to his grief. Not from the graveyard into the dance did He summon him, but from the smaller into the *larger* cemetery. Thither in thine hour of sorrow does He summon *thee.* He bids thee bury thy sorrow, not in

Cana, but in Gethsemane—not in the winecup, but in the common pain. It is by tears He would *heal* thy tears; it is by grief He would *cure* thy grief. Come out into the larger cemetery; come out to meet the common pain! By no frivolity will He dry thine eyes. To follow Him is to follow the cortege of all the Nains and Bethanys. To follow Him is to follow the stream of universal human suffering. Bury thy sorrow beside that stream!

George Matheson.

Go bury thy sorrow,
  The world hath its share;
Go bury it deeply,
  Go hide it with care;
Go think of it calmly,
  When curtained by night;
Go tell it to Jesus,
  And all will be right.

Hearts growing a-weary
  With heavier woe,
Now droop, 'mid the darkness,
  Go comfort them, go!
Go bury thy sorrows,
  Let others be blest;
Go give them the sunshine,
  Tell Jesus the rest.

Forget your own special cross for awhile— the Lord is thinking about it and you.

MARCH 2 _____

So He bringeth them unto their desired heaven (Psalm 107:30).

Death is home-coming. "I go," Christ says, "to prepare a place for you." We set sail upon an unknown sea, but we go not to a strange land. Here we are pilgrims and strangers; there we shall be at home.

When we are summoned to our departure, though the ship be strange and the sea unknown, we shall be embarking for a land where friends will be awaiting us. To fall asleep here, to wake up there and find ourselves at home—how strange will seem the sudden transition!

Picture death no longer as a skeleton with scythe and hourglass; that is pagan. See Him luminous and radiant, the Cross in His hand, a smile upon His lips, and from Him the invitation, "Come unto Me, ye that labor and are heavy laden, and I will give you rest, and I will give you life."

BON VOYAGE

Farewell, farewell! You sail away
  To where the lighted homelands are;
Your face is turned to radiant day
  From glimmers of the sea and star;
Close the tired eyes until you gain
God's heaven, where is no more pain.

The little boat will safely bear,
  The sea is quiet in the bay,
Not yours the trouble or the care,
  Dear heart, the boatman knows the way;
Lie still and sleep without a fear,
It is not long, for Home is near.

Be not afraid of hurt or loss,
  It is a peaceful way you take;
The night will see you safe across,
  And when you land the day will break.
Then ah! the dear ones gone before,
What welcomes wait along the shore!

Farewell! You vanish from my sight,
  And into shadow softly glide;
Oh, friend of mine, bound for the light,
  They watch you from the other side.
All joy and blessing go with you
Who go to God. Farewell, Adieu!

MARCH 3 ─────────────────────────────

For our good always (Deut. 6:24).

It is a great thing when our Gethsemane hours come, when the cup of bitterness is pressed to our lips, and when we pray that it may pass away, to feel that it is not fate, that it is not necessity, but divine love for good ends working upon us.

E. H. Chapin.

69

I KNOW

I know thy sorrow, child; I know it well,
Thou needst not try with broken voice to tell.
Just let Me lay thy head here on My breast,
And find here sweetest comfort, perfect rest;
Thou needst not bear the burden, child, thyself,
I yearn to take it all upon Myself;
Then trust it all to Me today—tomorrow,
Yes, e'en forever; for I know thy sorrow.

Long years ago I planned it all for thee;
Prepared it that thou mightst find need of Me.
Without it, child, thou wouldst not come to
Find this place of comfort in this love of Mine.
Hadst thou no cross like this for Me to bear,
Thou would not feel the need of My strong care;
But in thy weakness thou didst come to Me,
And through this plan I have won thee.

I know thy sorrow and I love thee more,
Because for such as thee I came and bore
The wrong, the shame, the pain of Calvary,
That I might comfort give to such as thee.
So, resting here, My child, thy hand in Mine,
Thy sorrow to My care today resign;
Dread not that some new care will come tomorrow—
What does it matter? I know all thy sorrow.

And I will gladly take it all for thee,
If only thou wilt trust it all to Me,
Thou needest not stir, but in My love lie still,
And learn the sweetness of thy Father's will—
That will has only planned for the best;
So, knowing this, lie still and sweetly rest.
Trust Me. The future shall not bring to thee
But that will bring thee closer still to Me. *Author Unknown.*

MARCH 4 ───────────────────────────

Thou hast guided them in Thy strength unto Thy holy habitation (Ex. 15:13).

Death is not a journey into an unknown land, it is a voyage Home. We are going not to a strange country, but to our Father's Home, and among our own kind and kin.

HEAVEN

In childhood's days our thoughts of heaven
Are pearly gates and streets of gold,
And all so very far away;
A place whose portals may unfold
To us—some far-off distant day.
But in the gathering of the years,
When life is in the fading leaf,
With eyes perchance dedimmed by tears,
And hearts oft overwhelmed with grief,
We look beyond the pearly gate,
Beyond the clouds of grief's dark night,
And see a place where loved ones wait,
Where all is blessedness and light.
And over all we see the face
Of Him who'll bring us to our own,—
Not to a far-off distant place,
For heaven is, after all, just Home!   *Sue H. McLane.*

MARCH 5 ——————————————————————

Now he is comforted (Luke 16:25).

God's Word withholds many details that we are impatient to learn. When our loved ones are taken from us we realize, perhaps as at no other time, that now we see through a glass darkly. We know far more of the events and scenes that will follow the return of our Lord and our gathering together unto Him than we do about the conditions that intervene between the grave and the rapture! How our eyes strain to pierce the gloom! We wake in the early morning and look out at the stars that we believe to be millions of miles away and we ask, Where are they now, those dear ones with whom yesterday we could talk and to whom we ministered? Can they look back in love upon our grief-stained faces? Do they long to be clothed upon with that form that is to be fashioned like unto our Lord's own glorious body? But while the revelations concerning the state of those loved ones who have fallen asleep may seem meager as to detail, yet are they exceedingly precious and reassuring. Paul says, "To die is gain;" and again, that to depart is to "be with Christ; which is far better." Since our loved ones are with the Lord we may lean hard upon the assurance, "In Thy presence is fulness of joy." Best of all, perhaps, comes the echo of our Lord's Word concerning the beggar Lazarus who had suffered so grievously from illness and poverty and this world's injustice: "Now he is comforted." Is it not enough? "Carried by the angels . . . with Christ . . . *comforted!*" What more could we ask for those to whose pain-racked bodies we have loved to minister? When our longing eyes try vainly to pierce the inscrutable depths of infinite blue that stretch above us, let us harken to the Saviour's gentle Word, "Now he is comforted," then wait with patience, knowing that if while we tarry the victory shout shall call us suddenly to meet Him in the air. "Them also that are fallen asleep in Jesus will God bring with Him." *Sunday School Times.*

MARCH 6 ───────────────────────────────────

God understandeth the way . . . and He knoweth (Job 28:23).

How can I go;
How rise, and take the path and know
I have no hand to hold, no face
To meet me on the way at any place!
  I stand
Just where I held his hand;
  I took—
Just here the wind hath shook
His gold curls, and his feet
This far came with me: then let me but repeat,
Just standing where I am,
All that his lips said—sacred as a psalm—
While we were moving on, before I knew
His footsteps would stop him. So new
The way looks on beyond; if I could stay,
If I could but live over day by day
The sweet gone-by; if I could be
Found waiting where he left me—but I see
A step ahead which I must take.
What that my heart should break;
  What that I cry—

Or am too mute to lift on high
A cry for pity—I must go;
Reach out for other hands; know
The bleak places of new hills; be strong:
Carry my burden all along
The uphill road; leave
All our footprints in the path that, in and out, weaves
On together until now; must take
The new step on alone, and make
My eyes lift to the sun, and look
At Purple hill, and throbbing brook,
    And make
My hands reach out again to take
Flowers, that will grow against my feet and keep
Reminding me I have no other hands to put them in!
    Steep
Be the way or level, can it matter now?
If I must leave his footprints does it matter how?
If I must go, walk just the same,
Without his love-lips murmuring my name
    I only know
It cannot matter much the way I go
So that the path leads high,
Leads closer, every day, toward the sky;
Leads, as God wills, toward the meeting-place
    Where I shall look upon my loved one's face.

George Kringle.

Round the next turn in the road Heaven awaits thee—therefore Traveler, forget thy weariness and cheerfully plod. Over the hill-crest it calls—so grasp thy staff and climb. Breast the storm—for at the end of the journey is Home.

MARCH 7

I shall be satisfied when I awake with thy likeness (Psalm 17:15).

Standing, O our God, upon the shrinking shores of time, where ever break and moan the waves of an eternal sea, we feel utterly homeless and afraid. Beneath our feet, crumbling rock and shifting sand; around us, scenes that change; before us, an ocean perilous, uncharted, and dark with storm. We have heard that far over the horizon, islands of the blest lift fronded palms in air. All we know for certain is that this is not our home. We cannot stand this restless change, this hurrying pace of life, the loss of loved ones, the terror of the shade which creeps around us. We must build our everlasting mansion, not here upon time's wooded shore, but in Thee, man's dwelling place in every generation.

Not here! not here! not where the sparkling waters
　　Fade into mocking sands as we draw near;
Where in the wilderness each footstep falters,
　　"I shall be satisfied"—but oh! not here.

Not here—where all the dreams of bliss deceive us,
　　Where the worn spirit never gains its goal;
Where, haunted ever by the thoughts that grieve us,
　　Across us floods of bitter memory roll.

There is a land where every pulse is thrilling
　　With rapture earth's sojourners may not know,
Where Heaven's repose the weary heart is stilling,
　　And peacefully life's time-tossed currents flow.

Thither my weak and weary steps are tending;
　　"Saviour and Lord! with Thy frail child abide;
Guide me toward Home, where, all my wondering ending,
　　I shall see Thee, and shall be satisfied!"

MARCH 8 _____

He giveth quietness (Job 34:29).

I do not know when or how it may please God to give you the quiet of mind that you need, but I tell you I believe it is to be had; and, in the meantime, you must go on doing your work, trusting in God, even for this. Tell Him to look at your sorrow; ask Him to come and set it right, making the joy go up in your heart by His presence.　　　　　　　　　　　*George Macdonald.*

How shall I quiet my heart? How shall I keep it still?
How shall I hush its tremulous start, at tidings of good
　　or ill?
How shall I gather and hold contentment and peace
　　and rest,
Wrapping their sweetness, fold on fold, over my troubled
　　breast?

The Spirit of God is still and gentle and mild and sweet,
What time His omnipotent, glorious will guideth the worlds
    at His feet:
Controlling all lesser things, this turbulent heart of mine
He keepeth as under His folded wings in a peace
    serene—divine.

So shall I quiet my heart, so shall I keep it still,
So shall I hush its tremulous start at tidings of good or ill;
So shall I silence my soul with a peacefulness deep
    and broad,
So shall I gather divine control in the infinite quiet of God.

MARCH 9 _____

They that are Christ's at His coming (1 Cor. 15:23).

THE JOY OF THE RESURRECTION

We do not realize the joy of the resurrection victory pictured in the Scriptures. We note the seeming paucity of statement concerning it, and are misled thereby. For we do not realize that the highest, deepest joy of the heart finds utterance in the fewest words.

When that boy came home from the suffering, struggle, and death of that awful world-conflict was your joy a voluble one, of much speaking and many sentences? Nay, you could only throw your arms about him and cry out with quivering heart, "Oh my boy!" And your strong-armed, stout-hearted lad could only take you in his arms, and, with tearful voice and glad heart, cry out, "Mother!" The deepest emotions of a true heart, find vent in the fewest words. And is not this why we have failed to see the well-springs of joy in the resurrection and forty days of Christ's presence with His own? Think of that morning when He stood in the garden in the dimness of dawn. When the weeping Mary began to speak to Him, how did He reveal Himself? By a single word. It was the word by which love most richly and deeply expresses its joy toward a loved one—the name of the loved one. "Mary!" That seems terse, and barrenly brief to us. But the thrill of resurrection joy and glory back of it must have been such as never vibrated through that single mention of Mary's name in all the years of her earthly life. And then when doubting Thomas reached forth his hand and touched the scarred side, how much did he say? Only "My Lord and My God!"

Can any human imagination picture the joy that must have flooded Thomas' heart as he realized that Jesus Christ was really risen from the dead and that he was touching Him with his own hand! And when John, with spiritual instinct, was the first to recognize the risen Lord upon the lake-shore in the faint light of that momentous morning what did he say? Only *"It is the Lord!"* Yet that little sentence sent head-long into the waiting sea the man whose heart had been broken by his denial of his Master, and opened the flood-gates of a joy so boundless and ecstatic that no human being could possibly picture it.

And so may it be some glad, golden day with us. If, suddenly, radiant faces should swarm into our astounded presence; sweet familiar voices of long ago whisper our name as our Lord spoke Mary's; the thrill, uplift, and splendor of glorification sweep through our whole being in one jubilee instant of time; and then we should be "caught up together with them to meet the Lord in the air," resurrection joy would be no mere dream as it seems now to many, but the same marvelous, thrilling reality of bliss and glory that it was twenty centuries ago there on the quiet shore of Galilee.

Only then it was "Christ *the first fruits,*" but for us it would be "*they that are Christ's at His coming.*"   *James McConkey.*

Why put on mourning for the guests of God?

MARCH 10 ⸻⸻⸻⸻⸻⸻⸻⸻⸻⸻⸻

And the city had no need of the sun, neither of the moon, to shine in it: for the glory of God did lighten it, and the Lamb is the light thereof (Rev. 21:23).

Thou glorious spirit-land! Oh, that I could behold thee as thou art—the regions of life and light and love, and the dwelling place of those beloved ones whose being has flowed onward, like a silver-clear stream, into the solemn sounding main, into the ocean of eternity.   *H. W. Longfellow.*

"I hear thee speak of the better land;
Thou callest its children a happy band.
Mother! oh, where is that radiant shore?

Shall we not seek it, and weep no more?
Is it where the flower of the orange blows,
And the fire-flies glance through the myrtle boughs?"
"Not there, not there, my child!"

"Is it where the feathery palm-trees rise,
And the date grows ripe under sunny skies?
Or amidst the green islands of glittering seas,
Where fragrant forests perfume the breeze,
And strange, bright birds, on their starry wings,
Bear the rich hues of all glorious things?"
"Not there, not there, my child!"

"Is it far away in some region old,
Where the rivers wander o'er sands of gold,
Where the burning rays of the ruby shine,
And the diamond lights up the secret mine,
And the pearl gleams forth from the coral strand?
Is it there, sweet mother, that better land?"
"Not there, not there, my child!"

"Eye hath not seen it, my gentle boy!
Ear hath not heard its deep sound of joy;
Dreams cannot picture a world so fair—
Sorrow and death may not enter there;
Time doth not breathe on its fadeless bloom:
Far beyond the clouds, and beyond the tomb—
It is there, it is there, my child!"   *Felicia Dorothae Hemans.*

MARCH 11

For in that He Himself hath suffered being tempted, He is able to succour them that are tempted (Heb. 2:18).

Jesus deals very gently with those who find the cross heavy. He sympathizes, for He knows what it means to suffer. He sank under His own Cross, and had to be helped with it by a passer-by on the way to Calvary.

"Daughter, take up thy cross and follow Me,"
"I hear, O Master, and would follow still,
Did not my frame, grown weaker than my will,
Because my long-borne cross weighs heavily,
Most helpless sinks when I would most obey;
But Thou that in Gethsemane did pray

The cup might pass, if such His will might be,
Till Thou wast over-worn in agony,
And so didst sing, exhausted on the way
To Calvary, till they raised the cross from Thee—
Thou wilt not chide if for a while at length
Weakened by anxious vigil, wrestling, loss,
Sinking, and finding none to raise my cross,
I lie where fallen, and wait returning strength."

MARCH 12

Wherefore seeing we also are compassed about with so great a cloud of witnesses, let us lay aside every weight, . . . and let us run with patience the race that is set before us, looking unto Jesus, the Author and Finisher of our faith (Heb. 12:1).

In one of his fine essays, F. W. Boreham describes an old country cricketer who had lost his sight. It was the great grief of his declining years that he would never be able to see his son play the game of which he himself had been such a master. The boy became the leading batsman of his school, and used to lead his father to the cricket field every time a big match was played. Although the old man was unable to see his boy play, he shared in the applause of the crowd, and was proud of his son's prowess and triumph. One day he died suddenly. A few days following, an important match was to be played, and naturally no one expected the son to be present, but to the surprise of every one he appeared as usual in his flannels, and played as he had never played before.

After the match, on a friend's congratulating him, saying, "You played the game of your life this afternoon," he replied, "How could I help it? It was the first time my father ever *saw* me play."

In the *Bonnie Brier Bush,* Ian Maclaren beautifully describes the farewell of a dying mother to her devoted son. "Ye'll no forget me, John, I ken that weel, and I'll never forget ye. I've loved ye here, and I'll love ye yonder. Th'll be no 'oor when I'll no pray for ye, and I'll ken better what to ask than I did here, sae dinna be comfortless, ye'll follow Christ. He'll keep ye too, and, John, I'll be watchin' for ye. Ye'll no fail me. If God calls ye to the ministry ye'll no refuse, an' the first day ye preach in yer ain kirk, speak a gude word for Jesus Christ, *an' John, I'll hear ye that day, though ye'll no see me, and I'll be satisfied."*

78

MARCH 13

Rejoicing in hope (Rom. 12:12).

> The leaves are fading and falling,
>   The winds are rough and wild,
> The birds have ceased their calling,
>   But let me tell you, my child.
>
> Though day by day as it closes,
>   Doth darker and colder grow,
> The roots of the bright red roses,
>   Will keep alive in the snow.
>
> And when the winter is over,
>   The boughs will get back new leaves,
> The quail come back to the clover,
>   And the swallows back to the eaves;
>
> The robin will wear on his bosom,
>   A vest that is bright and new,
> And the loveliest wayside blossom
>   Will shine with the sun and dew.
>
> The leaves, today, are swishing,
>   The brooks are all dry and dumb;
> But let me tell you, darling,
>   The spring will surely come.
>
> There must be rough cold weather,
>   And winds and rains so wild;
> Not all good things together,
>   Come to us here, my child.
>
> So, when some dear joy loses
>   Its beauteous summer glow,
> Think how the roots of the roses
>   Are kept alive in the snow.   *Alice Cary.*

MARCH 14

And the streets of the city shall be full of boys and girls, playing in the streets thereof (Zech. 8:5).

79

A NEW LITTLE GIRL IN HEAVEN

"Oh! what do you think the angels say?"
    Said the children up in heaven,
"There's a dear little girl coming home today;
She's almost ready to fly away
    From the earth we used to live in;
Let's go and open the gates of pearl,
Open them wide for the new little girl,"
    Said the children up in heaven.

"God wanted her here, where His little ones meet,"
    Said the children up in heaven,
"She will play with us in the golden street!
She has grown too fair, she has grown too sweet,
She needs the sunshine, this dear girl,
That gilds this side of the gates of pearl,"
    Said the children up in heaven.

"So the King called down from the angel's dome,"
    Said the children up in heaven,
"My little darling, arise and come
To the place prepared in thy Father's home,
    To the home My children live in."
"Let's go and watch at the gates of pearl,
Ready to welcome the new little girl,"
    Said the children up in heaven.

"Far down on the earth do you hear them weep?"
    Said the children up in heaven,
"For the dear little girl has gone to sleep;
The shadows fall and the night clouds sweep
    O'er the earth we used to live in;
But we'll go and open the gates of pearl;
Oh! why do they weep for their dear little girl?"
    Said the children up in heaven.

"Fly with her quick, O, angels dear,"
    Said the children up in heaven,
"See—she is coming! Look there! Look there,
At the jasper light on her sunny hair,
    Where the veiling clouds are riven!
Ah-hush-hush-hush all the swift wings furl!
For the King Himself at the gates of pearl
Is taking her hand, dear, tired little girl,
    And leading her into heaven."

(In loving memory of little Patsy Parsons.)

80

"He shall gather the lambs with His Arm and carry them in His bosom" (Isa. 40:11).

MARCH 15

He shall come down like rain upon the mown grass (Psalm 72:6).

Have you observed how blue the sky is after a thunderstrom, and how the flowers reopen and the birds begin to sing? Thus it will be that a solemn confidence and a deep-seated assurance will change the aspect of life for you when the storm of the first days of your grief are past. The hurt at your heart and the loneliness will not be less, but the closer fellowship with your Father, which began amid your tears, will become a dynamic force to carry you forward into braver and better deeds.   *Selected.*

MARCH 16

The Lord hath His way in the whirlwind and in the storm (Nahum 1:3).

Before my window is a beautiful green branch of a tree now in full spring dress. Only a few weeks ago and that same branch was loaded with ice—it seemed as if it must break. I remember one hour in which it seemed as if it could not keep up. I expected to see it give way, but it did not break, and to-day it is beautiful. There are many in this sad world who are as my branch was—loaded with ice. It seems as if their sorrows are like hail storms; and how to keep up, how to hold on, seems to be the one vital question. If one such should read about my branch let me say to you, Don't break! Cling for your life to the one truth, that God has not forgotten you. He holds the wind in His fists, and the waves that now seem as if they would swallow you up, in the hollow of His hands. You may look up and say,

> Thou hast a charge no waves can wash away;
> And let the storm that does Thy work,
> Deal with me as it may.

And so by simple faith in God's goodness and love you hold on, and when in a future—like the branch near my window, it will be all spring with you—you will remember your sorrows as waters that have passed away. Hold on! It is not always winter; spring is coming. The birds are yet to sing on the very branch now loaded with ice; only *don't break!* My branch did not have a will of its own, but we have wills, and God can energize them, and we must use our wills and say, "Though He slay me yet will I trust Him," and He never slays but to make alive. Thus trusting, though you may bend to the blast, you will not break; you will hold on, and you will see your Spring.

> Hold on, my heart, in thy believing—
> The steadfast only wins the crown;
> He who, when stormy winds are heaving,
> Parts with his anchor, shall go down;
> But he who Jesus holds through all,
> Shall stand, though heaven and earth shall fall.
>
> Hold out! There comes an end to sorrow;
> Hope from the dust shall conquering rise;
> The storm foretells a summer's morrow
> The Cross points on to Paradise;
> The Father reigneth! cease all doubt;
> Hold on, my heart, hold on, hold out.

MARCH 17

His compassions fail not (Lam. 3:22).

It is a most blessed experience to have the conscious presence of God with us through the trials and tests of life. But it is another thing when the Father apparently abandons us to fate in the storms of life; when He seems to have utterly forgotten us:

> When sorrows fall like rain, and troubles swarm like bees about the hive,
> When our ships at sea come drifting home, with broken masts and sails,
> When we groan and writhe beneath our crosses,
> When He plants our path thick with thorns,
> When our feet are cut with sharp rocks as we climb the hill difficulty,

When He loads our back heavy with burdens,
When He wrests from our arms whatever we love.

But had we no tests, no great hedged-in experiences, we should never know the wonderful Deliverer and triumphant Guide we have. His eye is upon us. He is working out some infinite purpose. Let us say as did Job: "He knoweth the way that I take, when He hath tried me, I shall come forth as gold."

MARCH 18 ────────────────────────────────

Put on as the elect of God, kindness (Col. 3:12).

In some parts of Italy, as soon as a peasant girl is married she makes a fine muslin bag. In this bag she gathers rose leaves; and year after year other rose leaves are added until perhaps, she is an old woman. Then when she dies, that bag of rose leaves is the beautiful, fragrant pillow that her head lies on in the coffin.

It is possible for us, year after year, to gather the rose leaves of tender ministries, unselfish sacrifices, brave actions, loving deeds for Christ's sake. We cannot do this if we let the opportunities of our early years slip by. Little time will be left us, if we do, to find the pillow on which our dying head may rest. We shall lose the desire to gather good deeds, and our hearts become selfish and unresponsive to our Lord.

Let us be watchful to crowd into our lives the lovely, unselfish and helpful things, that we may show our love to Christ. And then at last, our heads shall rest on something more fragrant than rose leaves—the fragrant memories of good deeds, sweet to ourselves, sweet to others, and approved by our Lord.   *Selected.*

> Oh, may I join the choir invisible
> Of those immortal dead who live again
> In lives made better by their presence.
>
> Carve your name on hearts, not on marble.

MARCH 19 ────────────────────────────────

Peace always by all means (2 Thess. 3:16).

How full is the declaration contained in this verse! Always peace, this is the promise. Perhaps if one thing disturbs our peace more than another it is that disappointments and disasters happen which we cannot account for; nor do we see any reason why they should have been allowed. Let us wait and believe that all has happened for the best. If we knew all, we should probably be praising God for that for which we are now ready to chide Him. Yes, in the light of eternity many things that are now dark and mysterious will become clear. In the meantime, may all that is tangled and perplexing and disappointing in our life drive us nearer to the Lord of peace. Our troubles down here so often arise from a partial knowledge. We see only a little bit at a time of God's plan and purpose; and the way it is all being worked out unrolls but slowly. Did we know more, and especially did we know all, our fears and regrets would be gone. Those early disciples were troubled because their Lord was going away. This is why He prefaced His last discourse with the words, "Let not your heart be troubled." Yet had they known all the advantages which would accrue from His leaving them, they would have rejoiced instead of having mourned.   *Russell Elliott.*

> He writes in characters too grand
> For our short sight to understand;
> We catch but broken strokes, and try
> To fathom all the mystery
> Of withered hopes, of death, or life,
> The endless way, the useless strife—
> But there, with larger, clearer sight,
> We shall see this—His way was right.
>
> Will not the end explain
> The crosses endeavor, earnest purpose foiled,
> The strange bewilderment of good work spoiled,
> The clinging weariness, the inward strain—
>   Will not the end explain?

MARCH 20

For we know that if our earthly house of this tabernacle were dissolved, we have a building of God, an house not made with hands, eternal in the heavens (2 Cor. 5:1).

A few days before his death, Dr. F. B. Meyer wrote a very dear friend these words: "I have just heard, to my great surprise, that I have but a few days to live. It may be that before this reaches you, I shall have entered the palace. Don't trouble to write. *We shall meet in the morning.*"

IN THE BEAUTIFUL MORNING

The storm and the darkness—the desolate night—
But the ship saileth sure, and the harbor's in sight;
  And a melody swells
  From the chime o' the bells;—
"Home in the beautiful morning."

O, long was the seaway, with billows to breast;
But we dreamed on those billows of havens of rest;
  O'er the ocean's sad knells
  Still the chime o' the bells—
"Home in the beautiful morning."

'Mid the wrecks that were tossed by the storm and the strife
We had drifted so far from the love that is life;
  But the bells o'er the foam,
  Ever singing of home—
"Home in the beautiful morning."

O, storm, and black billows, not hopeless, we roam,
For love guides the ship to the white shores of home;
  And the melody swells
  From the jubilant bells—
"Home in the beautiful morning."
           Frank L. Stanton.

MARCH 21

And the city lieth foursquare, . . . and the gates of it shall not be shut at all by day: for there shall be no night there (Rev. 21:16, 25).

For the child of God, all long, straight roads, however dusty, lead to the Golden City; the sure anticipation, therefore, of the goal, which must be a happy one, since God is God, and our trust that He is bringing us thither by the shortest and wisest path, should gild with the light of expectant hope the tedium and monotony of the present.

MORNING-LAND

"Some day," we say, and turn our eyes
Toward the fair hills of Paradise;
Some day, some time, a sweet new rest
Shall blossom, flower-like, in each breast,
Some day, some time, our eyes shall see
The faces kept in memory;
Some day their hands shall clasp our hand,
Just over in the Morning-land—
O Morning-land. O Morning-land.   *Edward H. Phelps.*

MARCH 22

While we look not at the things which are seen, but at the things which are not seen (2 Cor. 4:18).

We speak of snow as of an image of death. It may be that; but it hides the everlasting life always under its robe—the life to be revealed in due time, when all cold shadows shall melt away before the ascending sun, and we shall be, not unclothed, but clothed upon, and mortality shall be swallowed up of life.

Robert Collyer.

UNDER THE SNOW

It is pleasant to think, just under the snow,
    That stretches so bleak and blank and cold,
Are beauty and warmth that we cannot know—
    Green fields and leaves and blossoms of gold.

Yes, under this frozen and dumb expanse,
    Ungladdened by bee or bird or flower,
A world where the leaping fountains glance,
    And the buds expand, is waiting its hour.

It is hidden now; not a glimmer breaks
    Through the hard blue ice and the sparkling drift,
The world shrinks back from the downy flakes
    Which out of the folds of night-cloud sift.

But as fair and real a world it is
    As any that rolls in the upper blue;
If you wait, you will hear its melodies,
    And see the sparkle of fount and dew.

And often now when the skies are wild,
   And hoarse and sullen the night winds blow.
And lanes and hollows with drifts are piled,
   I think of the violets under the snow.

I look in the wild-flower's tremulous eye,
   I hear the chirp of the ground bird brown;
A breath from the budding grove steals by,
   And the swallows are dipping above the town.

So there, from the outer sense concealed,
   It lies, shut in by a veil of snow;
But there, to the inward eye revealed,
   Are boughs that blossom, and flowers that glow.

The lily shines on its bending stem,
   The crocus opens its April gold,
And the rose up-tosses it diadem
   Against the floor of the winter's cold.

And that other world, to my soul I say,
   That veiled and mystic world of the dead,
Is no farther away on any day
   Than the lilies just under the snow we tread.

T. Hempstead.

MARCH 23

He shall come down like rain upon the mown grass (Psalm 72:6).

Amos speaks of the king's mowings. Our King has many scythes, and is perpetually mowing His lawns. The musical tinkle of the whetstone on the scythe portends the cutting down of myriads of green blades, daisies, and other flowers. Beautiful as they were in the morning, within an hour or two they lie in long, faded rows.

Thus in human life we make a brave show, before the scythe of pain, the shears of disappointment, the sickle of death.

There is no method of obtaining a velvety lawn but by repeated mowings; and there is no way of developing tenderness, evenness, sympathy, but by the passing of God's scythes. How constantly the Word of God compares man to grass, and His glory to its flower! But when grass is mown, and all the tender shoots are bleeding, and desolation reigns where flowers were bursting, it is the most acceptable time for showers of rain falling soft and warm.

O soul, thou hast been mown! Time after time the King has come to thee with His sharp scythe. Do not dread the scythe—it is sure to be followed by the shower.   *F. B. Meyer.*

> When across the heart deep waves of sorrow
>   Break, as on a dry and barren shore;
> When hope glistens with no bright tomorrow,
>   And the storm seems sweeping evermore;
>
> When the cup of every earthly gladness
>   Bears no taste of the life-giving stream;
> And high hopes, as though to mock our sadness,
>   Fade and die as in some fitful dream,
>
> Who shall hush the weary spirit's chiding?
>   Who the aching void within shall fill?
> Who shall whisper of a peace abiding,
>   And each surging billow calmly still?
>
> Only He whose wounded heart was broken
>   With the bitter cross and thorny crown;
> Whose dear love glad words of joy had spoken,
>   Who His life for us laid meekly down.

MARCH 24

Fear thou not, for I am with thee (Isa. 41:10).

A MISSIONARY UNAFRAID

John W. Vinson was captured by bandits in China not long ago and finally shot to death when physically unable to accompany them further. He was lately out of a hospital and was still weak and ill when captured, but the bandits took his overcoat from him, and when found, the body was clad only in pajamas and coat.

A Chinese girl told of the bandits threatening him with guns. "Aren't you afraid?" they asked him. "No," he answered. "I'm not afraid. If you shoot me I will go straight to Heaven. My loving Lord Jesus is waiting for me there."

> Afraid? Of what?
> To feel the spirit's glad release?

To pass from pain to perfect peace,
The strife and strain of life to cease?
    Afraid—of that?

    Afraid? Of what?
Afraid to see the Saviour's face,
To hear His welcome, and to trace
The glory gleam from wounds of grace?
    Afraid—of that?

    Afraid? Of what?
A flash—a crash—a pierced heart;
Darkness—light—O heaven's art!
A wound of His a counterpart!
    Afraid—of that?

    Afraid? Of what?
To enter into Heaven's rest,
And yet to serve the Master blest,
From service good to service best?
    Afraid—of that?

    Afraid? Of what?
To do by death what life could not—
Baptize with death a stony plot,
Till souls shall blossom from that spot?
    Afraid—of that?   *E. H. Hamilton.*

MARCH 25

And there appeared an angel unto Him from heaven, strengthening Him (Luke 22:43).

An angel ministered to our Lord when in Gethsemane He wrestled with His great and bitter sorrow. What a benediction to the mighty Sufferer was in the soft gliding to His side of that gentle presence, in the touch of that soothing, supporting hand laid upon Him, in the comfort of that gentle voice thrilling with sympathy as it spoke its strengthening message of love! Was it a mere coincidence that just at that time and in that place the radiant messenger came? No, it is always so. Angels choose such occasions to pay their visits to men.

    With silence only as their benediction,
      God's Angels come;

Where, in the shadow of a great affliction
   The soul sits dumb.

MARCH 26

The righteous is taken away from the evil to come (Isa. 57:1).

Often, when we can see no love or kindness or wisdom in these early graves, it is because the morrow to us is mercifully veiled. Who can tell, if the loved and early lost had been spared, what trials might have been in reserve for them?—aye more, what sins and temptations might have overtaken them? God, who forsees all, graciously saved a heritage of sorrow by an early removal. He "hastened their escape from the windy storm and tempest." Better the brief loan, with all its hallowed, undarkened memories, than the prolonged life, with its possible evils. Better the lamb early taken from the fold, with its fleece unstained, than left footsore and fleece-torn, to pine on blighted herbage, and wander amid dry and deserted channels.

Oh, how many a bitter tear-drop would be dried, and broken heart solaced and comforted, if, remembering all the perils of this world of sin and suffering, and with the bright retrospect of lives suddenly cut short, we would listen to the utterance of Isaiah like a sweet chime wafted from the Temple of Heaven—"The righteous is taken away from *the evil to come.*"

> My darling boy, so early snatched away
>   From arms still seeking thee in empty air,
> That thou shouldst come to me I do not pray,
>   Lest, by thy coming, heaven should be less fair.
>
> Stay, rather, in perennial flower of youth,
>   Such as the Master, looking on, must love;
> And send to me the Spirit of the truth,
>   To teach me of the wisdom from above.
>
> Beckon to guide my thoughts, as stumblingly
>   They seek the kingdom of the undefiled;
> And meet me at the gateway with thy key,
>   The unstained spirit of a little child,   *Dr. Peabody.*

"Our children gone home": that, in the language of angels, is the meaning of early deaths.

Because I live, ye shall live also (John 14:19).

Very beautiful, is it not?—the picture of the opening springtime which we gather from our Bible, catching here a glimpse and there a glimpse as it lies reflected in the song of psalmist and prophet, and of Jesus, who had so often watched it as a boy on the hills of Galilee. Doubtless He used to go out to gather early lilies, and note the green garments of the fresh young grass. Ten million tiny strugglers on our hills and in our fields today are trying to show us that ours, too, is holy land. The flowers have begun to greet us in our walks—dumb angels, with faces all ashine with the glad tidings that the Saviour-season hath arisen. Thank God for the resurrection thoughts which the spring months bring to us! We die to live again. We die that we may live again. Nothing is quickened save it die. Mortality is the condition of immortality. What echoes we have wakened of this truth! The opening spring prints it off on every hillside in illuminated text of leaf and flower. We find, as always with these central facts of nature, that the best and highest meaning of the truth belongs to ourselves—so completely is a man a part of all, so completely is all represented in man. Our word "resurrection" seems to concentrate the history of the universe, to whisper the secret of the life of God.

Rev. W. C. Gannett.

When we have passed into the twilight of life, and our sun seems to be setting, let us call back, "I live!"

He sitteth on the waterfloods (Psalm 29:10—P. B. V.).

The waves," says Chrysostom, "are many, and the storm is furious; but I fear not to be drowned, for I stand upon a Rock."

> "He sitteth on the waterfloods"; across the storm
>   swept tide
> I hear His voice, as in the secret place in Him I hide;

And though the waters roar and toss, and though the
waves roll high,
I will not fear, for Faith can hear, His whispered, "It is I."

"He sitteth on the waterfloods"; they cannot sweep away
That which is built upon the Rock and there I stand
to-day.
The Rock of Ages is my home, and in that Rock I hide,
My resting place—the heart of God, my Saviour's
riven side.

"He sitteth on the waterfloods"; therefore I cannot fear,
For through the raging storm I feel and know that He
is near;
Nothing can touch me but His will, and none can do
me harm;
He lets me prove how real and deep is God's unfailing
calm.

"He sitteth on the waterfloods"; and if to-day I stand
In the storm area, He is there, my Pilot close at hand,
To guide me through the raging flood that worketh out
His will,
And well I know my listening heart will hear His,
"Peace be still."

"He sitteth on the waterfloods," and so I calmly wait
God's time to end the stormy strife, He never is too late.
"Clear shining after rain," will come, after the storm
a calm,
And tears will make a rainbow fair, and sorrow end
in psalm.   *L. A. B. S.*

MARCH 29 ———————————————————

*Thy God hath sent forth strength for thee (Psalm 68:28). Prayer Book
Version.*

M y soul, why art thou perplexed about the future? Seest thou
clouds in to-morrow's sky which thy present strength is
inadequate to meet? God has not given thee thy present strength
to meet the future, but to meet the present. When thy morrow
shall become thy day thou shalt learn thy power over it. Why art
thou distressed about the unborn sorrow? Thou thyself art born
anew for each new day. Thine armour is freshly burnished to fight

each rising sun. In the hour of battle thou wilt laugh at the memory of thy fears. Thou wilt say even of the last enemy that shall be conquered, "Oh, death! where is thy sting? Oh, grave! where is thy victory!" Thou shalt marvel at thyself when thou passes through the valley; thou shalt tread it so lightly, so easily. Thou shalt ask, "Can this be death?"

Thou shalt wonder to hear its desert break into singing, to see its wilderness blossom like the rose. Thou shalt be surprised to find so many lights gleaming in the valley. But the lights will not be in the valley but in thee. God will illuminate thee for the dark day, and what shadows shall abide the blaze of His illumination? The light will not come till the shades come. Weaken not thy spirit by forebodings before battle, for in a moment, in the twinkling of an eye, when the battle-trump shall sound, thy power shall be raised incorruptible, and "as thy days, so shall thy strength be."

George Matheson.

I am tired, Lord: let me furl my sail,
I hear thro' the mists how the sad waves wail,
My heart is quailing, and sick with fear,
Ask me no more on yon course to steer.

    Child, take this word again for Me;
    As thy days, so shall thy strength be.

Lord, the storm is o'er—we have ridden it well,
Through all its tossings no harm befell,
'Twas Thine hand upon the helm, I know,
But the track is so lonely whereon we go!

    For the lonely hour, child, trust in Me;
    As thy days, so shall thy strength be.

The canvas is torn, and the rigging rent,
While I see the white sails gleam content
'Neath the golden light on a sheltered bay;
Let me drop my anchor there, Lord, I pray.

    Child, thou must leave the choice to Me;
    As thy days, so shall thy strength be;

Lord, the night is coming—I fear, I fear!
The roar of the breakers is drawing near.
And I cannot turn my bark aside;
Now must I perish at eventide?

They shall never perish who trust in Me;
As thy days, so shall thy strength be;

The billows are past and the harbour won—
We saw in the gleam of the setting sun,
The waters of peace that bark enfold,
And bear it afar into joys untold,

Now heart, be strong to ride life's sea,
As thy days, so shall thy strength be.

The Twilight Hour.

MARCH 30

When thou wast weary with the length of the way thou didst not say "There is no hope," but there did come a quickening of thy strength; therefore thou didst not faint (Isa. 67:10).

Do not cast a mournful look at the tombstone. The angel is already appointed who is to roll it away. And who shall describe the rapture with which you will gaze at the wonderfully glorious being who will then spring up from that corruptible grain of wheat which you with so many tears have committed to the earth? Do not look at your fatherless children with an expression of deep grief. They are more than ever the Lord's children now— the heritage of Him who drew the little children towards Him and blessed them. Neither should you fear the heavy burden of your cares, the difficulties that may arise, the dangers that may threaten; nor yet your own weakness, your want of wisdom, your short-sightedness, your lack of that strong army which hitherto supported you so faithfully. All your difficulties will pass away like a cloud, and you will find that as your day is so will your strength be. Only keep your eyes fixed upon Jesus, who goeth before you and will clear the way step by step. If a wall should rise, He will make you to leap over it. If a troop should come up, He will make you to run through it. Only keep close to Him, and, weak woman though you be, you will, with your children by your side, run and not be weary, walk and not faint.   *Benjamin Orme.*

JUST ONE STEP MORE!

Just one step more! Although your footsteps falter.
Just one step more! it will not be in vain.

Press bravely on, God's promise cannot alter,
   Strength day by day—peace follows after pain.

Just one step more! Look up! the clouds are breaking,
   Across the hilltop comes the radiant morn.
Just one step more, brave heart! new hope is waking,
   New joy, new courage, each new day, are born.
                                             Kate Hopkins

The way is long, my child, but it shall be
Not one step longer than is best for thee;
And thou shalt know at last, when thou shalt stand
Close to the gate, how I did take thy hand,
And quick and straight led thee to heaven's gate, My
child!

MARCH 31

Thou remainest (Lam. 5:19).

We can pass to and fro to one another the watchword through the shadows: "THOU REMAINEST," and therefore the eternal morning is on the way. Therefore we who trust in Christ, will yet be satisfied as we have never been on earth, satisfied—the broken ties re-knit, the wounds of life healed, the love which passed from earth given back, the sorrows as a dream when one awaketh. And Christ has done this for us! Do not call death the end—it is the beginning. "I am come that they might have life and that they might have it more abundantly."

THOU REMAINEST

When from my life the old-time joys have vanished—
   Treasures, once mine, I may no longer claim—
This truth may feed my hungry heart and famished—
   Lord, THOU REMAINEST! THOU art still the same!

When streams have dried, those streams of glad
      refreshing—
   Friendships so blest, so pure, so rich, so free;
When sun-kissed skies give place to clouds depressing—
   Lord, THOU REMAINEST! Still my heart hath THEE.

When strength hath failed, and feet, now worn and weary,
   On gladsome errands may no longer go;

Why should I sigh, or let the days be dreary?
　　Lord, THOU REMAINEST! Couldst Thou more bestow?

Thus through life's days—who'er or what may fail me—
　　Friends, friendships, joys—in small or great degree,
Songs may be mine—no sadness need assail me,
　　Since THOU REMAINEST, and my heart hath THEE.

J. Danson Smith.

APRIL 1 ────────────────────────────────

The oil of joy for mourning; the garment of praise for the spirit of heaviness (Isa. 61:3).

O I am so sure we have never fully comprehended all that is coming back to us! I wonder how the angels can endure our lack of faith. We do not act so in regard to the spring; we know it will come back, and we say to the March winds, "Blow on; your time is short! April and May are coming." But, alas! we do not act that way about the winter of the heart. We put on our mourning, and we look and act as if it were all gone forever; when, instead of that, spring is coming back, and the voices of nature, and the look of nature, all say, "Resurrection! Resurrection!" We do not heed. Our eyes are too dim with weeping; we have been so accustomed to looking down instead of looking up, that we do not see God's face or hear His voice in nature all around us. Now, this month, with the beautiful Easter in it, calls for hope; and will you not leave your tombs of sorrow and come forth to life and usefulness? We must leave our graves and graveclothes, and let others say of us in our measure, "She is risen! She is alive; a new creature!"

Weighted wings cannot soar.

APRIL 2 ────────────────────────────────

The memory of the just is blessed (Prov. 10:7).

TREASURES OF THE HEART

I n one of our magazines, the writer tells of a visit she once paid to the home of a man who had for years given himself to the development of a great mine in the mountains of the West.

Fortune had favored him; he was now worth millions. With evident delight he showed his visitor through the rooms of his beautiful mansion, dwelling with peculiar pleasure upon the many pieces of furniture he had gathered at great cost from lands far and near.

At last he led the way to his private study; and now a marked change came over his manner. No longer was he a man of millions. For a moment he seemed to forget the mines of which he was master; it was nothing to him, now, that his wealth had made his name known far and wide; he was only a pilgrim on life's way resting for a while by a singing-brook.

"I wish to show you something," he said, a peculiar glow of joy lighting up his face, at the same time opening the door of a safe at the side of the room. Then he took out a little box, heavily bound with steel. Surely, the visitor thought, this must contain precious jewels. Such care would not otherwise be given to this casket. But when the lid was lifted, not sparkling gems from faraway mines, not glittering jewels, costly, and rare, met the lady's gaze, but a little, old gray shawl, fringed with black! As if the thing were prized beyond all he had shown his visitors, he carefully unfolded the shawl.

"My Mother's shawl!" he said, softly. "She wore this about her shoulders; and when she died and the things were divided among us, I asked for this as my share! It never has left me. When I had nothing in which to carry it, during the hard days out there, I wore it folded across my chest, under my shirt! It kept me straight! It is going to lead me to Heaven! I do not know how nor when, but I can bank on it as a certainty. It is so full of home-memories that I never have been able to get away from them! It is mother's whole personality concentrated! She always made the best of me, even in my wrong-doing! She has kept on making the best of me ever since! Mother has fallen asleep, but I expect to meet her some day!"

> Ah, golden yesterdays now laid to sleep,
> What everlasting fragrance still ye keep!

APRIL 3 _____

Hope thou in God: for I shall yet praise Him (Psalm 42:5).

I have seen a farmer drive his plow-share through the velvet greensward, and it looked like a harsh and cruel process; but the farmer's eye foresaw the springing blades of wheart and knew that within a few months that torn soil would laugh with a golden harvest. Deep soul-plowings bring rich fruits of the Spirit. There are bitter mercies as well as sweet mercies; but they are all mercies, whether given in honey or given in wormwood. *Theodore Cuyler.*

Father, to Thee we look in all our sorrow.
    Thou art the fountain whence our healing flows;
Dark though the night, joy cometh with the morrow;
    Safely they rest who on Thy love respose.

When fond hopes fail, and skies are dark before us,
    When the vain cares that vex our life increase—
Comes with its calm the thought that Thou art o'er us,
    And we grow quiet, folded in Thy peace.

Nought shall affright us on Thy goodness leaning,
    Low in the heart faith singeth still her song;
Chastened by pain we learn life's deeper meaning,
    And in our weakness Thou dost make us strong.

Patient, O heart, though heavy be thy sorrows!
    Be not cast down, disquieted in vain;
Yet shalt thou praise Him when these darkened furrows,
    Where now He plougheth, wave with golden grain.
                                    Frederick L. Hosmer.

APRIL 4

Behold He cometh. . . . Watch ye therefore. (Rev. 1:7; Luke 21:36).

Oh, the dear dead days of the long ago! They went down in the glowing West and with tear-blinded eyes we watched them receding and ending. But we are moving towards the East. And a Day is about to break. Oh my aching heart cried, "God, how much off is the night?" and whispering through the darkness came sacred melody, "The morning cometh." Not "mornings" are coming, no, just *Morning!* For never then shall the twilight deepen into the dusk and the dusk be lost in the great Darkness; for that Morning of which God has told me is the Dawn of the Day whose Light shall never fade nor pass away, when we shall live in the Light of His countenance with our Friends at Home.

W. B. Hinson

It may be in the evening—
  When the work of the day is done,
And you have time to sit in the twilight
  And watch the sinking sun.
While the long bright day dies slowly
  Over the sea—
And the hour grows quiet and holy
  With thoughts of Me;—
While you hear the village children
  Passing along the street,
Among those thronging footsteps
  May come the sound of My feet:
Therefore I tell you: Watch!
  By the light of the evening star,
When the room is growing dusky
  As the clouds afar;
Let the door be on the latch
  In your home.
For it may be through the gloaming
  I Will Come!

It may be in the morning,
  When the sun is bright and strong,
And the dew is glittering sharply
  Over the little lawn;
When the waves are laughing loudly
  Along the shore,
And the little birds are singing sweetly
  About the door;
With the long day's work before you,
  You rise up with the sun,
And the neighbors come and talk a little
  Of all that must be done;
But remember that I may be the next
  To come in at the door,
To call you from all your busy work
  For evermore;
As you work your heart must watch,
  For the door is on the latch
    In your room;
And it may be in the morning
  I Will Come!

So I am watching quietly,
  Every day;
Whenever the sun shines brightly,
  I rise and say—
"Surely it is the shining of His face!"
And look unto the gates of His high place
  Beyond the sea;
For I know He is coming shortly
  To summon me;
And when a shadow falls across the window
  Of my room,
Where I am working my appointed task,
I lift my head to watch the door, and ask
  If He is come;
And the angel answers sweetly
  In my home,
"Only a few more shadows,
  And He Will Come!"   *Selected.*

APRIL 5 _____

The Father hath not left me alone (John 8:29).

The Christ on the Cross appeared to be deserted by His Father.
You may be tempted to think that you, too, have been
deserted. Our Lord's supreme triumph consisted in His implicit
trust in His Father through the shadows.

Your victory will be won on the same road. When He had
endured the loss of everything that could be taken from Him, and
still held fast to His God, He entered into His eternal glory. Your
separation from your dearest one is for a short time only. Trust
God; hold fast; the reunion of Paradise is just beyond.

                                        Frederick G. Budlong.

  Now, has the shadow touched your face?
    Are the days dark? the prospects gray?
  O heart, be brave! The time of grace
    Can never pass from you away.
  Your Friend is tender, wise and true
      For love of you.

  He walked for you earth's changeful ways,
    He bore for you the lonely hour,

100

He lived for you through toilsome days,
   He met for you the tempter's power,
And joy through sorrow this Friend knew,
    For love of you.

APRIL 6

The Lord shall give thee rest from thy sorrow and from thy fear (Isa. 14:3).

THE HUSH-TIMES OF LIFE

There is help in the still places of life, its retreats, its withdrawals for communion with God and one's own soul. Bereavement is one of the still places of life; disappointment is another; pain is another. Every time of trial, every time of spiritual awakening, is a time of withdrawal for the soul, when it meets with the angel of God and wrestles with him for a blessing. It is in the still places of life that we learn more perfectly God's will concerning us.

James Buckham.

Be still, O trembling heart of mine,
   And be thou blest;
There is a place of love divine,
Where thou canst lay that head of thine—
   Upon His breast:
Why shouldst thou still thy burdens bear?—
He lives thy sorrows all to share;
Then cast on Him thine ev'ry care,
   And be at rest.   *Dr. R. E. Neighbour.*

APRIL 7

Bear ye one another's burdens and so fulfil the law of Christ (Gal. 6:2).

"My burden is too heavy, Lord,"
   I tremblingly said.
"I can no farther carry it!"
   And tears I shed.
Then came a sudden cry for help
   From one sore pressed;
I ran to seek him, gladly gave
   Him of my best.
Then thought I of my heavy burden—

But, lo! 'twas gone!
The gloom and doubt had vanished quite
And Love's light shone.

A PRAYER

The way is long, our Father, and sometimes very weary. Start us forth, each day, with fresh courage and whisper in our hearts a little song to gladden our step as we take up our burdens anew. May we never be too laden with personal troubles to carry balm of sympathy for friend and foe. Above all grant us the gift of clear vision that we may pierce the doubts and fears of the passing moment and always dwell with unfaltering confidence on the ultimate fact of Thy love.

> ....May I reach
> That purest heaven, be to other souls
> The cup of strength in some great agony.   *George Eliot.*

APRIL 8 ─────────────────────────────────

I will lead them in paths that they have not known. (Isa. 42:16).

I do not know what is around that next turn in this winding trail of life, but I know this, whatever there is around that corner, I shall have my hand in Another's hand when I go and face it. And if I feel a little bit disturbed, I shall move my finger around in the palm of that hand till I find the scar, and then I shall know that Jesus Christ, who on the cross was wounded for my sins, is not going to leave me no matter what corner I go around on the winding road of life.   *W. B. Hinson.*

> If thou wouldst walk with me,
> Take up thy cross:
> I carried Mine—is thine, then, heavier?
> Step for step, I walk with thee:
> Lay thy tired hand in Mine;
> Love bare for this alone—
> The prints that press thy palm—
> That I and thou together mightest walk
> Thy Calvary!

Every branch in me that beareth fruit, He purgeth it, that it may bring forth more fruit (John 15:2).

It takes a thousand buds to make one American Beauty rose, consequently nine hundred and ninety-nine of the them must be suppressed. Think of this, dear one, when billows of trouble overwhelm you, and God seems to have hidden His face. He has in view the height to which He intends to carry the culture of your soul. He has in mind a work which your loftiest ambition has never even thought of. He wants some heroes and leaders for His work—men and women that can stand pruning and transplanting—and He may want *you*. Then think of the American Beauty and bloom out for God.

DISBUDDING

"Disbudding consists in removing the buds before they have time to grow into young branches. It is a species of pruning which has for its object not only the training but also economy with regard to the resources of a tree, in order that there may be a greater supply of nourishment for the development of those buds which are allowed to remain.

"If the roots are capable of absorbing a given quantity of nutritive matter for the supply of all the buds upon a stem, and if a number of those buds be removed, it must be evident that those which remain will be able to draw a greater supply of sap and grow more vigorously than they otherwise would have done. This fact has furnished the idea of DISBUDDING. It has been proved that a judicious thinning of the buds after they have been unfolded in spring is a great utility." *English Encyclopedia.*

We . . . shall be caught up together with them . . . wherefore comfort one another with these words (1 Thess. 4:17, 18).

MY DREAM OF HEAVEN

What Heaven is, I know not; but I long have dreamed of its purple hills and its field of light, blossoming with immortal beauty; of its brooks of laughter, and its rivers of song and its palace of eternal love. I long have dreamed that every bird which sings its life out here, may sing forever there in the tree of life; and every consecrated soul that suffers here may rest among its flowers, and live and love forever. I long have dreamed of opal towers and burnished domes; but what care I for gate of pearl or street of gold, if I can meet the loved ones who have blessed me here, and see the glorified faces of father and mother and the boy brother who died among the bursting buds of hope; and take in my arms again, my baby, who fell asleep ere his little tongue had learned to lisp, "Our Father who art in Heaven." What care I for crown of stars and harp of gold, if I can love and laugh and sing with them forever in the smile of my Saviour and my God!

"Bob" Taylor.

I know we shall behold them raised, complete,
The dust swept from their beauty, glorified.

Elizabeth Barrett Browning.

APRIL 11 ───────────────────────────────

That we through patience and comfort of the Scriptures might have hope (Rom 15:4).

Nearly one year ago," wrote one bereaved, "the dearest mother in the world, to me, passed to the life beyond. At the time I said 'she died,' now I know this is not true. I mourned as one without hope. She was all I had, and I refused to be comforted—yes, that is the word, *'refused.'* I would not admit the possibility of comfort. One day, after an especially trying time, I was impelled to open the big Bible which mother always kept on a small stand by her chair. She was a partial invalid, though you would never have suspected it from the cheer of her voice and her sunny smile; and often, when things seemed harder than usual, or she needed guidance and encouragement, she would open her 'Book of Comfort' as she called it, and read the first verse or chapter that caught her eye. Perhaps it was this memory that led me to do the same thing; at all events I did it. And there was the wonderful story of the Resurrection, the place marked by a little slip of worn, yellowed paper, evidently years old.

"I read it once, twice, many times, and my heart grew strangely lighter. It was a message, not from the grave, but from a loving, living mother to her child. The 'miss' was still there, as we must miss one who has been called to another field of action or some far country here, but I felt I could never grieve again as I had done; and as I sat there gazing at the open Bible, the thought came to me that I should pass the message—mother's message—on. Had it come to me in another way probably it would not have meant to me what it did; I might not have heeded it at all. As it was I could not help it. And I have proved its truth—the reality of it. My faith in the goodness of God, in the 'life more abundant' promised by the Master, has grown wonderfully; I cannot disbelieve if I would."

Selected.

One of the sweet old chapters,
  After a day like this—
The day brought tears and troubles,
  The evening brings no kiss,
Nor rest in the arms I long for—
  Rest and refuge and home;
Grieved and lonely and weary,
  Unto the Book I come.

One of the sweet old chapters,
  That always will avail,
So full of heavenly comfort,
  When earthly comforts fail,
A sweet and blessed message
  From God to His children dear,
So rich in precious promises,
  So full of love and cheer.

One of the sweet old chapters,
  When comes the lonely night
When all things earthly fail us;
  And tears have dimmed our sight,
This only can relieve us,
  A message from above,
Then we can rest so sweetly,
  In faith, and hope, and love.

Selected.

His touch has still its ancient power
No word from Him shall fruitless fall.

Like as a Father (Psalm 103:13).

My little four-year-old boy lay sick and reckless, fever-flushed at night, while I lay beside him in the dark. Every now and then the child half waking, would speak out, "Fadder!" "Yes, dear," the answer came, "Hello, Fadder," the little one would say and drop again to sleep. Thus it is that we, children all, fever-flushed and troubled, as if in dreams, call out "Father" in the dark. He answers, "Yes, dear, I am here," and in Him we find peace and rest.   *George L. Perin.*

"Like as a father,"—Oh, sometimes
    My heart is very sore,
Longing for one now gone—it seems
    I want him more and more!
But only in my dreams he lives,
    And oft I wake to hear
A voice—my own—cry out in vain
    For "Father! Father dear!"

Then come those blessed, healing words,
    And many, many times,
They've been to me like music sweet
    From heaven's echoing chimes:
"Like as a father"—Oh, it's just
    The love I want and need,
And well I know His list'ning ear
    My faintest call will heed.

"A Father to the fatherless,"—
    That's what He says He'll be;
A Father tender, strong and true—
    That's what He is to me!
A Father who knows all my heart,
    Yet loves me just the same;
Oh, do you wonder that I love
    To call Him this dear name?   *Edith Lillian Young.*

I give unto them eternal life (John 10:28).

We have the promises of God, as thick as daisies in summer meadows, that death, which men most fear, shall be to us the most blessed of experiences, if we trust in Him. Death is unclasping; joy breaking out in the desert; the heart come to its blossoming time! Do we call it dying when the bud bursts into flower? *H. W. Beecher.*

SEED CORN INTO GRAIN

We are too stupid about death. We will not learn
How it is wages paid to those who earn;
How it is the gift for which on earth we yearn—
   To be set free from bondage to the flesh;
How it is turning seed corn into grain,
How it is winning heaven's eternal gain,
How it means freedom evermore from pain,
   How it untangles every mortal mesh.

We are so selfish about death. We count our grief
Far more than we consider their relief,
When the great Reaper gathers in the sheaf,
   No more to know the seasons' constant change;
And we forget that it means only life—
Life with all joy, peace, rest and glory rife,
The victory won, and ended all the strife,
   And heaven no longer far away or strange.
The Watchman-Examiner.

APRIL 14 ———————————————————————————

Take root downward, and bear fruit upward (Isa. 37:31).

Why is it that the mountain hemlocks can attain such stateliness in spite of fierce winter gales and crushing snows? If you look at one of them closely you will see that it has foliage almost as delicate as a fir, its dark needles being as dainty as fairy feathers. Yet if you try to break a twig or a bough you will learn that therein lies the strength and the tenacious power of the hemlock. It will bend and yield—but it will not break. Winds may whip and toss it this way and that, but they cannot break it—nor can elements, however fierce, pull its roots out of the ground. Secure and undaunted it stands. For months it may have its graceful form held down by a mighty weight of snow, but when the warm breath of summer winds, and the melting influence of summer's sun, relieve it of its burden, it straightens up, as proud and as noble as it was before.

Beautiful, wonderful hemlock of the mountains—what a lesson you bring to us! Though we may be storm-tossed and bent by the winds of sorrow, we need not be crushed and broken, if our souls are anchored to the Rock of Ages.

STRENGTH

Lord, make me strong! Let my soul rooted be
    Afar from vales of rest,
    Flung close to heaven upon a great Rock's breast,
Unsheltered and alone, but strong in Thee.

What though the lashing tempests leave their scars?
    Has not the Rock been bruised?
    Mine, with the strength of ages deep infused,
To face the storms and triumph with the stars!

Lord, plant my spirit high upon the crest
    Of Thine eternal strength!
    Then, though life's breaking struggles come at length,
Their storms shall only bend me to Thy breast.

Dorothy Clark Wilson

Suffer and be strong, is the pilgrim's watchword.

APRIL 15 ———————————————————————————

Let them also that love Thy name be joyful in Thee (Psalm 5:11).

Did you ever hear a robin sing?—or rather, I mean, did you ever listen to a robin's song? . . . He sang about the sunshine breaking through the cloud; about the rainbow smiling over the weary, rainclogged earth; about the mild, still, hazy autumn days that soothe the September gale to sleep; he sang of the glory of the dawn after the dark night; sang, too about the crumbs that little children strew upon the ground when it is covered with snow; and about the moist, warm wind that releases the frozen streams, and unwraps the young buds from their winter swathing bands. And because he sang in praise of all these sweet things, and yet had known and felt all the sad and gloomy ones that came before, his song was so cheerful and yet so touching, so contented and yet so plaintive, that none might hear it unmoved, or ponder on it untaught.

I heard a robin singing in the rain,
Its bird-soul pleading low. Again, again
It called to those sore-spent with Life's dull sting
To open their soul-windows to the Spring.
Surely it seemed those vibrant notes might lend
Fresh courage; my tired heart defend
'Gainst utter numbness. Yet all sound
First touched my senses, sorrow-bound, in vain,
E'en as the tranquil cadence of the rain
Upon a home deserted, lone, remote.
And then there fell one low, pulsating note,
That jarred a slumbering hurt and freshly smote
My soul, awoke the old, insistent pain;—
New consciousness and heart to fight again. *Mary Baldwin.*

APRIL 16

For the Lord shall be thine everlasting light, and the days of thy mourning shall be ended (Isa. 60:20).

A VISION BY THE SEA

I pitched my tent one summer night on a point of land extending far out into the sea. As darkness settled down upon me, the storm-clouds that had been gathering all that day came rolling in upon the land. The wild winds swept the sea, hill, and vale, while great angry waves dashed themselves in fury on the shore.

It was an appalling storm!

As I peered out of my tent into the blackness of the night I saw a great lighthouse lifting its golden beacon far into the clouds. All night long the storm raged. All night long that flaming signal was exalted far into the clouds!

But soon the morning dawned. That wild, tumultuous sea had now become an imperial highway of royal purple, flecked by golden flashlights sparkling in the pathway of the sun. Flocks fed in the valleys and along peaceful streams, while the flowers of the fields lifted their heads, still glistening with the tear-drops of the night, that they might be kissed by the lips of the rising sun.

A great fleet of vessels was moored under the shelter of yonder reef, having found its way into port by following the light through the storm. Their anchors were cast, their sails were furled. No need of the lighthouse now, for the sun had become the light thereof: the waves had ceased their troubling, and the sailors were at rest!

Oh, Beulah Land, sweet Beulah Land! Oh, Paradise, sweet Paradise! May we hold aloft the glorious light of the Gospel of Jesus Christ above the raging seas of time; that the storm-tossed mariners may find their way, by its rays, into the port of peace, where "the Lamb is the light thereof";—where "the wicked cease from troubling and the weary are at rest!"

Oh, Golden Day! Speed thou thy glorious coming!   *Selected.*

> Christian, confronted by a thousand waves
> And woes innumerable—Jesus saves!
> A whole Red Sea His fiat cleft in twain,
> And saints with Him still tread the untrodden main.
> Though flesh and heart both fail, yet onward, true,
> "Rock of my heart," O God, Thou'lt bear me through!
> Though my poor vessel reel, yet Heaven's own "Come!"
> Fresh drives her shining bulwarks through the foam,
> Urged by the magic mystery of Home.   *Rev. C. A. Fox.*

APRIL 17 _____

He careth (1 Peter 5:7).

One morning early I had a 'phone call. A husband and father had been slain in battle. I knew that home. There was a little Scotch wife in it, with four or five bairnies, and she was a good Christian woman. All the way to her house I kept asking God to give me some word to say to her. When she opened the door she looked suspicious at once. She said, "Preacher, why so early? Is my husband dead?"

I said, "Yes, he's dead."

She backed down the hall into a little dining room and the children came and gathered around her. One little girl said, "Mamma, is daddy dead?" And then they all sobbed when the mother replied, "Yes, they've killed him."

I couldn't do a thing but weep with them. After a while the woman looked up and said, "Preacher, do you think God Almighty knows about all this? Does God care?"

You may think that a strange way for a Christian to speak. But, friends, have not our hearts, too, been wrung at times with that cry of anguish on dark nights and in bitter experiences through which we have passed? As I stood there almost dumb in the presence of such grief, I remembered that Jesus, our precious Saviour, passed through a night of great sorrow and that He cried out in anguish, *"My God, my God, why?"* I am so glad that Jesus went through that experience, because I could then say to the little Scotch woman, "Yes, He knows. Don't you remember in that dark hour when He was hanging on the cross He said, *'My God, why hast thou forsaken me?'*"   *Dr. Philpott.*

Does Jesus care when I've said good-by
    To the dearest on earth to me,
When my sad heart aches, till it nearly breaks,
    Is it aught to Him? Does He see?

Oh, yes, He cares,
I know He cares,
His heart is touched with my grief;
Though the days be weary,
The long nights dreary,
I know my Saviour cares.

APRIL 18 ───────────────────────────────

There hath not failed one word of all his good promise (1 Kings 8:56).

Some day we shall understand that God has a reason in every NO which He speaks through the slow movement of life. "Somehow God makes up to us." How often, when His people are worrying and perlexing themselves about their prayers not being answered, is God answering them in a far richer way! Glimpses of this we see occasionally, but the full revelation of it remains for the future.

Oh, for the faith that does not make haste, but waits patiently for the Lord, waits patiently for the explanation that shall come in the end, at the revelation of Jesus Christ! When did God take anything from a man, without giving him manifold more in return? Suppose that the return had not been made immediately manifest, what then? Is today the limit of God's working time? Has He no provinces beyond this little world? Does the door of the grave open upon nothing but infinite darkness and eternal silence? Yet, even confining the judgment within the hour of this life, it is true that God never touches the heart with a trial without intending to bring in upon it some grander gift, some tenderer benediction.

He has attained to an eminent degree of Christian grace who knows how to wait.   *Selected.*

THE FOLDED PAGE

Up in the quaint old attic, as the raindrops pattered down,
And I sat conning over a school book—dusty, worn,
    and brown—
I came to a leaf that was folded, and marked in
    a childish hand,
"The teacher says to leave this now, 'Tis hard to
understand."

What was so hard? I wondered. I opened it with a smile.
Only to read, at the problem's end: We learned "why"
    after a while.
My tears fell thick as the raindrops then, up in the
    attic old,
As I thought of leaves that are "folded down" till the days
    of our lives are told.

One was folded there with a tender hand to the sound of
    summer rain;
When the dust of years lies thick above, will we open this
    page again?
And can we write with steady hand, and on our lips
    a smile,
"At last our Teacher told us "why," and we learned it—
    after a while!"

APRIL 19 _____

My people . . . have forgotten their resting place (Jer. 50:6).

It is poor relief from sorrow to fly to the distraction of the world; as well might a lost and weary bird, suspended over the abyss of the tempestuous ocean, seek a resting-place on the topmost wave, as the child of sorrow to seek a place of repose amid the bustling cares and intoxicating pleasures of earth and time.

"Art thou weary, art thou languid, art thou sore distrest?"
"Come to me," saith One—"and, coming, be at rest!"

"Hath He marks to lead me to Him—if He be my Guide?"
"His feet and hands are wound-prints, and His side?"

"Is there diadem, as monarch, that His brow adorns?"
"Yes; a crown, in very surety—but of thorns!"

"If I find Him, if I follow, what His guerdon here?"
"Many a sorrow, many a labor, many a tear!"

"If I still hold closely to Him, what hath He at last?"
"Sorrow vanquished, labor ended, Jordan past!"

"If I ask Him to receive me, will He say me nay?"
"Not till earth, and not till heaven pass away!"

"Tending, following, keeping, struggling, is He sure
   to bless?"
"Angels, martyrs, prophets, pilgrims, answer, Yes!"

Hymns of Consecration and Faith.

APRIL 20

Yet a little while (John 14:19).

THE MORROW

Underneath the green grass the little bulbs are talking, telling of the Spring so near at hand, telling of the sunshine, when upon their beautiful stems the glory will wave in the bright light, and the perfume fill all the garden and their many colored bells go ringing to the sparrow's note.

And underneath the green grass I heard a voice that cheered me. For I heard the dead—so men will call them, though the Great Christ called them the Sleepers—telling how the night of their Winter has well-nigh waned, and the morn of their resurrection is about to break, and their voices were jubilant and strong.

Underneath the green grass I heard a prophet saying, "The Winter's ravages in life will soon be lost in the glories of the Spring Time."

Yes, and distinctly as Israel heard Sinai's trumpet peal, and clearly as did John the call of the King through the surging waves about Patmos Isle, and surely as the Magdalene the tones of the Great Gardener, I heard a voice saying, "The Winter of the world is well worn away, and soon the great prophecies will attain their fulfilment; soon the Rose shall bloom where the hot sands have long swept; soon shall the Anthem swell where the sob has been bravely hushed; soon the scattered notes shall be gathered into the Eternal melody; soon the tired foot shall forget its weariness, as it presses the golden pave of the City of Light and Beauty; soon from the brow shall drop the thorn-crown and a halo of glory take its place; soon shall the hand that wielded the sword possess the palm branch of final victory; soon shall Canaan succeed the Desert, and Heaven glorify Earth and Time give place to Eternity, and God make all things new.   *Dr. Hinson.*

The heavens shall glow with splendor,
    But brighter far than they,
The saints shall shine in glory
    As Christ shall them array:
The beauty of the Saviour,
    Shall dazzle every eye,
    In the crowning day that's coming by and by.

Our pain shall then be over,
    We'll sin and sigh no more;
Behind us all of sorrow,
    And naught but joy before,
A joy in our Redeemer,
    As we to Him are nigh,
    In the crowning day that's coming by and by.

APRIL 21 ―――――――――――――――――――――――――

And my people shall dwell in a peaceable habitation. . . . and in quiet resting places; when it shall hail (Isa. 32:18, 19).

Have you ever seen men and women whom some disaster drove to a great act of prayer, and by and by the disaster was forgotten, but the sweetness of religion remained and warmed their souls? So have I seen a storm in later spring, and all was black, save where the lightning tore a cloud with thundering rent.

114

The winds blew and the rains fell, as though heaven had opened its windows. What a devastation there was! Not a spider's web that was out of doors escaped the storm, which tore up even the strong-branched oak. But ere long the lightning had gone by, the thunder was spent and silent, the rain was over, the western wind came up with its sweet breath, the clouds were chased away, and the retreating storm threw a scarf of rainbows over her fair shoulders and resplendent neck, and looked back and smiled, and so withdrew and passed out of sight. But for weeks long, the fields held up their hands full of ambrosial flowers, and all the summer through the grass was greener, the brooks were fuller, and the trees cast a more umbrageous shade, *because the storm passed by* —though all the rest of the earth had long ago forgotten the storm, its rainbows and its rain.   *Theodore Parker.*

> The storm had passed me, and I lay
> Upon the bosom of Life's ocean, derelict;
> Far off the thunder echoed, and beyond
> I heard the sullen roar of angry surf
> Beating a rock-bound shore; nor hope had I
> That ever ray of dawn could penetrate the gloom.
> At length a star appeared—and through the night
> A tender voice I heard: "Fear not! Thou art
> Not all bereft. My child, come thou to Me;
> When earthly joys take flight, true peace is born!"
> Then from the deeps of my unmeasured woe,
> Stretching my empty hands, to Him I cried;
> And when from the darkness unto light I turned—
>   Lo! it was day!   *Mary Lloyd McConnell.*

There are many people that have storms, but there are few who know how to put rainbows over them.

APRIL 22 _____

What I do thou knowest not now, but thou shalt know hereafter (John 13:7).

W e want to know more than the silent God deems it good to tell; to understand the "why" which He bids us wait to ask; to *see* the path which He has spread on purpose in the dark. The

Infinite Father does not stand by us to be catechised and to explain
Himself to our vain mind; He is here for our trust.

I CANNOT TELL

I cannot tell why life should thus be shorn—
  O, heart thus emptied be;
  Why stricken, broken, desolate, forlorn,
  Should be my life's decree:
  Yet—through my blinding tears I fain would trace
  The unchanged outline of Thy tender face.

I cannot tell what life shall henceforth be—
  So dark—this vale of tears:
  The change—to human loneliness—such agony—
  'Gainst life's past golden years:
  I only ask, while in this vale I stand,
  To feel the warm, dear pressure of Thy hand.

I cannot tell what stretching years may bring—
  Nor need I crave to know;
  E'en sorrows fount can be a hallowed thing,
  In place of bitter woe.
  Perhaps Thou hast some grace to yet impart—
  And I would find my refuge in Thy heart.

I cannot tell! Nor would I if I might!
  It would not COMFORT bring:
  My COMFORT comes through sheltering in the night
  'Neath Thy protecting wing.
  And so, my God—my King—my Guide—my Friend—
  My heart in Thee would hide it—till the End.
                                    J. Danson Smith.

APRIL 23

Consider Him . . . lest ye be wearied and faint in your minds (Heb. 12:3).

Remember, Christian, that even in your downcast moods and
in your darkest days, you are not severed from the company
of the great and the good. They are a great multitude, which no
man can number; and as they, too, go along their several ways,
beset by difficulties, wearied with toil, they seem to hold out to you
invisible hands to sympathy, and to bid you be of good cheer.
Nay, in a sense, you come nearer to that company by your very

116

sorrows: Elijah under the juniper tree; David breaking the night-silence of the wilderness of Judah with his moans and cries; the great Apostle of the Gentiles going wearily along the Appian Way; the "Man of Sorrows" Himself—these are your companions. Fear not, the darkness will ere long begin to melt. The day is already born. Plod on, poor pilgrim still, and let not faith die within thee. God has not forgotten thee.

I FEAR NOT!

Be strong and brave, My child!
  Step boldly on;
The way is rough, I know,
  The sunshine gone.
But in the Blest Beyond,
  All, all is peace;
There you shall know My will,
  There shall your sorrows cease!

Fear not, I hold thine hand
  In Mine, clasped tight.
Where'er My footsteps lead
  Can be no night;
For I have bridged the gulf
  Across the years,
Turning to joyous morn
  The night of sighs and tears.

No tongue can ever tell
  Or human heart conceive
What joys I have in store
  For all who now believe;
Hold on, My child, in faith—
  There dawns a perfect day,
When "that which is in part"
  Shall all be done away!

Phoebe Hadley.

APRIL 24

The Lord gave, and the Lord hath taken away (Job 1:21).

WE GIVE THEE BUT THINE OWN!

Can you rise to the sublime height of thinking that instead of reluctantly letting your dear one leave you, you have

actually given him to God for the more wonderful task of
Paradise? It will bring such content to your troubled spirit that you
can almost be glad to bear your loneliness in order that he may go
on into that richer service which you shall some day share.

I WOULD NOT GRIEVE TOO MUCH

I would not grieve too much. The Promise tells
   That rest is his who sleeps so sweetly there;
Beyond the dull, slow tolling of the bells
   Which marks his passing, life is free from care.

You would not mourn if one you love should rise
   To wear the royal purple and the crown,
Should gain the glory of the great and wise
   And put the tools of humble service down.

Suppose that life should call some friend you know
   Out of the ranks, and end his days of care,
You would rejoice and smile to see him go,
   Though you remained to work and struggle there.

So when death comes, though hard it seems to bear,
   And long the years with all their loneliness,
The loved one has been called away from care
   To high promotion, rest and happiness.   *Edgar Guest.*

God forbid that we should bury anything. There is no earth that
can touch my companion. There is no earth that can touch my
child. The jewel is not in the ground. The jewel is gone from the
casket, and I have buried the casket, not the jewel.

APRIL 25

For I know that my Redeemer liveth (Job 19:25).

How wondrously beautiful it is, that in each opening spring,
when all things are waking into new life, we take into our
hearts afresh the blessed fact of our Lord's resurrection! Death is
stripped of its terrors; the grave is illumined with light. Because He
lives we shall live also. Ah, into how many of our homes hath the
death angel entered since one short year ago—Death, with his
unrelenting face, his unhearing ears, his sealed lips! So many of us
have gone close to the "valley of shadows" with our loved ones,

and left them there—*we* to turn back to the earth life, desolate, burdened, heartbroken; *they* to step into the heaven life, where there is no more death, neither sorrow, nor crying, nor pain. Surely, we cannot grieve for them; it is for ourselves we mourn, forgetting, mayhap, in our selfish sorrow that "it is well" with our beloved in that better country. But as the blessed Eastertide once more draws near, let us lift up our tear-blurred eyes to the One who hath brought life and immortality to us all, and ask Him to fill our empty hands with work for Him.

> Last Easter, when my voice was lifted up
>   To sing the praises of my Risen Lord,
> I had not tasted sorrow's bitter cup,
>   The music held for me no minor chord.
> This Eastertide my stricken heart sends up
>   The strains I lift in accents clear and strong;
> For I have drained the dregs of sorrow's cup,
>   And learned the meaning of the Easter song.
> I know the sweetness of the minor chord,
>   The glory of the major full and clear;
> I know the power of my Risen Lord—
>   He lives, and they shall live whom I hold dear.
> And though I cannot help the tears that flow,
>   And though my heart is sad as heart can be,
> I sing the Easter song because I know
>   The blessed Easter message is for me.

APRIL 26

He is not here: for He is risen (Matt. 28:6).

May this Easter be full of blessing and comfort unutterable to all whose hearts are bereaved! The still form, the sepulcher—these are of the earth. "He is not here, He is risen," is as true today of our precious dead as of Him whom Mary and the disciples mourned so hopelessly, but who broke the bonds of the grave, and flung wide the doors of the great prison house to show us that the abode of the dead is really a place of light and life and joy.

> How did the Lord keep Easter? With His own!
> Back to meet Mary where she grieved alone,

With face and mien all tenderly the same,
Unto the very sepulchre He came.

Ah, the dear message that He gave her then—
Said for the sake of all bruised hearts of men—
"Go, tell those friends who have believed on Me,
I go before them in Galilee!

"Into the life so poor and hard and plain,
That for a while they must take up again,
My presence passes! Where their feet toil slow,
Mine, shining swift with love, still foremost go!

"Say, Mary, I will meet them, by the way
To walk a little with them, where they stay,
To bring My peace. Watch! For ye do not know
The day, the hour, when I may find you so!"

And I do think, as He came back to her,
The many mansions may be all astir
With tender steps that hasten in the way,
Seeking their own upon this Easter Day.

Parting the veil that hideth them about,
I think they come, tenderly wistful, out
From homes of heaven that only seem so far,
And walk in gardens where the new tombs are!
                                        A. D. T. Whitney.

JUST FOR TODAY

O sad-faced mourners, who each day are wending
    Through churchyard paths of cypress and of yew,
Leave for today the low graves you are tending,
    And lift your eyes to God's eternal blue!

It is no time for bitterness or sadness;
    Twine Easter lilies, not pale asphodels;
Let your souls thrill to the cares of gladness,
    And answer the sweet chime of Easter bells.

If Christ were still within the grave's low prison,
    A captive of the enemy we dread;
If from the moldering cell He had not risen,
    Who then could chide the gloomy tears you shed?

If Christ were dead, there would be need to sorrow,
    But He has risen and vanquished death for aye;

Hush, then, your sigh, if only till the morrow,
At Easter give your grief a holiday.   *May Riley Smith.*

APRIL 27

Because I live ye shall live also (John 14:19).

To every created thing God has given a tongue that proclaims a resurrection. If the Father deigns to touch with divine power the cold and pulseless heart of the buried acorn and to make it burst forth from its prison walls, will he leave neglected in the earth the soul of man, made in the image of his Creator? If He stoops to give to the rose bush, whose withered blossoms float upon the autumn breezes, the sweet assurance of another springtime, will He refuse the words of hope to the sons of men when the frosts of winter come? If matter, mute and inanimate though changed by the forces of nature into the multitude of forms, can never die, will the spirit of man suffer annihilation when it has paid a brief visit like a royal guest to this tenement of clay? No, I am as sure that there is another life as I am that I live today!

William Jennings Bryan.

THE FIRST EASTER

Lonely in the house of John,
While the others slept—
Sensing nor cooling winds
Nor stars,
His mother wept—
Seeing alone
The wreathen thorns
About His head,
Hearing His words
Upon the Cross,
Mourning Him dead.

Lonely in the house of John,
His mother lay,
Though song was in the olive trees,
And all the east was gray.

Then—Light . . .
Light in the little room . . .
Wide arms . . . and answering . . .

Light. . . . and His voice . . .
"Be not afraid, O mother,
It is I."

Harry Lee.

_____

Unto the upright there ariseth light in the darkness: he is gracious (Psalm 112:4).

I t is my comfort to know that the darkest cloud is fringed with covenant love. I can repose on the blessed assurance that present discipline is needed discipline, and that all which is mystery now, will be cleared up hereafter. May it be mine cheerfully to follow the footsteps of the guiding Shepherd *through the darkest, loneliest road;* and *amidst thickening sorrows may I have* grace to trust Him fully. In the midst of mysterious providences I will be still—hushing every murmur, and breathing in lowly resignation, "Thy will be done." *Dr. J. R. Macduff.*

Remember, Soul, out of this deep sorrow thou shalt escape—
And thou shalt walk in soft, white light, with kings and priests abroad,
And thou shalt summer high in bliss upon the hills of God.

Those who know the path to God, can find it in the dark.
Maclaren.

APRIL 29 _____

Thou wilt keep him in perfect peace whose mind is stayed on Thee (Isa. 26:3).

A ll we need to do in time of sorrow and loneliness is to stay our minds upon God, to trust Him, to rest in Him, to nestle in His love. We remember where John was found the night of the Lord's last supper with His disciples—the darkest night the world ever saw, in the deepest sorrow men ever knew—he was leaning on Jesus' breast. He crept into that holy shelter to find quiet. John was kept in perfect peace during all those terrible hours.

122

Everything appeared to have slipped away and there was nothing that seemed abiding. But John crept into the shelter of love and simply trusted, and was kept in holy peace.

A beautiful story is told of Rudyard Kipling during a serious illness a few years since. The trained nurse was sitting at his bedside on one of the anxious nights when the sick man's condition was most critical. She was watching him intently and noticed that his lips began to move. She bent over him, and heard him whisper the words of the old familiar prayer of childhood, "Now I lay me down to sleep."

The nurse, realizing that her patient did not require her services, and that he was praying, said in apology for having intruded upon him, "I beg your pardon, Mr. Kipling; I thought you wanted something." "I do," faintly replied the sick man: "I want my heavenly Father. He only can care for me now." In his great weakness there was nothing that human help could do, and he turned to God and crept into His bosom, seeking the blessing and the care which none but God can give. That is what we need to do in every time of trial, of sorrow—when the gentlest human love can do nothing—creep into our heavenly Father's bosom, saying, "Now I lay me down to sleep." That is the way to peace. Earth has no shelter in which it can be found, but in God the feeblest may find it.   *Dr. Miller.*

> Peace, perfect peace, with sorrows surging round?
> On Jesus' bosom nought but calm is found.
>
> Peace, perfect peace, our future all unknown?
> Jesus we know, and He is on the throne.
>
> Peace, perfect peace, death shadowing us and ours?
> Jesus has vanquished death and all its powers.
>
> It is enough: earth's struggles soon shall cease,
> And Jesus call us to heaven's perfect peace.
>   *Bishop E. H. Bickersteth.*

APRIL 30 _____

Stablish, strengthen, settle you (1 Peter 5:10).

Does the storm blow? He maketh the storm a calm.

Is it night?
Unto the upright there ariseth light in the darkness.

BLESSED BE STORMS

Job said, "You should say, 'Why persecute we him seeing the ROOT OF THE MATTER is found in me?'"

It requires storms to produce this rooting business. No tree becomes great unless it is transplanted out on a meadow where the winds and storms can get at it. It remains small if sheltered in the forest.

Out on the meadow it stands to shelter the herds and the flocks. The earth about the tree hardens. The rains do little good for the water runs off.

But the terrific storm strikes. It twists, turns, wrenches and at times all but tears it out of its place. If the tree could speak it might bitterly complain. Should Nature listen and cease the storm process?

On and on the storm almost bends it double. It is wrath now. What can such seeming cruelty mean? Is that love? But wait.

All about the tree the soil is all loosened. Great cracks are opened up away down into the ground. Deep wounds they might appear to the inexperienced. The rain now comes in with its gentle ministry. The "WOUNDS" fill up. The moisture reaches away down deep even to the utmost root. The sun again shines. New and vigorous life bursts forth. The roots go deeper, ever deeper. The branches shoot forth. Now and again one hears something snap and crack like a pistol. It is the expansion of the bark of the tree. It is getting too big for its clothes. *It is growing into a giant.* It is rooting.   *Dean Dutton.*

The brightest souls which glory ever knew,
Were rocked in storms and nursed when tempests blew.

MAY 1 _____

He shall gather the lambs with his arm, and carry them in his bosom (Isa. 40:11).

The little children were in the garden. They would pull a flower for mother. With loving hearts, but lack of wisdom, they pulled a large bud, enfolded in green, velvety leaves. Poor bud, untimely plucked from the parent stem, never to unfold as "a thing of beauty," only left to wither and die!

In the afternoon there came a card, with a black border and a silver lining! A little one had been taken away—the child of godly parents; and at the foot of the card was written:—

> Forever with the Lord;
>   Amen, so let it be!

The thought came with wonderful sweetness, and we pass it on to comfort other sorrowing hearts—*"God's flowers are always wisely pulled."*

He wants the buds as well as the blossoms, but He guides His Hands "wittingly." He makes no mistakes. That lovely flower, as dear to you as life itself, is not left to wither and die. It is but transplanted to a sunnier land, to the King's own palace garden. Even the precious body has but fallen asleep in Christ. "Awaiting," as has been said, "the spring wind of the first resurrection."

My little card had a silver lining; it might have been a golden one, for the light from the Glory land was shining on it. There can be no wrath in the removal of a dear one to heaven.

When you mourn, "The Lord hath taken away," do not forget the first part of the verse, "The Lord gave"; and above all, do not forget the close, "Blessed be the name of the Lord."

MAY 2

They overcame him by the blood of the Lamb, and by the word of their testimony; and they loved not their lives unto the death (Rev. 12:11).

When James and John came to Christ with their mother, asking Him to give them the best places in the kingdom, He did not refuse their request; but told them that they would be given to them if they could do His work, drink His cup, and be baptized with His baptism. Do we want the competition? The greatest things are always hedged about by the hardest things; and we, too, shall find mountains, and forests, and chariots of iron, and giants. Triumphal arches are not woven out of rose blossoms and silken cords, but reared by hard blows and bloody scars. Hardship is the price of coronation. The very hardships that you are enduring in your life today are given by the Master for the explicit purpose of enabling you to win your crown. Do not wait for some ideal situation, some romantic difficulty, some far-away emergency; but rise to meet the actual conditions which the providence of God has placed around you today. Your crown of glory lies embedded in the very heart of those things—those hardships and trials that are pressing you this very hour. There, beloved, lies your crown. God help you to overcome, and sometime wear it!

Selected.

Brave little woman, trudging along
    Patiently, day after day—
Weaving a garment of shining light
    Out of the clouds of gray;
Bearing the burdens of vexing cares,
    Like one of the saints of old—
Making the best of a dull, hard life
    With it miseries all untold!

Long have I watched her with wondering eyes—
    Faithful and sweet and strong—
Doing the work that the Master sends,
    Making of sorrow, song;
Questioning never the wisdom that asks
    Self-abnegation complete,
Willingly treading the pathway of thorns
    That leads to the Master's feet.

Sometime a fair, sweet morn shall dawn,
    With a smile of infinite grace;
Somewhere, oh somewhere, fruition shall be,
    When the angel shall find her a place
Close to the Father, and she hears Him say,
    As He tenderly bids her come,
"Out of the valley of darkness and toil,
    My Child, thou art welcome Home!"   *Stanley J. Davis*

MAY 3

In quietness and in confidence shall be your strength (Isa 30:15).

STILLNESS IN SUFFERING

They say there is a hollow, safe and still,
    A point of coolness and repose
Within the center of a flame, where life might dwell

126

Unharmed and unconsumed, as in a luminous shell:
Which bright walls of fire inclose
In breathless splendor; barrier that no foes
    Could pass at will.

When there is entire resignation, a complete yielding of the will to God, the flames of His afflictive providence cannot really bring hurt to the soul, but becomes rather as a wall of fire round about it. As one has beautifully written, "He that fully consents to endure to suffer all the will of God; he that finds amid these central fires deep content, as his spirit lies down in the center of God's will *and is still,* is permanently at peace with God, and as a consequence, is fully prepared to be kept permanently by the peace of God which passeth all understanding."

"All dear to God," said Luther, "must learn to endure." Christians conquer when they suffer. When they resist they lose the day."

And *stillness in suffering* must belong to a full consecration. Let us joy, as we enter the furnace of trial and sorrow, in the thought that we can be nearer to God in the center of the flame than we could be in the open air on a bed of roses.

Oh to be *kept,* kept in that unspeakable stillness which belongs to the "secret place of the Most High."

MAY 4 _____

But thou, when thou fastest, anoint thine head, and wash thy face; that thou appear not unto men to fast, but unto thy Father which is in secret: and thy Father which seeth in secret, shall reward thee openly (Matt. 6:17, 18).

Christ's direction for observance of the Sacrament of the Washen Face, while part of His prohibition of ostentatious religion, has an obviously deeper meaning than that which lies upon the surface. Its real significance is: Do your business with God secretly, especially the business of your lowest hours. For fasting ideally expresses the concentration of a compelled soul upon some great crisis—some sorrow which blots out for the time being every other interest, and blurs the aspect of every fair thing that still lives. In such an hour we are to seek the Presence. And, having communed with Heaven, and having faced the whole thing with God, He bids us go forth to reflect upon others something of the brightness of a God-lit peace.

It is as though He says: "Remove all trace of your tears. Conceal your grief, lest it infect others and darken the light by which they have to live. Bear your sorrow loyally—that is Christianly—with faith in God." In this He is Himself the world's greatest and bravest example.

For we well know how consistently throughout His life He observed this Sacrament of the Washen Face. Mark well His nights of prayer, when He called upon God with strong crying and tears, and was heard in that He feared. Yet on the morrow no man marked any trace of tears from those mountain-side vigils. He came to the day's duties—to heal the sick, to preach the Gospel, to reveal Heaven to men—with a winsome smile which drew children to His arms, and recreated hope in lives broken and outcast.

It is altogether beyond the power of human nature to be self-forgetful in sorrow. Only he who has learned from Christ how to shut the door, to face his sorrow alone with its Author, and to "have it out" with Him, can wash his face, and come forth radiant with the light which never was on land or sea. Let us keep the Feast.   *J. Stuart Holden.*

Hast thou e'er a grief, dear?
  Lock it in thy heart!
Keep it, close it,
  Sacred and apart;
Lest another, at thy sigh,
Hear his sorrow stir and cry.
Wakeful watch doth sorrow keep;
Hush it! hide it! bid it sleep!

Hast thou e'er a joy, love?
  Bind it on thy brow,
Vaunt it, flaunt it,
  All the world to know.
Where the shade lies dim and gray,
Turn its glad and heartless ray.
Does thy sad-browed neighbor smile?
  So thy life was worth the while.

And in the night His song shall be with me (Psalm 42:8).

T he ear of God hears no sublimer music than a Christian's *songs in the night.* Before Gethsemane's midnight struggle Christ himself chanted a hymn; and happy is the man or woman who can go into life's hard battle *singing!*

While dark hours of calamity and bereavement bring to the ordinary man of the world distress and complaints, they bring to the Christ-possessed soul tranquil submission and often an uplift of triumphant joy. The path of trial may lead down into grim and gloomy gorges that no sunbeams can penetrate; but "Thou art with me," is the cheerful song that faith sings along the darksome road.

What a thrilling outbreak of triumphant faith was that which came from the brave old Thomas Halyburton of Scotland in the darkest hour of his bereavement. When a much-loved son was taken away he made this record: "This day has been a day to be remembered. Oh, my soul, never forget what I have reached this day. My soul had smiles that almost wasted nature. Jesus came to me in the third watch of the night, walking upon the waters, and He said unto me: 'I am Alpha and Omega, the beginning and the end, and I have the keys of hell and death.' He stilled the tempest in my soul and lo! there was a great calm."

AGAINST A THORN

Once I heard a song of sweetness,
  As it cleft the morning air,
Sounding in its blest completeness,
  Life a tender, pleading prayer;
And I sought to find the singer,
  Whence the wondrous song was borne;
And I found a bird, sore wounded,
  Pinioned by a cruel thorn.

I have seen a soul in sadness,
  While its wings with pain were furl'd,
Giving hope, and cheer and gladness
  That should bless a weeping world:
And I knew that life of sweetness,
  Was of pain and sorrow borne;

And a stricken soul was singing,
  With its heart against a thorn.

Ye are told of One who loved you,
  Of a Saviour crucified;
Ye are told of nails that pinioned,
  And a spear that pierced His side;
Ye are told of cruel scourging,
  Of a Saviour bearing scorn,
And He died for your salvation,
  With His brow against a thorn.

Ye "are not above the Master."
  Will you breathe a sweet refrain?
And His Grace will be sufficient,
  When your heart is pierced with pain.
Will you live to bless His loved ones,
  Tho' your life be bruised and torn,
Like the bird that sang so sweetly,
  With its heart against a thorn.   *Selected.*

MAY 6 _____

Who is among you that feareth the Lord, that obeyeth The voice of his servant, that walketh in the darkness, and hath no light? let him trust in the name of the Lord, and stay upon his God (Isa. 50:10).

This is trusting God in the dark. Sometimes we have an experience in life that seems like walking through a long dark tunnel. . . . When we reach heaven we may discover that the richest and deepest and most profitable experiences that we had in this world were those gained in the very roads from which we shrank back with dread. Let us be assured of this, that, if the lesson and the rod are of His appointing, and His all wise love has engineered the deep tunnels of trial on the heavenward road, He will never desert us during the discipline. *God owns you and me,* and He has a right to do with us what He pleases. He will not lay on one stroke of cruelty, or a single one that He cannot give us grace to bear. Tighten your loins with the promises, and keep the strong staff of faith well in hand. Trust God in the dark. We are safer with Him in the dark than without Him in the sunshine. He will not suffer your foot to stumble. His rod and staff will never break. *Why* He brought us here we know not now, but we shall know hereafter. At the end of the gloomy passage beams the heavenly light; then comes the exceeding and eternal weight of glory. *Theodore Cuyler.*

Remember that your Father is just ahead of you in the shadow.

MAY 7 ———————————————————————————

Let us offer the sacrifice of praise to God continually (Heb. 13:15).

I ce breaks many a branch, and so I see a great many persons bowed down and crushed by their afflictions. But now and then I meet one that *sings* in affliction, and then I thank God for my own sake as well as his. There is no such sweet singing as a song in the night. You recollect the story of the woman who, when her only child died, in rapture looked up as with the face of an angel, and said, "I give you joy, my darling." That single sentence has gone with me years and years down through my life, quickening and comforting me.

KEEP UP THE SONG OF FAITH

Keep up the song of faith,
However dark the night;
And as you praise, the Lord will work
To change your faith to sight.

Keep up the song of faith,
And let your heart be strong,
For God delights when faith can praise
Though dark the night and long.

Keep up the song of faith,
The foe will hear and flee;
Oh, let not Satan hush your song
For praise is victory.

Keep up the song of faith,
The dawn will break ere long,
And we shall go to meet the Lord,
And join the endless song. *M. E. Barber.*

It was too hard for me, until I went into the sanctuary of God (Psalm 73:16, 17).

Back and forth the plow was driven. The field was covered with grasses and lovely flowers, but remorselessly through them all the share tore its way, cutting furrow after furrow. It seemed that all the beauty was being hopelessly destroyed. But by and by harvest time came, and the field waved with golden wheat. That was what the plowman's faith saw from the beginning.

Sorrow seems to destroy the life of a child of God. Its rude share plows again and again through it, making many a deep furrow, gashing its beauty. But afterward a harvest of blessing and good grows up out of the crushed and broken life. That is what God intends always in trial and sorrow. Let us have the plowman's faith, and we shall not faint when the share is driven through our heart. Then by faith we shall see beyond the pain and trial the blessing of richer life, of whiter holiness, of larger fruitfulness. And to win that blessing will be worth all the pain and trial.   *Selected.*

"It is so hard!" I said,
    And sat within and told my troubles o'er;
A hand fell softly on my bowed head,
    Yet no one passed my door.

"A fancy!" then I said;
    "But, oh! to feel that touch forevermore!
Methinks, indeed, I could be comforted!"
    And sorrowed as before.

"No other heart can know!"
    Broke out my grief again with bitter cry;
"And God is far—so far my faith lets go
    Her hold on Heaven, to die!"

Then some one stooped low,
    His heart full throbbing, as with tears, close by:
"Lord! is it Thou so moved by my woe?"
    He answered: "It is I."

I know, O Lord that thy judgments are right, and that Thou in faithfulness hast afflicted me! (Psalm 119:75).

I think when life's fitful fever is over we shall find that the royal road to intimacy with God lay through this old, undramatic, gainful way of pain. That is why God himself came to us not with argument and barren philosophy, but in an experience, as incarnation. He Himself has suffered, and through His pain we are made alive. Some day, it may be here, it may be there, in or out of the body, I know not, He will answer me and explain my suffering.

Harris E. Kirk.

Let us try to take up the sealed sorrow that has been dropped into our hearts, saying trustfully, "God's angel left this for me. It will have some blessing inside.

> Even sorrow touched by Thee grows bright
>   With more than rapture's ray,
> As darkness shows us worlds of light
>   We never saw by day.

I will sing a new song unto Thee, O Lord (Psalm 144:9).

One spring a mocking bird and his mate built their nest in a little tree just outside the window of a ranch house on the plains of New Mexico. His song was a great joy to the kindly people on the ranch, and when he sang at night they were glad that the air could be so filled with music.

The work on the ranch progressed into early summer; the fields of grain gave promise of a bountiful harvest, and in the mocking birds' nest were tiny birds. Then one night there was a storm, the growing grain was destroyed, the work of planting and tending had all been for naught. The morning brought such discouragement to the hearts in that home that they felt it was not worth while to go on, to start over again and plant another crop. Suddenly the mocking bird's song was heard, more joyous than ever. How had the birds fared in the storm? They had lost their nest and their little ones—their home and their children—but they had not yielded to discouragement. They had decided to build a new nest in a larger tree, and then, of course, there had to a be a song. And so, encouraged by the mocking birds, the family on the ranch started again, and was rewarded with a plenteous harvest at the end of the season.

What lessons of courage and happiness may be learned from the birds that fly and sing, and how comforting is the thought of wings!

I heard a bird at break of day
    Sing from the autumn trees
A song so musical and calm,
    So full of certainties;
No man, I think, could listen long
    Except upon his knees.
Yet this was but a simple bird,
    Alone among dead trees.   *Wm. Alexander Percy.*

MAY 11 ————————————————————————

Even so them also which sleep in Jesus will God bring with Him. . . .
Wherefore comfort one another with these words (1 Thess. 4:14, 18).

RECOMPENSE

We are quite sure
That He will give them back—bright, pure, and beautiful.
We know He will but keep
Our own and His until we fall asleep.
We know He does not mean
To break the strands reaching between
The Here and There.
He does not mean—though heaven be fair—
To change the spirits entering there, that they forget
The eyes upraised and wet,
The lips too still for prayer,
The mute despair.
He will not take
The spirits which He gave, and make
The glorified so new
That they are lost to me and you.
I do believe
They will receive
Us—you and me—and be so glad

To meet us, that when most I would grow sad
I just begin to think about that gladness,
And the day
When they shall tell us all about the way
That they have learned to go—
Heaven's pathways show.

My lost, my own and I
Shall have so much to see together by and by;
I do believe that God assures a sweet face,
But glorified, is waiting in the place
Where we shall meet, if only I
Am counted worthy in that by and by.
I do believe that God will give a sweet surprise
To tear-stained, saddened eyes,
And that His heaven will be
Most glad, most tided through with joy for you and me,
As we have suffered most. God never made
Spirit for spirit, answering shade for shade,
And placed them side by side—
So wrought in one, though separate, mystified—
And meant to break
The quivering threads between. When we shall wake,
I am quite sure, we will be very glad
That for a little while we were so sad.   *George Klingle.*

MAY 12

That where I am, there ye may be also (John 14:3).

FATHER IS UP THERE

Writing of early days, when he was summoned to his father's deathbed, Mr. Charles M. Alexander said: "The night my father died there came to me, as never before, the worth of a human soul. He could not take any of us with him: he must go alone. And I saw how the thing that mattered was to be sure that the soul was safe in God's keeping.

"I cried to God: 'If there is any way that Thou revealest Thyself to people, give me the certainty that my father is with Thee, and safe,' and I promised Him that I would serve Him all my life.

"As clearly as anything I ever experienced, the impression came to me: 'Your father is up here, safe with Me.' There and then, looking up at the stars, I promised to serve Him all my life, and the

135

load lifted right off me. A great longing to win souls came to me that night, and has been with me ever since."

THE ETERNAL HOME

Alone! To land upon that shore!
With not one sight that we have seen before—
    Things of a different hue,
    And sounds all strange and new,
No forms of earth or fancies to arrange,
But to begin alone that mighty change!

Alone! to land alone upon that shore,
Knowing so well we can return no more;
    No voice or face of friend,
    None with us to attend
Our disembarking on that awful strand—
But to arrive alone in such a land!

Alone? No; God hath been there long before—
Eternally hath waited on that shore,
    For us who were to come
    To our eternal Home.
Oh! is He not the lifelong Friend we know
More privately than any friend below?

Alone? That God we trust is on that shore,
The faithful One, whom we have trusted more
    In trials and in woes.
    Than we have trusted those
On whom we leaned most in our earthly strife.
Oh! we shall trust Him more in that new life!

So not alone we land upon that shore—
'Twill be as if we had been there before;
    We shall meet more we know
    Than we can meet below,
And find our rest like some returning dove—
Our Home at once with Eternal Love.   *F. W. Faber.*

MAY 13

Tarry ye here (Mark 14:34).

These are the words still of the suffering Master. Yes, tarry under the shade of your Gethsemane, whatever it is, and "watch with Me." Thus will your severest sorrows endear to you the nearness and presence of Him of whom alone it can be said, from His own deep heartfelt, experience, "In all their afflictions He was afflicted!"

And then, trust this all-comforting God *for the future.* He will read, in His own good time and way, the typical parable of our present volume. Yes, the time will undoubtedly come when "in Thy light we shall see light." What now is like the tolling of funeral bells will then appear rather to have been preparatory and preparation—chimes, ringing in the festal worshippers to the Church of the glorified. No purpose of God regarding you will remain unfulfilled, no flower uncrowned with blossom.

SATISFIED

Only to know in the coming years,
To see the "why" of life's many tears,
To read its disappointment scheme,
And understand the fevered dream,
Look out with eyes of perfect sight,
With all revealed in heaven's own light.

Only to see the coming years,
The vision hidden by life's tears;
Then with angelic hosts to fall,
And crown our Master Lord of all—
Love's rain of tears forever dried,
The heart forever satisfied.   *Robert Hare.*

MAY 14 _____

They went and told Jesus (Matt. 14:12).

BE STILL

Do you know what Luther said? "Suffer and be still and tell no man thy sorrow; trust in God—His help will not fail thee." This is what Scripture calls keeping silence before God. To talk much of one's sorrows makes one weak, but to tell one's sorrows to Him who heareth in secret makes one strong and calm.

Tholuck.

It is SO sweet to know—when we are tired
And when the hand of pain

Lies on our hearts, and when we look in vain
For human comfort—that the heart divine
Still understands these cares of yours and mine.
NOT ONLY UNDERSTANDS, BUT DAY BY DAY,
LIVES WITH US while we tread the earthly way—
Bears with us ALL our weariness, and feels
Across our sunshine—ever learns again
The shadow of the faintest cloud that steals
The depth and bitterness of human pain.
There is NO sorrow that He will not share.
No cross, no burden for our hearts to bear
WITHOUT HIS HELP—NO CARE OF OURS TOO SMALL
TO CAST ON JESUS. Let us tell Him ALL,
Lay at His feet the story of our woes,
And in His sympathy find sweet repose.

MAY 15

Lo, these are parts of His ways (Job 26:14).

When the great violin-makers of the Middle Ages wished to form a perfect instrument, they caused the tree to be felled at a particular period of its growth. The wood was then planed and cut into small pieces. These were exposed to the heat of the sun and to the winter's storms; were bent, rubbed, polished, and finally fastened together with incomparable skill.

If the wood could have found a tongue, doubtless it would have begged to grow in the forest, to rustle its branches, and bear its fruit as its companions were left to do, becoming at last a part of the sodden earth. But it was this harsh treatment that made out of its common boards the Stradivari violin, whose music still charms the world.

So by countless touches of pain and sorrow, God fits us to bear our part in the great harmony with which true and earnest souls shall ultimately fill the world.

> Love thou thy sorrow, grief shall bring its own excuse in
> after years,
> The rainbow!—see how fair a thing God hath built up
> from tears.

Be silent unto God and let Him mould thee (Psalm 37:7—Herb.).

There are songs which can be learned only in the valley; no art can teach them; no rules of voice can make them perfectly sung. Their music is in the heart. They are songs of memory, of personal experience. Thus George Matheson has written; he continues: "And so, my soul, thou art receiving a music lesson from thy Father. Thou art being educated for the choir invisible. There are parts of the symphony that none can take but thee. There are chords too minor for the angels. There may be heights in the symphony which are beyond thy scale—heights which the angels alone can reach. But there are depths which belong to thee and can be touched only by thee. Thy Father is training thee for the part the angels cannot sing; and the school is sorrow. Despise not thy school of sorrow, O my soul; it will give thee a unique part in the universal song.

> I walk down the Valley of Silence—
>   Down the dim, voiceless valley—alone!
> And I hear not the fall of a footstep
>   Around me, save God's and my own;
> And the hush of my heart is as holy
>   As hovers when angels have flown!
>
> In the hush of the Valley of Silence
>   I hear all the songs that I sing,
> And the notes float down the dim Valley
>   Till each finds a word for a wing,
> That to man, like the Dove of the Deluge,
>   The message of peace they may bring.
>
> But far on the deep there are billows,
>   That never shall break on the beach;
> And I have heard songs in the silence
>   That never shall float into speech;
> And I have had dreams in the Valley
>   Too lofty for language to reach.
>
> Do you ask me the place of the Valley,
>   Ye hearts that are harrowed by care?
> It lieth afar between mountains,
>   And God and His angels are there;

And one is the dark mountain of Sorrow,
And one the bright mountain of Prayer.

_____

Where is God my maker, who giveth songs in the night? (Job 35:10).

Do you have sleepless nights tossing on the hot pillow, and watching for the first glint of dawn? Ask the divine Spirit to enable you to fix your thoughts on God your Maker, and believe that He can fill those lonely, dreary hours with song. *Is yours the night of bereavement?* Is it not often at such a time that God draws near, and assures the mourner that the Lord has need of the departed loved one, and called "the eager, earnest spirit to stand in the bright throng of the invisible, liberated, radiant, active, intent on some high mission"; and as the thought enters, is there not the beginning of a song? *Is yours the night of discouragement and fancied or actual failure?* No one understands you, your friends reproach; but your Maker draws nigh, and gives you a song—a song of hope, the song which is harmonious with the strong deep music of His providence. Be ready to sing the songs that your Maker gives.

SONGS IN THE NIGHT

Under every grief and pine
Runs a joy with silken twine.

My songs have been the songs of the daylight,
    Of the sunshine of His face,
Of the hours of blest communion,
    And the wonders of His grace.

In my song has been unremembered
    The touch of His hand in my plight.
Oh! how easy to sing in the sunshine—
    He alone can give songs in the night.

The weight of an awful darkness,
    Hung over my soul like a pall;
And everything round me seemed blackness—
    No help but to struggle and fall

But treasures are found in the darkenss,
  And riches are hidden in store;
And sorrow oft gives us a song to sing,
  Unknown to us heretofore.

Our God gives us songs in the midnight,
  When our feet are held fast in the stocks;
And sends with the praises He giveth,
  The unloosing of bars and locks.   *J. Lyall.*

Better the night, with song in it, than no night and no song.

MAY 18

At evening time it shall be light (Zech. 14:7).

AT EVENTIDE

I love to connect our word "serene" with the Latin word
evening, as well as with its own mother-word *serenus—*
clear, or bright.

Often, after a windy, stormy day, there comes at evening a
clear, bright stillness, so that at evening time there is serenity as
well as light. So often in life's evening there comes a lull, a time of
peaceful waiting "between the lights," the burden-weighted heat
of the day behind, the radiance of eternity before. Perhaps the day
has been in truth "life's little day," swiftly ebbing to its close;
perhaps the worn, tired pilgrim has lived even beyond the
measure of three score years and ten. In either case it is in truth the
evening.

The clear face reflects "eternity's wonderful beauty," the sweet,
serene spirit is freshened by dew from the heavenly Hermon, the
fragrance of evening flowers fills the air, the songs of birds come in
tender, satisfied cadences, and even the clouds which remain are
enriched and made radiant by rays from the Sun of righteousness.

We whose evening is not yet, are entranced with the exquisite
blending of the warm human affection with the celestial flame
kindled from the sacred altar. With hushed souls we minister and
are ministered unto, until, too soon, the twilight time is past, and
the evening and the morning have become the eternal day.

Christian Observer.

There is but a step between me and death (1 Samuel 20:3).

C ould any experience have a more ennobling influence upon the life than the keen realization of the unseen world!

What a spur it proves to tireless zeal in the cause of Christ! What a blessed inspiration it provides when earth's storms threaten to extinguish the gleaming lights of hope and joy!

Training ourselves to cherish this thought of its nearness does not shadow our lives, while it does rob death of its dread.

BEYOND

It seemeth such a little way to me
    Across to that strange country—the Beyond;
And yet, not strange, for it has grown to be
    The home of those of whom I am so fond;
They make it seem familiar and most dear,
As journeying friends bring distant regions near.

I cannot make it seem a day to dread,
    When from this dear earth I shall journey out
To that still dearer country of the dead,
    And join the lost ones, so long dreamed about.
I love this world, yet shall I love to go
And meet the friends who wait for me, I know.

I never stand above a bier and see
    The seal of death set on some well-loved face
But that I think, "One more to welcome me
    When I shall cross the intervening space
Between this land and that one "over there";—
One more to make the strange Beyond seem fair.

And so for me there is no sting in death,
    And so the grave has lost its victory.
It is but crossing—with a bated breath
    And white, set face—a little strip of sea
To find the loved ones waiting on the shore,
More beautiful, more precious than before.

                                   Ella Wheeler Wilcox.

For I reckon that the sufferings of this present time are not worthy to be compared with the glory which shall be revealed in us (Rom. 8:18).

COMPENSATION IN HEAVEN

It will not take long for God to make up to you in the next world for all you have suffered in this. As you enter Heaven He may say: "Give this man one of those towered and colonnaded palaces on that ridge of gold overlooking the Sea of Glass.

"Give this woman a home among the amaranthine blooms and between those fountains tossing in everlasting sunlight. Give her a couch canopied with rainbows to pay her for all the fatigues of wifehood and motherhood, and housekeeping, from which she had no rest for forty years.

"Give these newly-arrived souls from earth the costliest things and roll to their door the grandest chariots, and hang on their walls the sweetest harps that ever responded to singers seraphic. Give to them rapture on rapture, jubilee on jubilee, heaven on heaven. They had a hard time on earth earning a livelihood, or nursing sick children, or waiting on querulous old age, or were compelled to work after they got short-breathed, and rheumatic, and dim-sighted.

"Chamberlains of Heaven, keepers of the King's robe, banqueters of eternal royalty, make up to them a hundredfold, a thousandfold, a millionfold for all they suffered from swaddling clothes to shroud, and let all those who, whether on the hills or in the temples, or on the throne or on Jasper wall, were helped and sanctified and prepared for this heavenly realm by trial and pain, stand up and wave their scepters!"

And I looked, and behold! nine-tenths of the ransomed rose to their feet, and nine-tenths of the scepters swayed to and fro in the light of the sun that never sets; and then I understood better than before that trouble comes for beneficent purposes, and that on the coldest nights the aurora is brightest in the northern heavens.

T. DeWitt Talmage.

She goeth unto the grave to weep there (John 11:31).

Comfort is not the only thing we need, if the graves of our beloved are to be made places of true blessing to our souls. Standing there, many solemn thoughts may well stir within us, many serious self-questionings, many deep heart-searchings may come.

To stand at the grave is a very solemn thing. It brings us closer to eternal realities than almost anything else can do.

A CALL

To the comforting, beautiful churchyard,
  To be with my dead and to pray,
World-weary and lonely and longing,
  I slipped in the gloaming today.
The face of sweet heaven bent o'er me,
  A light with the tenderest glow,
And something—the smile of the angels—
  Fell soft on the sleepers below.

Their harps were enmeshed in the tree tops,
  Light fingers were sweeping the strings,
I drank in the music seraphic,
  And marked the soft flutter of wings,
Those wings fanned invisible censers,
  So perfect the perfume they shed,
It seemed like a mantle of sweetness,
  Descending to cover the dead.

I looked on the couches of velvet,
  Embroidered with aster and rose,
And garnished with hand painted lilies—
  God's hand—where the sleepers repose;
I thought on the things they had toiled for,
  Had longed for and ventured to pray,
And knew that up yonder in heaven
  They enjoyed the fruition today.

I wept—for my own destitution—
  Then lifted my face to the skies,
The smile of the angels had faded,
  They looked down with pitying eyes.
Soft, soft fell their tears in the twilight,
  I felt that for me they were shed,
Compassionate tears for the living,
  But smiles for the fortunate dead.

Then lo! from the east came a brilliance,
   A glory illumined the air,
And I, in admiring wonder,
   Forgot all my grief and despair.
Hope flashed through my trembling heartstrings,
   A something spoke low to my soul,
It fluttered its quivering white wings
   In yearnings that baffled control.

And then to my spirit lethargic
   A wonderful miracle came,
A hunger and thirst for achievement,
   For battle, in Victory's name.
A longing to fill up the breaches,
   To man all the guns in the strife,
To scatter the perfume of lilies,
   Like yon, in the pathway of life.

To play upon harps that are human,
   With fingers so vibrant with love
That, raptured, the listening angels
   Would pause in the music above.
I rose in the golden effulgence
   That flooded the world with its light,
And knew that the God of the living
   Had smiled on His servant tonight.　　*May Elliott Hutson.*

MAY 22 ───────────────────────────

His compassions fail not (Lam. 3:22).

He comforted! "The Lord will command his loving-kindness in the day-time, and in the night his song shall be with me, and my prayer to the God of my life." Yes! "O thou afflicted, tossed with tempest and not comforted," unschooled and undisciplined in these fiery trials;—He who brought you into the furnace will lead you through! He has never failed in the case of any of His "poor afflicted ones" to realize His own precious promise, "As thy day is, so shall thy strength be." All is mystery and enigma to you *now,* —nothing but crossed plans, and blighted hopes, and a future of unutterable desolation. But He will yet vindicate His dealings. I believe even on earth He often leads us to see and learn "the need be"; and if *not* on earth, at least in glory, there will be a grand revelation of ineffable wisdom and love in this very trial which is now bowing your head like a bulrush, and making your eyes a very fountain of tears. *Dr. Macduff.*

IN MEMORY

What mean you by this weeping
  To break my very heart?
We both are in Christ's keeping,
  And therefore cannot part.
You there, I here, though parted
  We still at heart are one;
I only just in sunshine,
  The shadow scarcely gone.
What though the clouds surround you,
  You can the brightness see,
'Tis only a little way
  That leads from you to me.
I was so very weary,
  Surely you would not mourn,
That I a little sooner
  Should lay my burden down.
Then weep not, weep not Darling,
  God wipes away all tears;
'Tis only a little way
  Though you may call it years. *Author Unknown.*

MAY 23 _____

Hide me under the shadow of Thy wings (Psalm 17:8).

Let us not fill the night of sorrow with fretting cares, borrowing grief from remembrance and anticipation, but let us look away from all else to the Lord, remembering Him amid the night watches, and breathing: "Calm me, my God, and keep me calm." Like the nightdews will His comfort and His peace distil, and the heart stayed upon Him shall understand the loving-kindness of the Lord.

CALM ME, MY GOD

Calm me, my God, and keep me calm,
  While these hot breezes blow;

Be like the night-dew's cooling balm
   Upon earth's fevered brow!

Calm me, my God, and keep me calm,
   Soft resting on Thy breast;
Soothe me with holy hymn and psalm,
   And bid my spirit rest.

Calm me, my God, and keep me calm.
   Let Thine outstretched wing
Be like the shade of Elim's palm
   Beside her desert-spring.

Yes, keep me calm, though loud and rude
   The sounds my ear that greet—
Calm in the closet's solitude,
   Calm in the bustling street;

Calm as the ray of sun or star
   Which storms assail in vain—
Moving unruffled through earth's war,
   The eternal calm to gain.   *Horatius Bonar.*

MAY 24

Others (Phil. 2:4).

A Hindu woman, the beautiful Eastern legend tells us, lost her only child. Wild with grief, she implored her teacher to give her back her little one to love her. He looked at her for a long while tenderly, and said, "Go, my daughter, bring me a handful of rice from a house into which Death has never entered, and I will do as thou desirest." The woman at once began her search. She went from dwelling to dwelling, asking if there were members of the home missing. Far and wide she wandered but there was always a vacant seat by the hearth. Gradually the waves of her grief subsided before the spectacle of sorrow everywhere, and her heart, ceasing to be occupied with its own pangs, flowed out in strong yearning sympathy with the universal suffering. Tears of anguish softened to pity, passion melted away in compassion, she forgot herself in the general interest, and found redemption in redeeming.

I had a tiny box, a precious box
Of human love—my spikenard of great price;
I kept it close within my heart of hearts,
And scarce would lift the lid lest it should waste
Its perfume on the air. One day a strange
Deep sorrow came with crushing weight, and fell
Upon my costly treasure, sweet and rare,
And brake the box to atoms. All my heart
Rose in dismay and sorrow at this waste;
But, as I mourned, behold a miracle
Of grace divine. My human love was changed
To Heaven's own, and poured in healing streams
On other broken hearts, while soft and clear
A voice above me whispered, "Child of Mine,
With comfort wherewith thou are comforted,
From this time forth, go comfort others,
And thou shalt know blest fellowship with Me,
Whose broken heart of love hath healed the world."

Selected.

There is no fragrance like that of my alabaster box—the box I break for Thee.

MAY 25 ────────────────────────────

We would see Jesus (John 12:21).

HOMESICK MOUNT

In the neighborhood of Interlaken, Switzerland, there is a prominent point called "Homesick Mount." It is so called because it is generally the last spot which the traveler visits before leaving that part of Switzerland, and at a time when his thoughts are turning homeward. It commands a view of the whole beautiful valley of Interlaken, but the heart of the tourist is not there, but thinking of the friends and loved ones at home.

So it is with many to whom faith makes the invisible most real, as they near the end of their earthly pilgrimage. They reach the mount of homesickness and while they acknowledge all the beauty and gladness of this world, their hearts are not here. This sight does not enthrall them for their faces are turned toward home and their hearts dwell in the land of Promise.

148

WE WOULD SEE JESUS

We would see Jesus, for the shadows lengthen
 Across the little landscape of our life;
We would see Jesus, our weak faith to strengthen
 For the last weariness, the final strife.

We would see Jesus, for life's hand hath rested
 With its dark touch upon both heart and brow;
And though our souls have many a billow breasted,
 Others are rising in the distance now.

We would see Jesus, the great rock foundation
 Whereon our feet were set by sovereign grace;
Not life, nor death, with all their agitation,
 Can thence remove us till we see His face.

We would see Jesus; other lights are paling
 Which for long years we have rejoiced to see;
The blessings of our pilgrimage are failing—
 We would not mourn them, for we go to Thee.

We would see Jesus; yet the spirit lingers
 Round the dear objects it has loved so long;
And earth from earth can scarce unclose its fingers,
 Our love to Thee makes not this love less strong.

We would see Jesus; this is all we're needing
 Strength, joy and willingness come with the sight:
We would see Jesus, dying, risen, pleading;
 Then welcome day, and farewell mortal night!

MAY 26 _____

Let not your heart be troubled . . . in My Father's House are many mansions (John 14:1, 2).

A fierce storm was sweeping the Great Lakes. A steam tug towing a barge began to founder. The captain and his mates took to a small boat. All night long they tossed to and fro, every instant in jeopardy of their lives. In the morning they were rescued by a passing ship. The captain afterward testified that all the long night as they were beaten and tossed by the tempest there was one thing which nerved their arms and kept their hearts from

149

sinking in despair. It was this—shining through the darkness and the storm they saw the lights of home.

We are sailing on a stormy sea. Often our frail boat is tossed and beaten with the tempest. Sometimes the gales seem too fierce for us to weather, and we are sorely tempted to give way to the troubled heart that so easily besets us in such an hour. But the Captain of our salvation knows the sore and frequent temptation to be troubled in heart. His remedy is simple. Let not your heart be troubled. Think about the Father's House! Think of its peace, its joy; its glory; its reunions and fellowship; its sureness; its eternalness; and as you think, the troubled heart will vanish. You will be like the tempest-tossed sea captain. *You see the lights of home.*

James H. McConkey.

MAY 27 _____

There remaineth therefore a rest to the people of God (Heb. 4:9).

OUR LOVED ONES THERE

Heaven will be sweeter and more beautiful, more to be desired because of the entrance through its shining portals of our loved ones. It will be easy for us some day to let go of this life and go to be with the multitude of the redeemed who have "washed their robes and made them white in the blood of the Lamb." Let us think of the last and sweetest home-coming in the Father's house of many mansions, where our dear ones are waiting for us; and some night, God knows how soon it may come, they will meet us with outstretched hands. May the blessed Christ come into our hearts more completely, and may we rest our weary souls on Him.

> Bid me good-bye now,
>   As going at night to my room:
> If I may, I will open the door, love,
>   And call to you out of the gloom.
>
> If I may not, the Lord is our keeper,
>   And still we are both in His care—
> You on earth, I in heaven—both guarded,
>   Both safe, till you follow me there.   *Alfred Norris.*

150

_____

The mountains shall depart, and the hills be removed; but My kindness shall not depart from thee, neither shall the covenant of My peace be removed (Isa. 54:10).

W e should never see the stars if the sun did not go down. We should never discover the grace and loving-kindness of God if there were never a break in our earthly joy. We should never know the wonder of God's comfort if we had not sorrow. It is when the visible mountains depart, and we have them no longer to hide in, that our hearts find the mountains of God, with their eternal refuges.

> 'Twas in love I poured upon thee
>   Sunshine, joy, and sweet content,
> But the shadows—just believe Me,
>   They in greater love were sent.
>   Wounding thee, the would cut deeper
>   Into My heart e'en than thine.
> Grieving thee, oh child believe it,
>   That the greater grief was Mine.

_____

Jesus Himself stood in the midst of them, and saith unto them, Peace be unto you (Luke 24:36).

THE SMILE OF THE PILOT

R obert Louis Stevenson's story of a storm that caught a vessel off a rocky coast and threatened to drive it and its passengers to destruction is thrilling. In the midst of the terror one daring man, contrary to orders, went to the deck, made a dangerous passage to the pilot house, saw the steersman lashed fast at his post holding the wheel unwaveringly and inch by inch turning the ship out once more to sea. The pilot saw the watcher and smiled. Then the daring passenger went below and gave out a note of cheer. "I have seen the face of the pilot and he smiled. It is all well."

Blessed is he who in the midst of earthly stress and storm can say with equal assurance, "I have seen the face of my Pilot and He smiled!"

The story tells its own tale to us just now. It *is* a terrible storm that is on in your heart's experience. You can only think of the wreckage on the beach of your life, but listen! *There's the Pilot.* His Hand is on the wheel steady and firm. And if we may, in the venture of child's simple faith, creep out and look, *we can see His face.* It is always turned toward us. And He is smiling quietly down into our bewildered eyes. And we can say, in the words of the venturesome passenger, *"I have seen the face of the Pilot—and— He smiled."* He has our beloved ones up in the sunlight of the homeland with the Father.

And He Himself walks close by, saying in a quiet voice with a thrill of soft music in it, *"Be of good cheer, I am here."*

I sit alone and watch the darkning years,
    And all my heart grows dim with doubts and fear,
Till out of deepest gloom a Face appears—
    The only one of all that shineth clear.

Make white thy wedding-garments, O my soul!
    And sigh no longer for thy scanty dower;
For if He loves thee, He will crown thee whole
    With nobler beauty and immortal power.

O mighty Angel of the secret name!
    Come, for my heart doth answer Thy All-hail:
Come with the new name and the mystic stone,
    And speak so low that none shall hear the call—
O beautiful, beloved, and still unknown,
    I ask Thee naught:—Thy look hath promised all!"

Spencer.

MAY 30 _____

God is love (1 John 4:16).

Your child dies. Your heart is broken, your home is desolate, the half worn shoe she used to wear, the toy with which she played, will awaken your slumbering sorrow again and again, when time has partially healed the wound. Be patient: He doeth all things well. If you were walking along the street holding your child by the hand, in the holy pride and unspeakable joy of motherhood; and when you reached an unpleasant or dangerous place, you took the little one in your arms and carried her over and set her safely down beyond the unpleasant or dangerous place, you have done a kindness. So it may be that the Great Father of us all, as He held your child by the hand, saw some place of discomfort or pain or danger or loss, and in infinite tenderness took the little one up in His loving arms and placed her safely down on the other shore. You may some day see clearly where you are in darkness now, and in the clearer light of heaven thank Him for that act which almost excites rebellious feelings now. *Rev. Robert Forbes.*

TWO LITTLE FEET

Two little feet went pattering by
    Years ago,
They wandered off to the sunny sky
    Years ago,
They crept not back to the love they left,
They climbed nevermore to the arms bereft—
    Years ago.

Again I shall hear those two little feet
    Pattering by;
Their music a thousand times more sweet
    In the sky;
I joy to think that the Father's care
Will hold them safe till I meet them there
    By and by.   *Anon.*

MAY 31 ———————————————————————

I am the Lord . . . which leadeth thee by the way that thou shouldest go (Isa. 48:17).

"When I am weary and disappointed," says a sympathetic writer, "when the skies lower into the sombre night, when there is no song of bird, and the perfume of flowers is but dying breath; when all is unsetting and autumn; *then I yearn for Him* who sits with the summer of love in His soul and feel that earthly affection is but a glow-worm light, compared to that which blazes with such effulgence in the heart of God."

Other lights may be obscured or missing; yours may possibly even now be either the mourner's watch, with its hushed vigils, or you may be sundered by death from dearly loved ones, yearning for "the touch of the vanished hand." You cannot get away from the touch of God. "The Lord thy God is with thee whithersoever thou goest." He loves thee through thine anguish, and will yet assuredly vindicate the rectitude of all His procedure.

THROUGH THE GARDEN

He leadeth me, tho' by a way unknown,
Upward but onward toward the great white throne.
No path have I; the way is rough and wild;
But I can hear the clear, sweet voice,
    "I hold thy hand, My child."

O'er desert drear, the storm-blown drifting sand,
Fills eyes tear-laden till I scarce can stand.
Then He bends down and whispers soft and low,
"Just lean on Me, I know the way; I know."

"I know how long the march, the loneliness,
The deep soul-anguish with no friend to bless;
Just close thine eyes, My child, and lean on Me;
I walked alone this dark Gethsemane.

JUNE 1

I will lead the blind in a way they have not known; in paths they knew not I will make them tread: I turn dark spaces before them into light and the rugged ways into a smooth plain. These things will I do for them, and not forsake them (Isa. 42:16—Delitzsch).

Suppose you are bewildered and know not which way to turn. Death has suddenly robbed you of your loved one, and it all seems so inexplicable. The age-old question, "Why?" comes to your mind continually. You cry out, but there is no answer, no explanation. Cannot you take this trial into your heart and be ignorant, not because you are obliged, but because that being God's will, it is yours also? Cannot you utterly and perfectly love God and rejoice to be in the dark, and gloom-beset, because that very thing is the fact of God's Infinite Being as it is to you?

Faith can sit down before mysteries and say, "The Lord is good."

Dear Heart!
    Stop planning for thyself tonight,
    When darkness seems to hide the light;

For He who holds the universe
Has planned it all aright.

Florence M. Schmidt.

JUNE 2 _____

*In peace will I lie down and at once sleep . . . For Thou, Jehovah in my
loneliness, maketh me to dwell in safety (Psalm 4:4. Original Greek.)*

How have I learned to sleep? He bade me rest
In the charmed circle of His loving arms;
I found there was no pillow like His breast,
And here I sleep, secure from all alarms;
OUTSIDE are storms, "deep calleth unto deep"—
But HERE, "He giveth His beloved sleep."

GOD KEEP YOU!

God keep you, dearest, all the lonely night;
   The winds are still,
The moon drops down behind the western hill;—
   God keep you, dearest, till the light.

God keep you then when slumbers melt away,
   And care and strife
Take up new arms to fret our waking life,
   And keep you through the battle of the day.

God keep you! Nay, beloved soul, how vain,
   How poor is prayer!
I can but say again, and yet again,
   God keep you every time and everywhere!

Mary Aigne de Vere.

JUNE 3 _____

He rode—upon the wings of the wind (2 Samuel 22:11).

O ur God does not *beat down* the storms that rise against Him:
He rides upon them; He works through them. You are often
surprised that so many thorny paths are allowed to open for the
good—how that aspiring boy Joseph is put in the dungeon; how
that beautiful child Moses is cast into the Nile. You would have
expected Providence to have interrupted the opening of those pits
destined for destruction. Well, He might have done so; He might

155

have said to the storm, "Peace, be still!" But there was a more
excellent way—to ride upon it. God said, "I will not shut up the
pit, but I will make it the road to the throne of Egypt; I will not dry
the Nile, but I will make it a channel to a great sea; I will not
prevent the cross, but I will make it the world's crown."

You too should ride upon the wings of the wind. Say not, "I
must take shelter till the storm passes." Say not, "God will sweep
it away that I may come nearer to Himself." Nay, it is the storm
that will *bring* you nearer. He maketh the clouds His chariot. Leap
into His chariot! Commit yourself to the black horses! Go out to
meet the storm! Recline upon the bosom of the cloud! Ride upon
the wings of the wind! And they will bear you home. Your cross
will make your crown.   *George Matheson.*

JUNE 4 _____

Blessed are the dead which die in the Lord (Rev. 14:13).

>   No more trouble, or toil, no more head care,
>   Or heart ache, no goodbye spoken, no sigh heard,
>   No more pain, no more weariness, no woe of
>   Any kind—no sickness, no sorrow—
>   Blessed are the dead.
>
>   No storm upon the Sea, no bitterness in the cup,
>   No shadow on the landscape, no thorn beside
>   The flower, no clouded Sky, no opening Grave,
>   No Death, and no more sin—
>   Blessed are the dead.
>
>   The Battles of life fought, the Storms of life
>   Weathered, the lessons of life learned,
>   The pilgrimage of life trodden, Marahs,
>   Burning sands all past—
>   Blessed are the dead.
>
>   Thrones, harps, Crowns all present, Pearly
>   Gates and Jasper walls, Golden pavements and
>   Harps of Triumph, Palm branches for Victors—
>   Blessed are the dead.
>
>   The eternal ministries of Glory, the Home of
>   Abiding-places, the Foursquare City, the

Unsetting Sunlight of God's face—
  Blessed are the dead.

The twelve fruited Trees of healing, the crystal
Sea of glass, the Hallelujah Chorus of the
Redeemed and the Eulogy of God.
  Blessed are the dead.

And over there by the silver river where flowers bloom and
where God reigns, they will await us. Linger for us, dear ones, at
the pearly gate, for we shall soon be at home over there.

W. B. Hinson.

JUNE 5

*For I the Lord thy God will hold thy right hand, saying unto thee, Fear not;
I will help thee (Isa. 41:13).*

There is something in bereavement which makes it mean a
great deal in a woman's life. It is a sore disppointment.
Dreams of love's happiness are shattered. The beauty which had
only begun to be realized in her home, in her wedded joy, in the
development of her plans and hopes is suddenly left to wither.
Very great is the sorrow when one of two lovers is taken and the
other left. Widowhood is very desolate and lonely.

Just how shall she meet her perplexities. She is a Christian. She
is comforted in her grief by the truth of Divine love, that her
sorrow was no accident, that her bereavement was not the plan of
God to break up the goodness and beauty of her life, that nothing
has really gone wrong in the plan of Christ for her. But the
question presses itself upon her mind—I am sure it has done so a
thousand times—How am I to go on in this broken life of mine?
What am I to do in my shattering bereavement? Her life is not yet
finished. She is only a girl in years. She may live—she probably
will live—forty years or more. What does Christ want her to do
with her broken life?

God's plan for her was not spoiled when her sorrow came
interrupting everything leaving her in darkness. The sorrow was
not a surprise to God, and His plan for her life runs on to the end
of her years. What the remainder of the plan is she does not know
for the present. She must go on in faith and confidence. Believe

that all these broken things are in His hands. "Gather up the broken pieces that remain that nothing be lost"—that is what Christ is saying to her today. Let her gather up the broken pieces from this miracle of love and happiness. Let her keep all the fragments.

The next thing is for her to recommit her life, with its grief, its desolation, its broken things, all to Christ. She must not undertake to rebuild it. She must not make plans of her own for the years to come. She must let Christ lead her, let Him plan for her, mark out the way. He must build the life for her. He must have much of the love she has to give. Be brave dear soul! God's help is near!

Dr. Miller.

Lean not to thine own understanding,
But let the Lord manage for thee.

Oft when I seem to tread alone
Some barren waste with thorns o'ergrown,
Thy voice of love, in tenderest tone,
Whispers, "Still cling to ME!"

JUNE 6

They that dwell under His shadow shall return; they shall revive as the corn and grow as the vine (Hosea 14:7).

The day closed with heavy showers. The plants in my garden were beaten down before the pelting storm, and I saw one flower that I had admired for its beauty and loved for its fragrance exposed to the pitiless storm. The flower fell, shut up its petals, dropped its head; and I saw that all its glory was gone. "I must wait till next year," I said, "before I see that beautiful thing again."

That night passed, and morning came; the sun shone again, and the morning brought strength to the flower. The light looked at it, and the flower looked at the light. There was contact and communion, and power passed into the flower. It held up its head, opened its petals, regained its glory, and seemed fairer than before. I wonder how it took place—this feeble thing coming into contact with the strong thing, and gaining strength!

I cannot tell how it is that I should be able to receive into my being a power to do and to bear my communion with God, but I know it is a fact.

Are you in peril through some crushing, heavy trial? Seek this communion with Christ, and you will receive strength and be able to conquer. "I will strengthen thee."

YESTERDAY'S GRIEF

The rain that fell a-yesterday is ruby on the roses
    Silver on the poplar leaf, and gold on willow stem;
The grief that chanced a-yesterday is silence that incloses
    Holy loves when time and change shall never trouble
      them.

The rain that fell a-yesterday makes all the hillsides
      glisten,
    Coral on the laurel and beryl on the grass;
The grief that chanced a-yesterday has taught the soul
    to listen
    For whispers of eternity in all the winds that pass.

O faint-of-heart, storm-beaten, this rain will gleam
      tomorrow,
    Flame within the columbine and jewels on the thorn,
Heaven in the forget-me-not; though sorrow now
      be sorrow,
    Yet sorrow shall be beauty in the magic of the morn.
Katherine Lee Bates.

JUNE 7

He woundeth and His hands make whole (Job 5:18).

GOD'S BIRD

There is a story of an Indian child who came in one day from the wheat-field with a hurt bird in her hand. Running to the old chief, she said: "See! This is my bird. I found it in the wheat. It is hurt." The old man looked at the wounded bird and replied slowly: "No, it is not your bird, my child—it is God's bird. Take it back and lay it down where you found it. If you keep it, it will die. If you give it back into God's hands, He will heal its hurt and it will live."

What the old Indian said of hurt birds is true of hearts hurt by

159

sorrow. No human hand can heal them—the only safe thing to do in time of grief is to put our lives into God's hands, to commit them to Him. His hands are gentle and skillful. They will not break a bruised reed nor quench the smoking flax. He will give us just the help we need and just when we need it.

> How oft at the touch of that nail-scarred palm,
> My storm-troubled soul has at once grown calm.
> The tempest that surges I will not fear,
> For how can I sink if that Hand is near!

JUNE 8

The Lord will be a refuge unto His people, and a stronghold to the children of Israel (Joel 3:16).

In the tropics, we are told, the raging storms have a patch of clear blue sky over the central calm, and poets call this *"the whirlwind's heart of peace."* But the quietude means dread and danger to the mariner, for no wind moves the sailing ship, yet the blast around drives in heavy, troublous billows: the sailor would fain avoid that perilous center.

There is no *false* peace in the calm the Christian knows *even at the whirlwind time.* There are seasons when it seems to us the Lord thundereth in the heavens, and the Highest gives forth His voice in terror and in wrath; but higher than the storms our vision must look—even to our Father's face—which promises love and rest and protection.

Be of comfort, my soul! His arms are around thee in the tempest-hour; He will stay His rough wind from which thou tremblest; He will be to thee a covert from the storm, an everlasting shelter.

JUNE 9

Am I not better to thee (1 Samuel 1:8).

> The evening shadows fall. The day is done—
> Glad day of service, till the setting sun
> Sinks in the reddening west, then work is o'er;
> And entering my hut I close the door.

The evening shadows steal across the room,
And all is still, enwrapped in deepening gloom.
No human voice to break the stillness, here
I dwell alone, and all I hold most dear
Are far removed beyond the trackless sea—
So very far they seem to-night from me!
Yet for a moment brief methinks I hear
The echo of loved voices in mine ear;
The dear home faces seem to shine again,
Then swiftly vanish in a mist of pain.
And dearest ones now long since "gone before"
Thus seem to come and disappear once more.
Yet 'tis but for a moment that I turn,
And with heart-longings for beloved ones yearn.
Hush! I am not alone, a Presence blest
Fills all my chamber with a sense of rest!
A moment's darkness, then a flood of light!
A moment's sadness, then a great delight!
A well-known Voice is whispering unto me,
"Am not I better, O beloved, to thee?"
"Am not I better far to thee than all?"

Low at His feet I now adoring fall,
Out-breathing there in speechless love and praise
The song the heart is 'most too full to raise.

Thou art enough, my own beloved ONE!
And work with Thee is sweet till day is done;
And when at eventide I close my door,
Shut in with Jesus, what can I need more?
Mine is a joy, a satisfaction rare,
Which only "separated ones" may share.

The evening shades may fall about my room,
But brighter glows the glory.
        Till He come
I'll wait and work, and praise Him all the way,
And so "in Him" be found at dawn of Day;
Then through a long Eternity to prove
The satisfying power of Jesus' love!   *E. May Grimes.*

JUNE 10 _____

His right hand presseth me to His heart (Isa. 41:10—German).

Every great sorrow is in a certain sense a lonely sorrow. It drives a man into the fastnesses of himself. . . . Christ is the one Guest who can enter the sacred chamber of a great sorrow. The soul's sense of loneliness yields to Him. The heart's sensitive reserve gives way. Christ enters, and thenceforth sorrow takes on a new meaning and aspect. The blinding bereavement, and crushing loss or disappointment, the trial that has wrenched the very heart strings asunder, the awful temptation that has swept the soul at last from its moorings—all these crises of life fall into harmony with the divine love and the divine purpose when the Saviour enters the hidden Chamber of our griefs. We never know what sorrow means, or what it can do for the soul till then. "Lo!" says Christ to the spirit brooding in lonely grief, "lo, I am with you alway, even unto the end of the world." Blessed promise! Lord Jesus, come Thou into all our sorrow-burdened hearts; fill them with Thy divine sympathy, and help us to learn through Thy love the sacred meaning and uses of all life's dark and painful experiences!   *James Buckham, Ph.D.*

GOD EVER CARES

God ever cares! Not only in life's summer,
    When skies are bright and days are long and glad:
He cares as much when life is draped in winter,
    And heart doth feel bereft, and lone, and sad.

God ever cares! His heart is ever tender;
    His love doth never fail nor show decay:
The loves of earth, though strong and deep, may perish—
    But His shall never, never pass away.

God ever cares! And thus when life is lonely,
    When blessings one time prized are growing dim—
The heart may find a sweet and sunny shelter—
    A refuge and a resting-place in Him.

God ever cares! And time can never change Him—
    His nature is to care, and love, and bless;
And drearest, darkest, emptiest days afford Him
    But means to make more sweet His own caress.
                                        J. D. Smith.

I am He that liveth, and was dead; and behold I am alive forevermore, Amen; and have the keys of hell and of death (Rev. 1:18).

Have I been so long time with you, and yet hast thou not known Me? Have I ever failed you yet? I know when and how you are to die, and where I shall keep your dust till the day of resurrection. I know how it will fare with your loved ones; my providence is not going to die when you die. I have sounded all the depths of death, and risen with the key of every grave in my hand. The dark which you fear is but the way home. "Be of good cheer; it is I; be not afraid."

Why should you weep and grieve and sigh?
As those who have no hope brought nigh?
   Let Christ your comfort be:
By Him thy sorrows all were borne,
And death of all its terrors shorn,
   From death and Hell he took the sting,
   Rejoice, O sorrowing, and sing—
      He is thy victory.

Down into death the Saviour went,
Threw back its bars, the tomb He rent;
   He went to set thee free:
He hold the keys of death and hell,
He saith, "Trust, all things are well;
   Come, unto me your burden bring,
   Come, learn to trust in Me, and sing—
      I am thy victory."   *Dr. R. E. Neighbour.*

Dost thou know the balancings of the clouds, the wondrous works of Him which is perfect in knowledge? (Job 37:16).

THE CLOUDS THAT ARE FULL OF RAIN

What a comfort it is to know that no stranger-hand hath veiled our sky! The shadows have gathered, at the will of Him we trust, and love to "break in blessings" overhead. Not one sorrow hath befallen us, or can befall, save by His appointing and for the fulfillment of His merciful purpose; we are too blind, too feeble, to *understand* "the balancings of the clouds, the wondrous works of Him which is perfect in knowledge," but we know His name is Love, and behind all mystery is the Light that changeth not.

The clouds of sorrow mean for *us* abundance of rain; shall we not sing in thanksgiving and joy, since the Lord hath been mindful of us, and prepared for us the help and blessing His wisdom knows we need?

"Sore trial makes common Christians into uncommon saints, and fits them for being used in uncommon service."

JUNE 13 ─────────────────────────

Whosoever liveth and believeth in Me shall never die (John 11:26).

We thank Thee for the dear and faithful dead, for those who have made the distant Heavens a Home for us, and whose truth and beauty are even now in our hearts. One by one Thou dost gather the scattered families out of the earthly light into the Heavenly glory, from the distractions and strife and weariness of time to the peace of eternity. We thank Thee for the labors and the joys of these mortal years. We thank Thee for our deep sense of the mysteries that lie beyond our dust, and for the eye of faith which Thou hast opened for all who believe in Thy Son to outlook that mark. May we live altogether in Thy Faith and Love, and in that Hope which is full of Immortality. Amen!   *Rufus Ellis.*

AWAY

I cannot say and I will not say
That he is dead—he is just away.

With a cheery smile and a wave of the hand
He has wandered into an unknown land;

And left us dreaming how very fair
It needs must be since he lingers there.

And you—O you, who the wildest yearn
For the old-time step and the glad return,

Think of him faring on, as dear
In the love of There as the love of Here.

Mild and gentle as he was brave—
When the sweetest love of his life he gave

To simple things; where the violets grew
Blue as the eyes they were likened to,

The touches of his hands have strayed
As reverently as his lips have prayed;

When the little brown thrush that harshly chirred
Was as dear to him as the mocking bird;

And he pitied as much as a man in pain
A writhing honey-bee wet with rain.

Think of him still as the same, I say:
He is not dead—he is just away!   *James Whitcomb Riley.*

JUNE 14 _____

The maid is not dead, but sleepeth (Matt. 9:24).

THE MAIDEN, GOD'S FLOWER

It sometimes happens that the sun arises with unusual splendor. In golden armor it battles with the forces of darkness and sends them flying beyond the western hills. Each leaf hangs stuck with diamond dewdrops, each drop burning like the sun himself.

Men said, this is a fair day, and hope and joy beamed from their eyes. All nature was aglow with the light. The little birds caught the day spirit and sang their sweetest carols. The sky, blue and June-like, laid its warm ear close to earth to hear if it were in tune. O, what is so rare as a morn in June!

But before the morning was scarce begun, a cloud arose. It came up very fast, and grew thicker and thicker. The day drew darker and darker. Not one gleam of gold could push through that stormcloud to give man one ray of hope. The day became very dark. Then came the storm—terrible, furious. It whirled through the valley of oaks and writhed and twisted their great trunks until all was waste and desolation.

Once there was a life that came in like a new-born day. It brought golden light into one home, yea, many homes. There was never a day in June so rare as that bright life. It gave hope and happiness to everyone. The birds sang merrier for her presence.

Flowers seemed to give out their sweetest perfume for her pleasure. It was easy to be good when she was near. All was happiness, all was light.

But the storm arose suddenly. There was no warning but a heart-pain, sharp as a lightning flash. Then all grew dark. Great hearts were torn and mangled. Strong men broke down and cried. It was like a battlefield of wounded, a valley of oaks after a storm. It is all lost, we say. But wait! That bright sunlit morn gave hope to a little seed. It took root and grew into a vine with luxuriant foliage, and covered over the wounded hearts with its healing leaves of memory. And, as the oak looks richer with the ivy clinging to it, so our lives will be made richer and sweeter because of the clinging love-memory of our little girl.

Nothing can be lost. This is the law of physics. If no energy can be lost, how can love, sweetness, and purity be lost? There was real worth in this young life—worth to her home, worth to the Sunday School, worth to the "Helping Hands," worth to the C. E. society, worth to the public schools; and I say it with all seriousness, worth to God. If there is anything earthly that would picture her character, it is sunlight and roses. If there is anything heavenly that portrays her nature, it is love. What more does earth need? What more can heaven demand? Sunlight, roses and love—they give joy to man; they will give joy to God. Her life has been a blessing to us, though it was so very short, but

'Tis better to have loved and lost,
Than never to have loved at all.   *Rev. Wm. Rainey Bennett.*

JUNE 15 _____

In my Father's house are many mansions: if it were not so, I would have told you (John 14:2).

THE FATHER'S HOUSE IS A SURE HOUSE

These are days of doubt. Men are doubting the Godhood of our Lord; doubting His atonement; His resurrection; His glorious return; doubting hell; doubting heaven. Naturally the thought arises—Can we possibly be deceived? Is it all true? Is it true that He shall change the body of our humiliation and fashion it like unto the body of His glory; that His servants shall serve Him in a service that sweeps the universe; that they shall forever live in the glory of His face to face presence; that they shall "stand in their lot" through all the ages; that they shall share His kingship and follow Him whithersoever He goeth; that their tears shall be wiped away, their sufferings forgotten, their separation ended?

It is surely, unshakably, and eternally true. For He who never deceived a soul in earth or heaven; He who is "full of grace and truth"; He who is the truth Himself, has said with a voice of assurance which rings out from the heart of this fourteenth of John from two thousand years ago—

If it were not so, I would have told you!   *James McConkey.*

JUNE 16 ────────────────────────────────

God meant it unto good (Gen. 50:20).

There is a beautiful figure in one of Wordsworth's poems, of a bird that is swept from Norway by storm. And it battles against the storm with desperate effort, eager to wing back again to Norway. But all is vain, and so at last it yields, thinking that the gale will carry it to death—and the gale carries it to sunny England, with its green meadows and its forest glades.

Ah, how many of us have been like that little voyager, fretting and fighting against the will of God! And we thought that life could never be the same again when we were carried seaward by the storm. Until at last, finding all was useless, perhaps, yielding to the wind that bloweth where it listeth, we have been carried to a land that was far richer, where there were green pastures and still waters.

> I'd like a way
> To change the clouds that bring us sorrow,
> And build today a bright tomorrow;
> To banish cares that tarry long,
> And have the days like the blue-bird's song—
> I'd like a way.
>
> I'll find a way—
> I'll set sail when the breeze is high
> And calmly drift when pleasure's nigh;
> I'll steer a course afar from tears,

And take in joy the coming years—
   I'll find a way.

   I've lost the way!
Out through the gloom a beam of light
Looks like a purpose looming bright!
Up with the sail! I'll out to sea,
And bring that purpose back to me,
   Or go its way.   *M. B. S.*

JUNE 17

Thy will be done (Matt. 6:10).

When the heart has been wrung by anguish, when the waters have overwhelmed us—the proud waters have gone over our soul—when we have been beaten back and trampled down and when the sun has darkened our sky, and the stars have forgot their shining, in the wreck of our career, in the blight of hope, when the unforeseen and the unlooked-for have made mock of our ambitions, when death has robbed us of that which has given us the best joy we have known on earth, and left us, as it seemed, friendless, unpitied, homeless in the night—then we have tried to stay our faltering faith on God with this prayer of fathomless pain: They will be done.   *Dr. Aked.*

One may be quiescent, yet not acquiescent. There must be the folded will, as well as the folded heart.

THE FOLDED WILL
O fluttering heart that, like a bird imprisoned,
   Beateth itself against life's circling bars;
Lift thou a song to Him who sees clear-visioned
   Thy home beyond the stars.
Trust thou in God, to whom the night and day
Shine as one light that never fades away.

Fold thou thy wings and wait the time appointed,
   When, to thy joy, from earthly bonds set free,
Thine eyes behold, with heavenly powers anointed,
   Green fields of liberty.
O prisoner of hope, in patience wait,
Till God's hour strike—and opened is the gate.

Thus shalt thou know, e'en now, the satisfaction
  Of hearts that trust the Faithful and the True,
The freedom of the soul, of faith in action,
  Soaring beyond the blue.
Thou need'st not wait for liberty until
The day shall break, if thou but fold thy will.

O blessed peace, the peace of simply taking
  The yoke of Christ to learn His promised rest;
The peace of lying still, thy choice forsaking,
  To lean upon His breast;
The rest of folded hands from work self-wove,
The peace of folded will in His great love.   *J. H. S.*

JUNE 18

*Saul and Jonathan were lovely and pleasant in their lives, and in their
death they were not divided (2 Samuel 1:23).*

They that live beyond the world cannot be separated by it.
Death cannot kill what never dies. Nor can spirits ever be
divided that live and love in the same divine principle, the root and
record of their friendship.

Death is but crossing the world as friends do the seas; they live
in one another still.

This is the comfort of friends, that though they may be said to
die, yet their friendship and society are, in the best sense, ever
present, because immortal.   *William Penn.*

THE ULTIMATE

How far together? Till the road
  Ends at some churchyard wall; until the bell
Tolls for the entrance to the lone abode;
  Until the only whisper is "Farewell"?

How far together? Till the light
  No longer wakens in the loving eyes;
Until the shadow of the final night
  Has swept the last star-glimmer from the skies?

How far together? Past the end
  Of this short road, beyond the starry gleam;
Till day and night and time and space shall blend
  Into the vast Forever of our Dream.   *Eldredge Denison.*

169

The dear ones left behind?
Oh, foolish ones and blind—
A day and you will meet,
A night and you will greet.

JUNE 19

Blessed is he whosoever is not offended in Me (Matt. 11:6).

In many ways our confidence in God is tested; amongst others, by the multiplication of occasions when it is possible to be offended in Him. God can bring us into strong faith only by taking great liberties with our confidence. John is in a miserable prison and hears that Jesus is raising the dead and healing the sick. Most naturally he must think that if Jesus can do that He can surely get him out of this prison. *Why* does He not do it? What grace it must have taken not to question *why* He who possessed such mighty resources should leave him there undelivered in that dungeon! But Jesus left him right there with no explanation. One word would have opened those doors and let him free.

If we are to enjoy a close walk with God, we have to leave many things unexplained. We do not understand everything, but "what I do Thou knowest not now, but thou shalt know hereafter." God *could* take burdens out of our lives and yet He does not. These are the hours which peculiarly fit us for the inheritance of the saints in light, when Jesus puts all around us the message: "I can do it; but trust Me, though I do not do it." That is just the point where hearts break. He has all power and yet He does not mention one word to you of deliverance. These are the hours that we will study with delight and amazement in the light of eternity: no explanation; faith nourished; the prison doors left closed; and then the message, "Blessed is he whosoever is not offended in Me."— That is all!

Try not to misinterpret Him.

JUNE 20

After the fire a still small voice (1 Kings 19:12).

It is easy with the lip to speak of the duty of lying dumb under the rod—the nobleness of submission. This exhortation, glibly spoken, comes too often from those who have never themselves entered the inner depths of trial; who, however meaning kindly, venture to address the smitten heart with conventional phrases of solace. They, unwittingly but unskilfully, probe the wound; in ignorance of how their words of intended condolence only lacerate. Resignation, aided with the soothing influence of time, *does* generally, and in due course, manifest itself. In the deepest night-watches of sorrow, the lullabies not of man but of God, come in to soothe to rest, and to still the surges of the soul.

> Did I hear Him whisper to me
>   Sweet and low?
> Did His voice go thrilling through me?
>   Did I know
> That His precious self was near me,
> That He'd brought His love to cheer me
>   As I go?
>
> When my bleeding heart was aching
>   For my loss,
> And my clinging love was making
>   Gold of dross;
> When my heart with pain was throbbing,
> Then Thy love the weight was robbing
>   From my cross.   *J. A. W. H.*

JUNE 21 _____

Let patience have her perfect work (James 1:4).

How can I believe in any good coming out of this long, dark, lingering trouble?" some weary heart may ask. "All is barren, unlovely, unpromising; there is no flower of hope that can blossom from out this sorrow." Let us hear what the sweet-brier under our window has to say.

"When I was planted in this garden I was only a bare brown root, feeling very different from the golden crocus near me, and the laughing daffodils that rejoiced in the sunlight. I had no beauty, no balm, no grace; I was anything but an ornament, and I could scarcely understand why the gardener should set me here at all.

Yet something within me said, " *Wait!* " I could do nothing else; so I was content simply to do what I *could.* The gardener evidently *meant* me to wait, and I saw his kind face look down upon me sometimes with a smile as I drank the rain and stretched out of my life to the light. Circumstances seemed all against me; but a Power worked within me that was greater than circumstances. By and by sweet influences stole from out me; Heaven made my rod to blossom, and people turned with yearning looks to touch my leaves, and the old memories and new aspirations were born through the brier that waited alone and unnoticed for its crown of glory.

"Is anything too hard for the Lord?" Dwell within His light through the waiting-time; drink in the dews of His gracious Spirit, the Comforter; and thou, weary heart! shalt be used to breathe influences that shall be sweet and blest to eternity; thy memory shall be fragrant even when thy place is known no more. *Selected.*

JUNE 22 ─────────────────────────────────

I reckon that the sufferings of this present time are not worthy to be compared with the glory which shall be revealed in us (Rom 8:18).

It is the testimony of universal Christian experience, that, from the grave-side of our hardest trials, we have risen to the grandest achievements of the divine life. And so it is, not only with us of this generation, but across the long and weary centuries; for from prison cells and fiery stakes, from disappointed hopes and from beside open graves, there have come the richest experience of the love of God and of His supporting power, the noblest witnesses of resignation to His will, and the fullest consciousness and assurance that He doeth all things well! Blessed be His name!

And then, when the morning of Eternity has dawned upon us at last, and we shall have come, through God's good grace, to stand forth as children newly risen at the break of day to behold the beauty of the dawn—strong in the consciousness of the life forever freed from the bondage of corruption, and made beautiful and complete in the image of God—then, ah, then, our bitterest woe of earth, forever past, shall seem of "as little moment to us as the tear which glistens in the eye of childhood even while the laugh leaps to the lips." Then shall the soul be forever freed from the ills that now assail and afflict it; then shall the fact and experience of suffering be over; and then shall the final end of suffering be attained, and attained forever. Weeping may endure for the night—and the night may be long and dark—but joy cometh in the morning. "Wherefore, comfort one another with these words."

> The easy path in the lowland hath little of grand or new,
> But a toilsome ascent leads on to a wide and glorious view!
> Peopled and warm is the valley, lonely and chill the height,
> But the peak that is nearer the storm cloud is nearer the stars of light.
> F. R. Havergal.

JUNE 23

It shall turn to you for a testimony (Luke 21:13).

Two young people went to the mission field to give their lives to the work of evangelism. When they were getting control of the language, and when they were dreaming and planning for work in a new station they were to open, the husband was smitten with a serious malady. The devoted wife was by his side in the hospital as his strength waned, and together they talked of the high hopes, the sure mercies and the unfailing wisdom of God. They talked especially of one great hope, so near to fulfillment for them, but which his eyes were not to behold here.

When the wife had held the Lover's head in her arms and kissed him farewell at the border of the two worlds, she turned to go into the valley of the shadow of death and bring back their son, child of prayer and promise. The burial of one Love and the birth of a new Love came thus together.

What would the young missionary widow do? Surely she would seek the comfort and support of loved ones in the homeland. Not so with this brave little woman. Her Lord had brought her to the mission field and He had not changed. She must carry on. In that year of waiting there was prayer, there was meditation; there was a new getting acquainted with God. In it all the bruised heart was being bound up and made greater in God's grace.

Later on she wrote: "In a hospital in a strange land, I sat

watching and waiting, while he who was not only husband but all relatives and friends in one, was entering the valley of the shadow. In unconsiousness once he called the name of his boyhood friend, who had sung at our wedding. Then memories! Ah, memories! I was hearing again the song of that sacred night, 'The Sweetest Story Ever Told,' and walking again a flower-petalled aisle, and feeling the thrill of the song that closed that holy hour:

> We've a Saviour to show to the nations,
>   Who the path of sorrow has trod,
> That all of the world's great people
>   Might come to the truth of God.

"Then memories of happy days that followed! Of moonlight nights from the top deck on the ocean; of fair days and beautiful nights with a star-lit heaven above, and rolling waves beneath! Memories of entering the first time the land of our adoption, of plans for a bright future in the greatest cause in all the world! Memories of home life so fragrant and sacred; of dreams for our child in the Master's service!

"In that quiet hour in the morning when the finer, bigger, fuller life opened to him, it seemed to me that every hope was being torn out of my life. Yet, he had said, when I told him I could not go on without him, 'We are not just for each other, but for our Lord. Though you should be called away from me today, tomorrow I should pick up the threads, and carry on in the Master's service the best I could without you. You must do the same'."

No, we are not here just for ourselves. Love must be strong and unselfish. It must look away from its own torn heart to a needy world, forward to the day when it shall be joyous forever, up to the wise Father who does all things well. If the Weaver of our life's pattern chooses another plan than the one we thought to use, is He not wiser than we? Surely it will be a pattern more beautiful than our fondest dreams.

> *"The Life Beautiful," by Rosalie Mills Appleby.*

"This shall turn" (Phil. 1:19).

> THIS SHALL TURN! This thing which speaks denial
> To cherished hopes and prayers of many years;
> This heavy blow—this overweight of trial,
> This, this shall turn, though now there falleth tears.

THIS SHALL TURN! This sudden, swift disaster,
This rapid wreckage of life's planned-out way—
Yes, this shall turn, and heart may beat e'en faster
In contemplation of the brighter day.

Yes,—"THIS WILL TURN!" We'll say it and believe it!
This, this shall turn, how soon we cannot say!
And happy sight shall truly yet perceive it,
That God HATH TURNED it all in His own way.

J. Danson Smith.

JUNE 24

*And they sang a new song, saying, Thou art worthy to take the book . . .
for Thou wast slain, and hast redeemed us to God by Thy blood, out of
every kindred, and tongue, and people, and nation (Rev. 5:9).*

What is the most inspiring music you ever heard? An old man
wrote me a letter a few days ago; he told me of being in
Boston in 1869 for the great Peace Jubilee, sung in praise of the
ending of the Civil War. There was a chorus of 10,000 voices, and
an orchestra of 1000 pieces; two hundred anvils had been placed
on the platform for use in the "Anvil Chorus." There were huge
bells; and outside, in the park, was artillery to be fired by
electricity, in harmony with the chorus.

At the head of the two hundred violins stood the world's
greatest violinist, Ole Bull, who had them so trained that their
bows worked as in the hand of one man. Parepa Rosa was the
soloist, of whose singing that day Dr. Talmadge said, "It will never
be equalled again on earth." When in the "Star-Spangled
Banner" she sang the high "C," with the fortefortissimo
accompaniment of the full chorus and orchestra, the bells and
cannon, it was so loud and clear that it seemed to bury the
accompaniment. Nothing like it was ever heard before, and never
will be again. The letter closed, "I am an old man now, but am
looking forward to the music of Heaven, where there will be music
infinitely superior to the marvelous chorus I listened to that day."

Days of Devotion.

What a wonderful chorus through the skies shall ring.
When the saints are marching in!

Lord, if Thou hast provided such music for the people of earth, what hast Thou in store for Thy saints in Heaven!

> There all the millions of His saints
>   Shall in one song unite,
> And each the bliss of all shall view
>   With infinite delight.   *Philip Doddridge.*

Even now I can hear its deep diapason, the ebb and flow of its deathless music.   *Bishop Foster.*

> When we've been there ten thousand years.
>   Bright shining as the sun,
> We've no less days to sing His praise,
>   Then when we first begun!

JUNE 25

Afterward (Heb. 12:11).

FIREWEED

A stretch of ragged, burnt-over woodland clearing turned into a purple blaze of glory; the ranks of summer bloom marching like an army with banners. Only a little while before, the fire-swept space had showed dark and unsightly, full of charred stumps and moss, all its beauty of strong, living green turned to desolation. Now, over the flame's blackened path surged the conquering hosts of the fireweed. Flame and ruin and desolation were as if they had not been, and the summer grew more glorious for the wealth of royal bloom. A terrible and searching grief had yielded a sure and beautiful joy.

"Tribulation worketh patience," wrote the author of the Epistle to the Romans. A strong soul, faced by disaster, grief, death, sets itself first of all not to cry out. Holding steady against the shock, it sits alone in silence and takes counsel with itself, striving for nothing beyond its power. Being strong it knows its own weakness. Here is no place for the sudden display of evanescent heroisms.

Now is the moment for self-containment. Down in the dark, below the desolation wrought by the flame of suffering, the roots of the bloom that shall be are striving for life. This the strong soul knows as its moment of growth; for only a strong soul retains through every stupefying trial, ever overwhelming sorrow, its consciousness of the import and significance of the immediate. The lesson to be learned is inaction, repression, growth below ground. "Tribulation," he said—and he used the all-embracing word that leaves nothing unexpressed—"Tribulation worketh patience."

Observation alone would have caused him to omit that, and seeing how soon the blackened wastes of the high-hearted burst into bloom he might have written, "Tribulation worketh experience." But this was from the pen of one whose life had known the oft-unmarked pause for patience. He knew the processes of the dark and the silence, when the night closes in, and the stars shine too near for lack of the shielding branches; he knew the workings of the day and the renewed stir and throb of living when the sun beats upon the unprotected ground; he knew of the dew of the tears and of the healing breath of prayer; and, above all, he knew of the life below death, of the push of the roots, nourished by sun and wind and dew and star-shine, into the potency and promise of splendor.

And now the strong soul, having adjusted itself in these hours of patience, may use its slowly garnered power. Unconscious of acquisition, it has acquired; bent only on enduring, it has steadied itself to swift achievement; now is the crowning moment. It needs all its forces to meet the demand, endure the strain. All the flame-blackened wastes of suffering are to be clothed with green. To the eye of the world desolation must be hidden; herein is the heroism of experience wrought by patience, when, grown stronger through silence, the soul covers its scars with verdure, and the world forgets.

But verdure is not all. Consciously, every faculty intent, the strong soul has lived in the significance of the immediate; nothing has been lost in the confusion of apprehension or the daze of retrospect. "Where'er thou art, be all there," was written for us who must bring blossom out of blackness.

And the apostle writes after experience, hope. Blossom follows hard upon the new green of experience—the bloom that is hope; for this transition from scar to beauty is but the evolution of hope. All the once desolate spaces are in a wonder and wealth of purple; never could they flaunt the red of untried joy, the gold of gladness, or the brave blue of unassaulted courage; purple is for that which is born of conquest over pain, and the fireweed, emblem of that

hope which maketh not ashamed, must forever wear purple.
There are those who know whereof this is written; there are spaces
in lives around us—nay, perhaps, in your life and mine—that
gleam in a glory of color, but the purple is the purple of the
fireweed.   *The Congregationalist.*

A fire swept the forest growth away—
  All the green thicket deeds of tender Earth;
  And every sapling Hope had given birth
Burned red, then white, and crumbled to decay;
While blackened trees stood stark in mute dismay.

So like our lives, consumed by some distress,
  When trusting hearts, blithe in the spirit of youth,
  Are blasted by the flames of sorrow's truth,
And withered in Pain's fire of faithlessness—
Until where Beauty bloomed no man can guess.

Yet, lo! a miracle when time is told—
  As trees and flowers shall bless that sod again,
  And lift their fervent lips to summer's rain,
So may our hearts arise from ashes cold
To give new growth to God a thousandfold.
                                          Edith Livingston Smith.

JUNE 26 ───

I will tell thee what the Lord hath said to me this night (1 Samuel 15:16).

BE STILL AND SLEEP

Be still and sleep, my soul!
  Now gentle-footed night,
In softly shadowed stole,
  Holds all the day from sight.

Why shouldst thou lie and stare
  Against the dark, and toss,
And live again thy care,
  Thine agony and loss?

'Twas given thee to live,
  And thou hast lived it all;
Let that suffice, nor give
  One thought what may befall.

Thou has no need to wake,
   Thou art no sentinel;
Love all the care will take,
   And Wisdom watcheth well.

Weep not, think not, but rest!
   The stars in silence roll;
On the world's mother-breast,
   Be still and sleep, my soul!

Edward Rowland Sill.

Much might be said on the wisdom of taking a constantly fresh view of life. It is one of the moral uses of the night that it gives the world anew to us every morning, and of sleep that it makes life a daily re-creation. If we always saw the world we might grow weary of it. If a third of life were not spent in unconsciousness, the rest might become tedious. God is thus all the while presenting the cup of life afresh to our lips. Thus, after a night of peaceful sleep we behold the world as new and fresh and wonderful as it was on the first morning of creation, when God pronounced it "very good." And sleep itself has a divine alchemy that gives us to ourselves with our primitive energy of body and mind. The days are not mere repetitions of themselves: to-morrow will have another meaning; I shall come to it with large vision than I have to-day.

T. T. Munger.

Rest, beloved, sleep on calmly,
   Love and trust Me—this your part;
Through the night of doubt and sorrow
   You are hidden in My heart.
Fear no evil—"look not round thee,"
   Walk by faith and not by sight,
Stars shine brightest through the darkness—
   I am with you day and night.

JUNE 27

Break forth in singing, O mountains, for the Lord hath comforted His people (Isa. 49:13).

There is a story of song birds being brought over the sea. There were thirty-six thousand of them, mostly canaries. At first, after the ship sailed, the sea was calm and the birds were silent.

They kept their little heads under their wings and not a note was heard. But the third day out the ship struck a furious gale. The passengers were terrified, the children wept. Then the strange thing happened. As the tempest reached its height, the birds all began to sing, first one, then another, till the whole thirty-six thousand were singing as if their little throats would burst.

When the clouds of sorrow gather and break, when the storm rises in its fury—do we then begin to sing?

If we fully understood the covenant of our God and believed His promises, should not our song break forth in tenfold joy when the tempest begins?

> A sweeter song my soul has heard
> Than angel anthem, lay of bird.
>
> It cheers my heart in storm and night,
> And makes both storm and darkness bright.
>
> The sweetest song that comes to me—
> The Song of Hope—It may yet be!
>
> Is Winter here? Have song-birds fled?
> They have but flown; they are not dead.
>
> The snows will melt, and with the spring
> The birds return on joyous wing;
>
> The flowers that faded long ago
> Will bloom again in summer's glow.
>
> So faces that have vanished here
> In heaven's bright morn will reappear.
>
> Sweet voices that are hushed and still
> Will there again our spirit's thrill.
>
> Hope may have flown, but not for aye,
> True hope will live a deathless day.
>
> Above the clouds, beyond the night,
> Faith soars and sings in living light.
>
> There comes the sweetest songs to me,
> The Song of Hope—It yet shall be!

Selected.

Now, after the death of Moses, the servant of the Lord, it came to pass that the Lord spake unto Joshua the son of Nun, Moses' minister, saying, "Moses My servant is dead; now therefore arise, go over this Jordan, thou, and all this people (Josh. 1:1, 2).

S orrow came to you yesterday and emptied your home. Your first impulse now is to give up, and sit down in despair amid the wrecks of your hopes. But you dare not do that. You are in the lines of battle, and the crisis is at hand. To falter a moment would be to imperil some holy interest. Other lives would be harmed by your pausing. Holy interests would suffer should your hands be folded. You must not linger even to indulge your grief.

Sorrows are but incidents in life, and must not interrupt us. We must leave them behind, while we press on to things that are before. God has so ordered that in pressing on in duty we shall find the truest, richest comfort for ourselves.

Sitting down to brood over our sorrows, the darkness deepens about us and creeps into our hearts, and our strength changes to weakness. But if we turn away from the gloom, and take up the tasks and duties to which God calls us, the light will come again and we shall grow stronger.

> When all our hopes are gone,
> 'Tis well our hands must still keep toiling on
>   For others' sake;
> For strength to bear is found in duty done;
> And he is blest indeed who learns to make
> The joy of others cure his own heartache.

THEY BEST CAN BIND WHO HAVE BEEN BRUISED OFT.

And a man shall be as an hiding place from the wind, and a covert from the tempest; as rivers of water in a dry place, as the shadow of a great rock in a weary land (Isa. 32:2).

O Lord God, Thou art our refuge and our hope; on Thee alone we rest, for we find all to be weak and insufficient but Thee. Many friends cannot profit, nor strong helpers assist, nor prudent counsellors advise, nor the books of the learned afford comfort, nor any precious substance deliver, nor any place give shelter, unless Thou Thyself dost assist, strengthen, console, instruct, and guard us. *James Martineau.*

PRAYER

Father! in Thy mysterious presence kneeling,
  Fain would our souls feel all Thy kindling love,
For we are weak, and need some deep revealing
  Of trust and strength and calmness from above.

Lord! we have wandered forth through doubt and sorrow,
  And Thou hast made each step an onward one;
And we will ever trust each unknown morrow—
  Thou wilt sustain us till its work is done.

In the heart's depths a peace serene and holy
  Abides; and when pain seems to have her will,
Or we despair, oh, may that peace rise slowly,
  Stronger than agony, and we be still.

Now, Father, now, in Thy dear presence kneeling,
  Our spirits yearn to feel Thy kindling love;
Now make us strong, we need Thy deep revealing
  Of trust and strength and calmness from above.

Selected.

JUNE 30 ———————————————————————————————

But now they desire a better country (Heb. 11:16).

Shortly before his death, the Rev. Robert J. Burdette wrote a personal letter to the editor of a paper, in which he said:
"I watch the sunset as I look out over the rim of the blue Pacific, and there is no mystery beyond the horizon line, because I know what there is over there. I have been there. I have journeyed in those lands. Over there where the sun is just sinking is Japan. That star is rising over China. In that direction lie the Philippines. I know all that.

"Well, there is another land that I look toward as I watch the sunset. I have never seen it. I have never seen any one who has been there, but it has a more abiding reality than any of those lands which I do know.

182

"This land is beyond the sunset—this land of immortality, this fair and blessed country of the soul—why, this heaven of ours is the one thing in the world which I know with absolute, unshaken, unchangeable certainty. This I know with a knowledge that is never shadowed by a passing cloud of doubt. I may not always be certain about this world; my geographical locations may sometimes become confused, but the other world—*that* I know.

"And as the afternoon sun sinks lower, faith shines more clearly and hope, lifting her voice in a higher key, sings the songs of fruition. My work is about ended, I think. The best of it I have done poorly; any of it I might have done better, but I have done it. And in the fairer land, with finer material and a better working light, I will do better work."

MY AIN COUNTRIE

I'm far frae my hame, and I'm weary aftenwhiles
For the langed-for hame-bringing, an' my Father's welcome
     smiles;
I'll ne'er be fu' content until my een do see
The gowden gates o' Heaven, an' my ain countrie.
The earth is flecked wi' flowers—money-tinted, fresh
     an' gay—
The birdies warble blithely, for my Father make them sae,
But these sichts an' these soun's will as naething be
     to me
When I hear the angels singing in my ain countrie.

I've His gude word o' promise, that, some gladsome day,
     the King.
To His ain royal palace His banished hame will bring;
Wi' een an' wi' hearts running o'wer we shall see
"The King in His beauty," an' our ain countrie.
My sins hae been mony, an' my sorrows hae been mair,
But there they'll never vex me, nor be remembered mair;
His bluid hath made me white, His hands shall dry
     mine e'e,
When He brings me hame at last to my ain countrie.

Like a bairn to its mither, a wee birdie to its nest,
I would fain be ganging noo unto by Saviour's breast;
For He gathers in His bosom witless, worthless lambs
     like me,
And carries them Himsel' to His ain countrie.

He's faithful that hath promised—He'll surely come
    again—
He'll keep His tryst wi' me, at what hour I dinna ken;
But He bids me still to wait, an' ready aye to be
To gang at ony moment to my ain countrie.

Mary Lee Demarest.

JULY 1

Thy daughter is dead: why troublest thou the Master any further? (Mark 5:35).

What hopelessness! They had watched the sweet flower fade, till no color was left on the pale cheek, and the merry voice was still; and then they thought of the Galilean Teacher: Why cost Him time and trouble? His visit will be useless now! It was very kind of Him to be willing to come! But is now of no use! Very kind; but no use."

Are there not times when we, too, say, it is no use troubling further; we must just bear our trial as well as we can, God Himself cannot help us. Can He give back the twin-soul? Can he restore the love that has died out? It is no use to trouble God or man. We have no alternate but to suffer till eternity explains the mysteries of time.

But Jesus knows the way out. He says, in His sweet undertone, *"Fear not! only believe." He has the keys of death.* He never would have let things come to this awful pass by His delay unless He had known, that, even if the worse came to worst, all would end well. He has purposely delayed till this, that He might have the better opportunity of showing you what God can do.

Fear not! the hand of the Almighty Saviour has yours within its grasp. He will not let you stumble as you go down this dark staircase by His side. Only believe! Have faith in Him. All may seem mysterious now, but you will come to see that it was wisest and best after all. You shall yet clasp to your heart the lost one arrayed in resurrection beauty.   *F. B. Meyer.*

Because He heard my voice and answered me,
    Because He listened, ah, so patiently,
In those dark days, when sorrowful, alone,
    I knelt with tears, and prayed Him for a stone.

I paused a moment in my work to pray
   And then and there
All life seemed suddenly made new and fair;
   For like the psalmist's dove among the pots,
My spirit found her wings.

Because He said me "Nay" and then instead,
   Oh, wonderful sweet truth, He gave me bread,
Set my heart singing in sweet accord;
   Because of this I love—I love the Lord.

JULY 2

For the Lord Himself shall descend from heaven with a shout, with the voice of the archangel, and with the trump of God: and the dead in Christ shall rise first.

Then we which are alive and remain shall be caught up together with them in the clouds, to met the Lord in the air: and so shall we ever be with the Lord (1 Thess. 4:16, 17).

Those *who died in Christ will come with Him.* They are now waiting around Him till He give the final order for the whole heavenly cortege, which has been collecting for ages, to move. The holy angels will accompany; but the beloved saints shall ride in the chariots of God as the bride beside the bridegroom.

Those who died in Christ shall be forever re-united with us who wait for Him and them. They shall come with Him. "God will bring them." We, on the other hand, if we are living at the supreme moment, shall be changed and caught up to meet Him, and then, all one in Christ, we shall be forever with Him to go out no more forever.

"Wherefore comfort one another with THESE words" (1 Thess. 4:18).

Sometimes you went away
For just a little while,
And I could scarcely wait
To see again your smile.
I listened for your step,
My hand was on the door,
And what a joy it was
To have you back once more.

One day you said "Goodbye,"
And went to see the King,
His beauty to behold
And precious sheaves to bring;
In eagerness I wait
The while I feel my lack.
I'm looking hour by hour
To see you both come back.

Edith L. Mapes.

JULY 3

Jesus wept (John 11:35).

It is an affecting thing to see a great man in tears! "Jesus wept." It was ever His delight to tread in the footsteps of sorrow—to heal the broken-hearted—turning aside from His own path of suffering to "weep with those that weep."

Bethany! That scene, that *word,* is a condensed volume of consolation for yearning and desolate hearts. What a majesty in those tears! He had just before been discoursing on Himself as the Resurrection and the Life—the next moment He is a Weeping Man by a human grave melted in anguished sorrow at a bereaved one's side! Think of the funeral at the gate of Nain, reading its lesson to dejected myriads—"Let thy widows trust in Me!"

Think of the farewell discourse to His disciples, when, muffling all His own foreseen and anticipated sorrows, He thought only of soothing and mitigating theirs! Think of the affecting pause in that silent procession to Calvary, when He turns round and stills the sobs of those who are tracking His steps with their weeping! Think of that wondrous epitome of human tenderness, just ere His eyes close in their sleep of agony—in the mightiest crisis of all time—when filial love looked down on an anguished mother, and provided her a son and a home!

Ah, was there ever sympathy like that ! Son! Brother! Kinsman! Saviour! all in one! The majesty of the Godhead almost lost in the tenderness of the Friend. But so it *was,* and so it *is.* The heart of the new enthroned King beats responsive to the humblest of His sorrow-stricken people.

"I am poor and needy, yet the Lord *carries me on His Heart!*" (Psalm 40:17, margin).

186

What is the use of the man of Sorrows,
  If you do not turn to Him in your need?
When your home is shadowed and your heart is breaking,
  Then is the time to trust indeed;
He has never been known to fail in giving
  The oil and wine for the open sore,
And the Heart that wept with the lonely sisters
  Is the same today and forevermore.

JULY 4

Parted asunder . . . And Elisha . . . saw him no more (2 Kings 2:11, 12).

Yes, that is the way of it. "Parted asunder!" We all know what that means. "And Elisha saw Him no more!" We all know what that means. Mothers taken away from their children, fathers taken away from their household, husbands taken away from the arms of their wives, little children, whose laughter was the sweetest music of the household. Oft 'tis so. Parted asunder.

But what matters it all—all this parting asunder—as when Elijah went up by a whirlwind into heaven—if for a little while we do *not* see them, and in a little while we *shall* see them? What sadness hath our being parted asunder from our loved ones here if it is to greet other redeemed loved ones in the other world? What sting hath our going if it is God's whirlwind that comes for us? Why bitter tears when one of God's days we shall have them forever—if God sent for them to be with Him?

Darling baby of the heart, I shall have you and love you forever. Think of that—when the chariot and the whirlwind goeth up. Mother, you whose going up was like a soldier from hard warfare, I shall love you and have you forever. Father, you whose leaving was, to you, like a sailor home from a stormy sea, I shall have you forever.

Friend of mine, you whose leaving me stopped the singing of the birds, I shall have you forever. Lover, you whose going plucked the sun out of Life's sky, I shall have you forever. And it shall be when the chariot comes for me, even as it came for you.

And, in this thought, in this belief, we shall face the farewell of our friends and the goodbye from our loved ones in the spirit of old Elijah as he went from Gilgal with Elisha, as he came to Bethel with Elisha.

As it was with Elijah when the whirlwind from heaven brought him home, so shall our farewells here be changed into greetings yonder.   *The Whirlwinds of God.*

"Tell my father," said Lincoln, "that if it be his lot to go now, he will soon have a joyous meeting with the many loved ones gone before, and where the rest of us, through the help of God, hope ere long to join them."

> Over the river they beckon to me,
>   Loved ones who've crossed to the farther side;
> The gleam of their snowy robes I see,
>   But their voices are lost in the rushing tide.
> There's one with ringlets of sunny gold,
>   And eyes the reflection of heaven's own blue;
> He crossed in the twilight gray and cold,
>   And the pale mist hid him from mortal view.
> We saw not the angels who met him there;
>   The gates of the city we could not see;
> Over the river, over the river,
>   My brother stands waiting to welcome me.
>
> Over the river the boatman pale
>   Carried another, the household pet;
> Her brown curls waved in the gentle gale,
>   Darling lassie! I see her yet.
> She crossed on her bosom her dimpled hands,
>   And fearlessly entered the phantom bark;
> We felt it glide from the silver sands,
>   And all our sunshine grew strangely dark.
> We know she is safe on the farther side,
>   Where all the ransomed and angels be:
> Over the river, the mystic river,
>   My childhood's idol is waiting for me.
>
> For none return from those quiet shores,
>   Who cross with the boatman cold and pale;
> We hear the dip of the golden oars
>   And catch a gleam of the snowy sail—
> And lo! they have passed from our yearning hearts;
>   They cross the stream and are gone for aye.
> We may not sunder the veil apart
>   That hides from our vision the gates of day;
> We only know that their barks no more
>   May sail with us o'er life's stormy sea;

188

Yet somewhere, I know, on the unseen shore,
　　They watch, and beckon, and wait for me.

And I sit and think, when the sunset's gold
　　Is flushing river and hill and shore,
I shall one day stand by the water cold,
　　And list for the sound of the boatman's oar;
I shall watch for a gleam of the flapping sail;
　　I shall hear the boat as it gains the strand;
I shall pass from sight with the boatman pale,
　　To the better shore of the spirit land.
I shall know the loved who have gone before,
　　And joyfully sweet will the meeting be,
When over the river, the peaceful river,
　　The angel of death shall carry me.

Nancy Woodbury Priest.

JULY 5

Blessed is the man who, nerved by Thee, hath set his heart on ascents (Psalm 84:5—Vulgate).

Each Christian had his own dark seasons, to which God sent His own light; and these times of needfulness and of deliverance are known, perhaps, to no one but himself—not even, it may be, to his very dearest. There is an inner world of thought and feeling in which each of us lives, wherein we are profoundly alone; and many a light and shadow may sweep over that little world, many a twilight gloominess may come, and many a heaven-sent light may scatter it, of which none save ourselves will ever know."

　　If I stoop
Into the dark, tremendous sea of cloud,
It is but for a time; I press God's lamp
Close to my breast—its splendour soon or late
Will pierce the gloom: I shall emerge one day.

Robert Browning.

A PRAYER FOR COURAGE

God make me brave for Life—
Oh, braver than this!
Let me straighten after pain,

189

As a tree straightens after the rain,
Shining and lovely again.

God make me brave for Life.
Much braver than this!
As the blown grass lifts, let us rise
From sorrow with quiet eyes,
Knowing Thy way is wise.

God make me brave—Life brings
Such blinding things,
Help me to keep my sight,
Help me to see aright
That out of the dark comes Light.

Grace Noll Crowell.

JULY 6

Seek Him that . . . turneth the shadow of death into the morning (Amos 5:8).

Why will ye call it "Death's dark night?"
Death is the entrace into light!

When I was about seven or eight years old, there fell into my hands a little book containing, among other similar ones, an account of "Dr. Doddridge's "Dream of Heaven." I was fascinated with it and read it over and over. Night after night when I said my prayers, I prayed that I might dream of heaven "tonight." Strange, for I was a little girl—one perhaps wouldn't think that thoughts of heaven ever found place in my mind. As years went on I ceased to pray that prayer, and the story of the dream of heaven went out of my mind. Something else took its place. Whenever thoughts of death came, a most terrifying fear possessed me. And even after I was saved, that fear tormented and tempted me whenever I allowed myself to think about it. But God always gave me peace at last in believing His promise that He will go with me through the dark waters when He calls me to go through them.

Well, not long after my marriage, I was called upon to sing at a funeral, and when I at last reached home I lay down on the couch to rest. I don't know whether it was a dream or a vision, whether I was awake or asleep, but something came, beyond all words to express. I thought death had come; Jesus was near, dimly seen, but He was surely there; something seemed to enfold me, wonderful, indescribable—I called it glory. I said, "If this is death, how wonderful! how wonderful!" I think I must have said it aloud.

I have never felt one tremor of the fear of death since that time. And—the prayer of the little girl who wanted so earnestly to dream of heaven was answered.   *Mrs. T. Stuart Kennedy.*

A Chrisitan soldier who was instantly killed in action during the late war left the following poem, which he had written, as his conception of a passing into the glory-world:

> Here the bright day glides tranquil to its close;
> I hear the kindly voices that I love,
> The water washing on the lonely crags,
> The evening call of loon and whip-poor-will.
> I feel the cool breath of God's holy night
> Breathed round me, on my hand the hand of one
> Best loved of all I leave behind. I see—
> O Heaven, pity those who cannot see!
> Glory on glory—glory on that face
> So near, so dear; gold glory on the wave,
> Purple and gold and darting tongues of flame;
> Calm glory on the cloud-piled dome of heaven;
> Glory of fire on the sun's great face.
> So slips my soul, scarce heeding of the change,
> From glory unto glory! Heaven breaks—
> Eternal glory, on the face of God!

Death is but a halting-place between two Eternities, a gentle wafting to Immortal life.

JULY 7 _____

Instead of the thorn shall come up the fir tree, and instead of the brier shall come up the myrtle tree: and it shall be to the Lord for a name, for an everlasting sign that shall not be cut off (Isa. 55:13).

An old legend relates that long ago some monks had found a crown of thorns which the Saviour wore on the day He was crucified. During Passion Week it was laid on the altar of the Chapel and the people looked upon the sacred crown with great reverence, awed as they saw the cruel thorns bearing still their stains of blood.

Very early on Easter morning, one of the monks entered the Chapel to remove the relic which would be so out of harmony with the glad thoughts of the day. When he opened the door he found the whole place filled with wondrous perfume. He could not understand it. As he went up to the altar, the early sunlight, coming in through the eastern window, showed him the crown still resting there, but it had become a crown of roses every rose pouring out its marvelous fragrance.

The beautiful legend is a parable of what Christ does with earth's sorrows for all who love and trust Him. Out of pain comes blessing. The crown of thorns must be worn by the Master's own, but the thorns burst into sweet flowers as the light of heaven's morning touches them.

AN ANGEL OF PATIENCE

Beside the toilsome way,
    Lowly and sad, by fruits and flowers unblest,
Which my worn feet tread sadly, day by day,
    Longing in vain for rest.

And angel softly walks,
    With pale, sweet face, and eyes cast meekly down,
The while, from withered leaves and flowerless stalks,
    She weaves my fitting crown.

A sweet and patient grace,
    A look of firm endurance true and tried,
Of suffering meekly borne, rests on her face,
    So pure, so glorified.

And when my fainting heart
    Desponds and murmurs at its adverse fate,
Then quietly the angel's bright lips part,
    Murmuring softly, "Wait!"

"Patience," she sweetly saith;
    "Thy Father's mercies never come too late;
Gird thee with patient strength and trusting faith
    And firm endurance. "Wait!"

Angel! behold, I wait,
    Wearing the thorny crown through all life's hours—
Wait till thy hand shall ope th' eternal gate,
    And change the thorns to flowers.

Thy years shall have no end (Psalm 102:27).

I t is never wise to *live* in the past. There are, indeed, some uses of our past which are helpful, and which bring blessing. We should remember past mercies, that we may have confidence in new needs or trials in the future. We should remember past comforts, that there may be stars in our sky when night comes again.

But while there are these true uses of memory, we should guard against *living* in the past. We should draw our life's inspirations not from memory, but from hope; not from what is gone, but from what is yet to come. Forgetting the things which are behind, we should reach forward into those things which are before. It is better farther on.

LOOKING BACK

Would you be young again?
  So would not I;
One tear to mem'ry given,
  Onward I'd hie.
Life's dark flood forded o'er,
All but at rest on shore—
Say, would you plunge once more,
  With Home so nigh?

If you might, would you now
  Retrace your way?
Wander through stormy wilds,
  Faint and astray?
Night's gloomy watches spread,
Morning all beaming red,
Hope's smiles around us shed,
  Heavenward—away!

Where, then, are those dear ones,
  Our joy and delight?
Dear, and more dear, though now
  Hidden from sight.
Where they rejoice to be.
There is the land for me;
Fly, time—fly speedily!
  Come, life and light!

Lady Nairn.

Look not mournfully into the Past. It comes not back again. Go forth in faith to meet the shadowy Future, without fear, and with a trusting heart.

JULY 9

When my father and my mother forsake me, then the Lord will take me up (Psalm 27:10).

I have no earthly parent," may the orphan say, "to look after me; but have I not God to take me up and carry me along the path of life? Beset as it is with many dangers, and exposed at every step as I am to temptations, who is able as He to point out these dangers, to warn me against them; or who can so effectually neutralize the power of tempter, and make a way for my escape? Can He not cause His angels to encamp around me, and peradventure commission even the glorified spirit of my departed parent, to act unseen, as a spiritual body-guard around my exposed career?"

But when I go
To my lone bed, I find no mother there;
And weeping kneel, to say the prayer she taught;
Or when I read the Bible that she loved,
Or to her vacant seat at church draw near,
And think of her, a voice is in my heart,
Bidding me early seek my God, and love
My blessed Saviour; and that voice is hers—
I know it is, because these were the words
She used to speak so tenderly, with tears,
At the still twilight hour—or when we walked
Forth in the spring, among rejoicing birds,
Or peaceful talked beside the winter hearth.

Mrs. Sigourney.

A MINISTERING ANGEL

Orphan, thou most sorely stricken
Of the mourners thronging earth,
Clouds half veil thy brightest sunshine,
Sadness mingles with thy mirth.
Yet although that gentle bosom,
Which has pillowed oft thy head,
Now is cold, thy mother's spirit

Can not rest among the dead.
Still her watchful eye is o'er thee
Through the day and still at night
Hers the eye that guards thy slumber,
Making thy young dreams so bright.
Oh! the friends, the friends, we've cherished,
How we weep to see them die!
All unthinking they're the angels
That will guide us to the sky!

Emily Judson.

JULY 10

When thou walkest through the fire thou shalt not be burned; neither shall the flame kindle upon thee (Isa. 43:2).

There is no profit in walking mournfully. All the profit a man ever gets is from his joy. The advantages of the fires of sorrow do not lie in the things they consume. The sweetest of all the uses of adversity is to show me the joy which it cannot take away. There is a substance which fire will not destroy; it is like the bush Moses saw, in the wilderness. I could never have its quality proved except by fire. Yet the blessing is not the fire but the unconsumedness. Shadrach, Meshach, and Abednego passed through the furnace and got no hurt. What was to them the benefit of the furnace? Percisely the limit of its power—what it could not do. Doubtless in things not vital there was damage done: the men were cast in bound and they came out loose; there was destruction to the environment.

But it was not this that made the furnace beneficial. It was the untouched thing, the unsinged thing, the unharmed thing. The glory of the furnace was its failure. I could not praise the setting of the sun if it did not bring out the beauty of the evening star.

George Matheson.

Life has it compensations and its joys. Still the hall-mark of our eternal distinction is our capability, through divine help, of rising above tragedy and sorrow. We have a right to fear but not to lose our faith and hope because of life's Gethsemanes. We must go, as did Christ, in the strength of the Lord. This is the only way to find a

> . . .solid standing place amid
> The wash and welter, whence all doubts are bid,
> Back to the ledge they break against in foam.

JULY 11

He hath prepared for them a city (Heb. 11:16).

One night, lying on my couch when very tired, my children all around me in full romp and hilarity and laughter, half awake and half asleep, I dreamed this dream: "I was in a country. It was not in Persia, although more than oriental luxuries crowned the cities. It was not in the tropics, although more than tropical fruitfulness filled the gardens. It was not in Italy, although more than Italian softness filled the air. And I wandered around looking for thorns and nettles, but I found that they did not grow there; and I saw the sun rise and watched to see it set, but it set not. And I saw people in holiday attire, and I said, 'When will they put off all this, and put on workman's garb, and delve in the mine or swelter at the forge? But they never put off the holiday attire.

"And I wandered in the suburbs of the city to find the place where the dead sleep, and I looked all along the line for beautiful hills—the place where the dead might most blissfully sleep—and I saw towers and castles, but not a mausoleum or a monument or a white slab was to be seen. And I went to the chapel of the great town, and I said: 'Where do the poor worship, and where are the benches on which they sit?' And the answer was made me: 'We have no poor in this country.'

"And then I wandered out to find the hovels of the destitute, and I found mansions of amber and ivory and gold; but not a tear could I see, not a sigh could I hear; and I was bewildered, and sat down under the branches of a great tree, and I said: 'Where am I, and whence comes all this scene?' And then out from among the leaves and up to the flowery paths and across the shifting streams, there came a beautiful group thronging about me, and as I saw them come I thought I knew their step, and as they shouted I thought I knew their voices, but they were so gloriously arrayed in apparel such as I had never before witnessed, that I bowed as stranger to stranger. But when again they clapped their hands and shouted, 'Welcome! Welcome!' the mystery all vanished, and I found that time had gone and eternity had come, and we were all together again in our new home in Heaven.

"And I looked around, and I said, 'Are we all here?' And the voices of many generations responded, 'All here!' And while tears of gladness were raining down our cheeks, and the branches of Lebanon cedars were clapping their hands, and the towers of the great city were chiming their welcome, we all together began to leap and shout and sing, 'Home, Home, Home, Home!' "

T. Dewitt Talmage.

JULY 12

They rest from their labors; and their works do follow them (Rev. 14:13).

Thou hast taught me, O Lord, that the work need not end when the life has closed. Thou hast taught me that the influence can outlive the hand that shed it. Thou hast taught me that much of this world's work is done by the departed, that we live by the afterglow of many vanished days. Help me to remember the afterglow. When I see lives interruped and am tempted to say, "To what purpose is this waste?" help me to remember the afterglow. Help me to remember that among the forces of earth there is none more potent than that of those whom we call dead.

George Matheson.

THE ROSE STILL GROWS

Near a shady wall a rose once grew,
Budded and blossomed in God's free light,
Watered and fed by morning dew,
Shedding its sweetness day and night.

As it grew and blossomed fair and tall,
Slowly rising to loftier heights,
It came to a crevice in the wall,
Through which there shone a beam of light.

Onward it crept with added strength;
With never a thought of fear or pride,
It followed the light through the crevice's length,
And unfolded itself on the other side.

The light, the dew, the broadening view,
Were found the same as they were before,

197

And it lost itself in beauties new,
Breathing the fragrance more and more.

Shall claim of death cause us to grieve,
And make our courage faint or fall?
Nay; let us faith and hope receive;
The rose still grows beyond the wall.

Scattering fragrance far and wide,
Just as it did in days of yore,
Just as it did on the other side,
Just as it will forevermore.   *A. L. Frinke.*

JULY 13

I will lift up mine eyes unto the hills; from whence cometh my help (Psalm 121:1).

There is a great difference in the way different people endure their sorrow. Some look only down, down into the grave, down into their own breaking hearts, down at the emptiness, the ruin, the darkness about them. These find no comfort. Others, with grief no less keen, with loss no less sore, look up into the face of God and see love there; look into Heaven where their loved ones are; look at the blessed stars of hope which shine above them, and are comforted.

Whittier, in "Snowbound," sets the two aspects of sorrow side by side:

No voice is heard, no sign is made,
No step in on the conscious floor.
Yet Love will dream, and Faith will trust,
Since He who knows our need is just,
That somehow, somewhere, meet we must.
Alas for him who never sees
The stars shine through his cypress trees,
Who hath not learned, in hours of faith,
The truth to flesh and sense unknown,
That Life is ever lord of Death,
And Love can never lose its own.

198

They wandered in the wilderness in a solitary way. . . . Then they cried unto the Lord in their trouble, and He delivered them out of their distresses (Psalm 107:4, 6).

A SOLITARY WAY

There is a mystery in human hearts;
And though we be encircled by a host
Of those who love us well, and are beloved,
To every one of us, from time to time,
There comes a sense of utter loneliness:
Our dearest friend is stranger to our joy,
And cannot realize our bitterness.
"There is not one who really understands,
Not one to enter into all I feel"
Such is the cry of each of us in turn;
We wander in "a solitary way."
No matter what or where our lot may be;
Each heart, mysterious even to itself,
Must live its inner life in solitude.

And would you know the reason why this is?
It is because the Lord desires our love:
In every heart He wishes to be first.
He therefore keeps the secret key Himself,
To open all its chambers and to bless
With perfect sympathy and holy peace,
Each solitary soul that comes to Him.
So when we feel this loneliness, it is
The voice of Jesus saying, "Come to Me";
And every time we are "not understood,"
It is a call to us to come again;
For Christ alone can satisfy the soul,
And those who walk with Him from day to day,
Can never have "a solitary way."

And when beneath some heavy cross you faint,
And say, "I cannot bear this load alone,"
You say the truth. Christ made it purposely
So heavy that you must return to Him.
The bitter grief, which "no one understands,"
Conveys a secret message from the King,
Entreating you to come to Him again.
"The Man of Sorrows" understands it well;
In all points tempted, He can feel with you.

You cannot come too often, or too near—
The Son of God is Infinite in grace,
His presence satisfied the longing coul,
And those who walk with Him from day to day,
Can never have "a solitary way."   *Selected.*

JULY 15

And He took them and went aside privately into a desert place (Luke 9:10).

ALONE WITH GOD

There are moments in our lives, and they come very often, too, when it becomes a necessity to be alone with God; when nothing will meet our spiritual requirements except silent communion with the Father. There are moments when, without this intimate and tender relationship with Him, the path of duty would be lost, and we would wander in the darkness without a guide.

The hight revelations come to us in those moments when we are alone with God. The presence of others sometimes appears to break the spell of sweetness that seems to exist around the spirit that seeks communion with Him. Even the presence of a very dear friend might cast a shadow between the seeking of soul and God, and in some degree drive away the Holy Spirit that comes to bless our lives. God never fails of meeting the one that comes to bless our lives. God never fails of meeting the one that seeks for the divine influence of His Spirit, whether it be in the glowing morning, the bright noontide, or in the holy hush of night.

When the human heart is full of cares and crushed almost to the earth by heavy sorrows; when every nerve and fiber groans with agony, there is no sweeter and surer relief than to fly to the sacred presence of Him who never fails to lift the load of sorrow from the suffering one. If the path of duty is lost to the tear-blinded eyes; if the wanderer is bewildered amid the shadows of the way, how oft has all been made plain by the sweet soul-communion with Jesus!

O ye who are weak and heavy burdened; ye who are sick and wounded in life's great battle; ye who with bleeding feet are journeying up life's rocky steep, seek God's blessed Spirit, and He will bear the burden for you.

Come ye yourselves apart and rest awhile,
 Weary, I know it, of the press and throng;
Wipe from your brow the sweat and dust of toil,
 And in My quiet strength again be strong.

JULY 16

I shall go to Him (2 Samuel 12:23).

And what a change is this! Yesterday, an infant in his mother's arms, or a child amused with a rattle or a straw; today a seraph in the midst of seraphims, burning with excessive glory in the presence of God.

Do you see in the midst of that bright and blessed throng the child you mourn? Would you call him back again? I fear you would! But I ask you, *what would tempt him back again?*

Bring out the playthings that he liked on earth, the toys that filled his childish heart with gladness, and pleased him on the nursery floor, the paradise that was ever bright when he smiled within it; hold them up, and ask him to throw away his harp, and the friends in heaven, the bosom of his loving Saviour; and would he come, to be a boy again, to live, and laugh and love again, to suffer, to die and *perhaps* be lost! I think that he would stay. I think I would shut the door if I saw him coming.

The child is happier now. Infinite love called the child. Infinite wisdom took him away. You shall have him again.

THE LITTLE BOY THAT DIED

I am all alone in my chamber now,
 And the midnight hour is near;
And the fagots crack, and the clock's dull tick,
 Are the only sounds I hear;
And over my soul in its solitude
 Sweet feelings of sadness glide,
For my heart and my eyes are full when I think
 Of the little boy that died.

I went one night to my father's house—
 Went home to the dear ones all—
And softly I opened the garden gate,
 And softly the door of the hall.
My mother came out to meet her son—

She kissed me and then she sighed,
And her head fell on my neck, and she wept
    For the little boy that died.

I shall miss him when the flowers come,
    In the garden where he played;
I shall miss him more by the fireside,
    When the flowers have all decayed.
I shall see the toys and his empty chair,
    And the horse he used to ride;
And they will speak with a silent speech
    Of the little boy that died.

We shall go home to our Father's house—
    To our Father's house in the skies—
Where the hope of our souls shall have no blight,
    Our love, no broken ties.
We shall roam on the banks of the river of peace,
    And bathe in its blissful tide,
And one of the joys of our heaven shall be
    The little boy that died.

"The mother's heart remembers, though all the world forget."

JULY 17 ─────────────────────────────────

The Lord sitteth upon the flood; yea the Lord sitteth King for ever. The Lord will bless His people with peace (Psalm 29:10, 11).

Several years ago in autumn, the eve of harvest, I was present at a musical service in the Cathedral of Lucerne, where the notes of the organ, played by a skilled musician, rolled through the building, interpreting Nature in her diversified moods, from the wild and grand to the soft and beautiful. It was an evident "adaptation" of Beethoven's *Pastoral Symphony.* It began with the birth of the storm, which seemed slowly to brood over the far horizon. Now it was heralded by pattering rain-drops; now it was the sighing of the wind through "the forest primeval"; now it was the thunder tones waking the echoes of the neighboring Alps, the torrents which the rain had swelled rushing through their gorges. In the vivid words of Lowell, almost as if written for the occasion:

    You can hear the quick heart of the tempest beat.
    And then a total lull.

Yes, the lull, and what followed was the most impressive of all. The revel of these forces, which spoke only too audibly of terror and dismay, ruined harvests and blighted crops, was followed by a soft cadence. At first, it resembled the ripple of brook or twitter of lark. The dulcet sounds wax sweeter and lovelier. The spirit of the storm was exorcised; and the culmination of all was the Reapers', or the Villagers', "Hymn of Thanksgiving," rising like a canticle of angels.

These final notes alone remained, leaving on the ear the peace and calm of heaven. With that the performance ceased.

Many a soul knows too well what, in another sense, after the quiet of "summer in the life"—a blissful calm—is the devastation of autumn storm with its rain, and flood, and hurricane. But "the Lord sitteth on the flood; yea, the Lord sitteth King forever. . . . He will bless His people with peace."

THROUGH THE STORM

I heard a voice, a tender voice, soft falling
  Through the storm;
The waves were high, the bitter winds were calling,
  Yet breathing warm.

Of skies serene, of sunny uplands lying
  In peace beyond;
This tender voice, unto my voice replying,
  Made answer fond.

Sometimes, indeed, like crash of armies meeting
  Arose the gale—
But, over all, that sweet voice kept repeating
  "I shall not fail."   *At Dawn of Day.*

JULY 18 ⸺⸺⸺⸺⸺⸺⸺⸺⸺⸺⸺⸺⸺

Joy cometh in the morning (Psalm 30:5).

Farther on, you will find no thorns, but in every step you will tread out the fragrance of the sweetest flowers. Farther on, you will meet with no foe; but kindred spirits with their great thoughts, wise and loving, will cheer you on the way. Farther on, and no dark cloud will throw its gloomy shadows over you; you shall have the brightest stars at night, and nought but sunshine in the day. Farther on, the prospect improves; the valleys are more rich and the mountains more grand; flowers of lovelier hue and fragrance are there; trees of statelier mould deck the landscape and rivers, and lakes more pellucid and more majestic refresh and beautify the scene. Take courage, my brother, it is better farther on!

HOPE'S SONG

I hear it singing, singing sweetly,
  Softly in an undertone—
Singing as if God had taught it,
  "It is better farther on!"

Night and day it sings the same song,
  Sings it while I sit alone,
Sings so that the heart may hear it,
  "It is better farther on!"

Sits upon the grave and sings it,
  Sings it when the heart would groan,
Sings it when the shadows darken,
  "It is better farther on!"

Farther on? Oh, how much farther?
  Count the milestones one by one—
No, not counting, only trusting,
  "It is better farther on!"

JULY 19 _____

I will not leave you comfortless; I will come to you (John 14:18).

A re you afraid of loneliness? Jesus Christ comes to us and says, "My child, you are not to live your life on this earth *alone;* you are not to emerge upon the other side *alone.*" If we saw it, how it would comfort us! Jesus Christ leads us along the path of life, and leads us into the dark valley, and leads us into the very heart of God.

Are we not making a mistake when we are talking of the "other world?" It is not another world after all. It is all God's world. Our loved ones are not going into some place which is all strange to them. What is the light of heaven? The face of Jesus. What is the service of heaven? The praise of Jesus. What is the center of heaven? Jesus. It is not a new world. You and I will feel at home the first moment we get there. There is nothing strange about it. It has a greater brightness and a brighter glory and a more rapturous peace, and it all gathers around the presence of our beloved Lord.

> The way was long, and the shadows spread, far as the
> eye could see.
> I stretched my hands to a human Christ, who walked
> through the night with me.
> Out of the darkness we came at last, our feet on the
> dawn-warm sod,
> And I knew by the light in His wondrous eye, that I
> walked with the Son of God.

JULY 20

Is it well with the child? And she answered, it is well (2 Kings 4:26).

A greater love than yours watched over him and has taken him away. Why he was taken in the dawn of his being, we cannot tell. The secrets of that world which he has entered can alone explain it. Our world does not seem to have been intended for the education of all. To many it is only a birthplace. They are born to be translated, to receive their education elsewhere. Can we not trust our loving Father to choose the place where His children shall be trained? Is it not enough that they are in His Hands?

LIFTED OVER

> As tender mothers guiding baby steps,
> Where places come at which the tiny feet
> Would trip, lift up the little ones in arms
> Of love, and set them down beyond all harm—
> So did our Father watch the precious boy,
> Led o'er the stones by me, who stumbled oft
> Myself, but strove to help my darling on:
> He saw the sweet limbs faltering, and saw
> Rough ways before us, where my arms would fail;
> So reached from Heaven, lifting the dear child,
> Who smiled in leaving me; He put him down,
> Beyond all hurt, beyond my sight, and bade
> Him wait for me! Shall I not then be glad,
> And, thanking God, press on to overtake?   *H. H.*

And the city had no need of the sun, neither of the moon to shine in it: for the glory of God did lighten it, and the Lamb is the light thereof (Rev. 21:23).

A VISION-DREAM

I dreamed a sweet and happy dream
About life's troubled and swollen stream,
That emptied into the river broad,
Which flows very close to the throne of God.

I dreamed of the land of the fairer sky,
Where the old grow young, and never die;
Of the land of peace, and of sweet repose—
And the just are saved from all their woes.

I dreamed that the weary left their cares
At the outer gate, where they ceased their prayers;
Heard the Master say: "Lay your burdens down
Where you drop your cross to receive your crown."

I dreamed that I met the friends of my youth
Who had walked in the light of the precious truth;
I beheld their crowns, and their scepters fair,
And talked with the Blood-washed gathered there.

I dreamed that I saw the small and great,
As they streamed in through the open gate,
And I saw and greeted my own again,
As the anthem swelled to the grand Amen!

I dreamed that Mother stretched forth her hands
In greeting her son in the heavenly lands;
And my own dear boy came running fast,
And said: "O daddy! You've come at last!"

I dreamed that we sat by the river fair,
And breathed the healing, heavenly air,
And ate of the fruit of life's fair tree
With the thrill and the peace of eternity.

I dreamed that my loved ones took my hands
To lead me, and show me the heavenly lands;
They told me the secrets of suffering time,
And poured in my wounds the oil and wine.

I dreamed that the crown on the Savior's brow,
Bedecked with stars—someway, somehow—
Was in part my own, and my name was there
Writ out in gold in His snowy hair.

I dreamed that the Savior came to me
As we stood beholding the glassy sea,
And the city of light, with its sparkling dome,
And He said: "My Child, this is Home, Sweet Home!"

William J. Meredith.

And then, the quiet of the green inland valleys of our Father's land, where no tempest comes any more, nor, the loud winds are ever heard, nor the salt sea is ever seen; but perpetual calm and blessedness; all mystery gone and all rebellion hushed and silenced and all unrest at an end forever! "No more sea"; but, instead of that wild yeasty chaos of turbulent waters, there shall be the river that make glad the city of God, the river of the water of life that proceedeth "out of the throne of God and the Lamb."

JULY 22

Why art thou cast down, O my soul? Hope in God; for I shall yet praise Him (Psalm 43:5).

E verything seems changed," wrote one in deep sorrow. "The Bible has lost its inspiration. Prayer seems empty, futile, and comfortless. I am in a maze of aching doubts and questionings, and know not where to turn."

Hold fast, beloved! The pain will not be less, but the light will come. Soon you will begin to realize that each day brings you nearer the reunion you crave. You want to be ready and you want to be worthy. Keep on trusting—that is all that matters.

When the storms of life are raging, tempests wild on sea and land,
I will seek a place of refuge, in the shadow of God's Hand.
Though He may permit affliction, 'twill but make me long for Home,
For in love, and not in anger, all His chastisements will come.

207

Faith can firmly trust Him,
Come what may.

JULY 23 _____

How precious also are Thy thoughts unto me, O God (Psalm 139:17).

Not long ago I was in the home of a dear friend whose husband
had been suddenly snatched from her embrace. Always a
frail little body, we all wondered if she could bear up against this
great sorrow. Would it not crush her to the earth?

Far in the deep watches of that awful night, when her loved one
lay in the peace of death, I would hear this child of God, as I vainly
tried to sleep, repeating sweet passages from the Word—songs of
comfort and precious promises for her hour of trouble. Then
would come words of her own—low, calm, strong, and full of
hope and trust in the Father who doeth all things well. She fail?
Her faith was grounded on the Rock! In the morning I spoke of
having caught something of the midnight talk with Jesus. "Yes,"
came the answer, "I would die if I did not have God's Book—and
God!"   *Edgar L. Vincent.*

I opened the old, old Bible,
    And looked at a page of Psalms,
Till the wintry sea of my troubles
    Was soothed as by summer calms;
For the words that have helped so many,
    And that ages have made more dear,
Seemed new in their power to comfort,
    As they brought me their word of cheer.

JULY 24_____

*There appeared an angel unto Him from heaven, strengthening Him
(Luke 22:43).*

The Lord Jesus, in the Garden of Gethsemane, has shown us
how to suffer. He chose His Father's will. He looked right
beyond His suffering to His Father, and said: "If this cup may not
pass from me, except I drink it, Thy will be done." He gave up His

208

own way and will, saying, "I will Thy will, O My Father; Thy will, and not Mine, be done."

Let all sufferers who read these lines go apart and dare to say the same words: "Thy will be done in the earth of my life, as in the heaven of Thy purpose; I choose Thy will." Say this thoughtfully and deliberately, not because you can feel it, not because the way of the Cross is pleasant, but because it must be right. Say it repeatedly, whenever the surge of pain sweeps through you, whenever the wound begins to bleed afresh: "Not my will, but Thine be done." *Dare to say yes to God.* "Even so, Father, for so it seemeth good in Thy sight."

And so you will be led to feel that all is right and well; and a great calm will settle down on your heart, a peace that passeth understanding, a sense of rest, which is not inconsistent with suffering, but walks in the midst of it as the three young men in the fiery furnace, to whom the burning coals must have been like the dewy grass of a forest glade. "The doctor told us my little child was dying. I felt like a stone. But *in a moment* I seemed to give up my hold on her. She appeared no longer mine, but God's." *Selected.*

Afflictions cannot injure when blended with submission.

"I can't!" despairingly I cried!
  This gentle whisper sounded at my side,
"Of course not, child, Thou wast not fashioned so,
  But I, thy Father, CAN and WILL. I know
Thy weakness, all thy longing see,
  And I am always strong to strengthen thee."

Mary O'Hara.

JULY 25 ─────────────────────────────────

Praise ye the Lord (Psalm 150:6).

When the soldiers of Napoleon were weak and discouraged on the Alpine ascent, we are told their leader ordered: "Sound the French *Gloria*"; and the music gave the men new heart, and triumphantly they pressed forward. Christian, whatever be your cross, look up to your Master and sound the *Gloria* . In the years to come, some troubled heart, remembering the victory of your own unchanging trust, shall give thanks to God and take courage.

> Don't let the song go out of your life,
>   Though it chance sometimes to flow
> In a minor strain: it will blend again
>   With the major tone, you know.
>
> What though shadows rise to obscure life's skies,
>   And hide for a time the sun,
> The sooner they'll lift and reveal the rift,
>   If you let the melody run.
>
> Don't let the song go out of your life,
>   Though the voice may have lost it trill;
> Though the tremulous note may die in your throat,
>   Let it sing in your spirit still.
>
> Don't let the song go out of your life;
>   Let it ring in the soul while here;
> And when you go hence, 'twill follow you thence,
>   And live on in another sphere.

JULY 26

The time of my departure is at hand (2 Tim. 4:6).

Paul used a word which carries with it the idea of lifting anchor, spreading sail and going out of the land-locked harbor into the open sea. It may be rendered "The time of my loosing is at hand." Death is the launch of the ship. Death is going out of the dock.

I am standing upon the seashore. A ship at my side spreads her white sails to the morning breeze and starts for the blue ocean. She is an object of beauty and strength, and I stand and watch her until at length she hangs like a speck of white cloud just where the sea and sky come down to meet and mingle with each other. Then someone at my side says, "There! she's gone!" Gone where? Gone from my sight—that is all. She is just as large in the mast and hull and spar as she was when she left my side, and just as able to bear her load of living freight to the place of destination. Her diminished size is in me, and not in her. And just at that moment, when someone at my side says, "There! she's gone!"

there are other eyes that are watching for her coming and other voices ready to take up the glad shout, "There she comes!" And that is—dying.

Oh, safe in port where the billows break not!

Horatius Bonar.

I watched a sail until it dropped from sight
Over the rounding sea. A gleam of white,
A last far-flashed farewell, and, like a thought
Slipt out of mind, it vanished and was not.

Yet to the helmsman standing at the wheel
Broad seas still stretched beneath the gliding keel.
Disaster? Change? He felt no slightest sign,
Nor dreamed he of that far horizon line.

So may it be, perchance, when down the tide
Our dear ones vanish. Peacefully they glide
On level seas, nor mark the unknown bound.
We call it death—to them 'tis life beyond.   *Anonymous.*

Hide your thorn in the rose. Bury your sigh in the song. Keep your cross, if you will, but keep it under a wreath of flowers. It is the singing of your heart that will make you forget your sorrow. He will give you a "song in your desert night." It may be that your loved one in the Glory-land will hear and be glad.

JULY 27

O Lord God, Thou knowest (Psalm 139:4).

Here is the response of faith. *"Thou knowest!"* —what a pillow for the heart to repose upon! *"Thou knowest!"*— what few but comprehensive words to sum up and express the heart's difficulties and perplexities and trials. *"Thou knowest!"*— what an inexpressibly sweet resting-place in the midst of life's tumultuous heavings; in the midst of a sea that knows no calm; in the midst of a sea in which tossings to and fro are the hourly history!

What an answer they contain for every heart that can find no words to express its big emotions; for a heart whose sorrows are too deep for language to find its way to God. Oh, that they were ever uppermost in the soul, as the response to every difficulty in our path! They are God's answer to everything we cannot fathom; God's answer for our hearts to rest upon, and our lips to utter, when every way is hedged up, so that we cannot pass. *"O Lord, Thou knowest!"* Rest here, believer. Lean thy soul on these words. Repose calmly on the bosom of thy God, and carry them with thee into every scene of life. *"O Lord, Thou knowest."*

Frederick Whitfield.

JULY 28

And ye now therefore have sorrow: but I will see you again, and your heart shall rejoice, and your joy no man taketh from you (John 16:22).

SHOULD YOU GO FIRST

Should you go first and I remain
   To walk the road alone,
I'll live in memory's garden, dear,
   With happy days we've known.
In Spring I'll wait for roses red,
   In Summer—lilacs blue;
In Autumn when the brown leaves call
   I'll catch a breath of you.

Should you go first and I remain
   For battles to be fought,
Each thing you've touched along the way
   Will be a hallowed spot.
I'll hear your voice, I'll see your smile,
   Though blindly I may grope,
The memory of your helping hand
   Will buoy me on with hope.

Should you go first and I remain
   To finish with the scroll,
No length'ning shadows shall creep in
   To make this life seem droll.
We've known so much of happiness,
   We've had our cup of joy;
Ah, memory is one gift of God
   That death cannot destroy.

Should you go first and I remain,
   One thing I'd have you do:

Walk slowly down the path of death,
  For soon I'll follow you.
I'll want to know each step you take,
  That I may walk the same,
For some day down that lonely road
  You'll hear me call your name.   *A. K. Rowswell.*

Give me courage to go on alone!

JULY 29 ────────────────────────────────

How precious also are Thy thoughts unto me, O God! how great is the sum of them! (Psalm 139:17).

For I know the thoughts that I think toward you, saith the Lord, thoughts of peace, and not of evil, to give you an expected end (Jer. 29:11).

In a certain old town was a great cathedral. And in that cathedral was a wondrous stained glass window. Its fame had gone abroad over the land. From miles around people pilgrimaged to gaze upon the splendor of this masterpiece of art. One day there came a great storm. The violence of the tempest forced the window, and it crashed to the marble floor, shattered into a hundred pieces. Great was the grief of the people at the catastrophe which had suddenly bereft the town of its proudest work of art. They gathered up the fragments, huddled them in a box, and carried them to the cellar of the church. One day there came along a stranger and craved permission to see the beautiful window. They told him of its fate. He asked what they had done with the fragments. And they took him to the vault and showed him the broken pieces of glass. "Would you mind giving these to me?" said the stranger. "Take them along," was the reply , "they are no longer of any use to us." And the visitor carefully lifted the box and carried it away in his arms. Weeks passed by; then one day there came an invitation to the custodians of the cathedral. It was from a famous artist, noted for his master-skill in glass-craft. It summoned them to his study to inspect a stained glass window, the work of his genius. Ushering them into his studio he stood them before a great veil of canvass. At the touch of his hand upon a cord the canvass dropped. And there before their astonished gaze shone a stained glass window surpassing in beauty all their eyes had ever beheld. As they gazed entraced upon its rich tints, wondrous patterns, and cunning workmanship the artist turned and said: "This window I have wrought from the fragments of your shattered one, and it is now ready to be replaced." Once more a great window shed its beauteous light into the dim aisles of the old cathedral. But the splendor of the new far surpassed the glory of the old, and the fame of its strange fashioning filled the land.

Do you say that your plans have been crushed? Have joy and sweetness vanished from life? Does there seem nought left for you but to walk its weary treadmill until its days of darkness and drudgery shall end? Then know this. Jesus Christ is a matchless life-mender. *Try Him.* He will take that seemingly shattered life and fashion a far more beautiful one from its fragments than you yourself could ever have wrought from the whole. In Him your weary soul shall find its longed-for rest. And the fragments that remain of God's heritage of life to you shall mean in gladsome days to come, more than all the vanished years that are crooning their sad lament in your innermost soul tonight.

James McConkey.

JULY 30 ⎯⎯⎯⎯⎯⎯⎯⎯⎯⎯⎯⎯⎯⎯⎯⎯⎯⎯⎯ ⎯

He purgeth it, that it may bring forth more fruit (John 15:2).

> Never sit me down and say,
>   "There's nothing left but sorrow"
> We walk the wilderness today,
>   The promised land tomorrow.
>
> Bring up heroic lives, and all
>   Be like a sheathen sabre,
> Ready to flash out God's call,
>   O chivalry of Labor!
>
> Triumph and toil and time and aye,
>   Joy suns the clouds of sorrow;
> And 'tis the martyrdom today
>   Brings victory tomorrow.

Don't let yourself wither in sorrows, like one without hope, but ever learn the ever widening field of duties that is opening up.

Jowett.

214

The dark brown mold's upturned
  By the sharp pointed plow,
And I've a lesson learned:

My life is but a field
  Stretched out beneath God's sky,
Some harvest rich to yield.

Where grows the golden grain?
  Where faith? where sympathy?—
In a furrow cut by pain.
                                    Maltbie D. Babcock.

JULY 31

*For now I know that thou fearest God, seeing that thou hast not withheld
thy son, thine only son from me (Gen. 22:12).*

THINE AND MINE

I closely held within my arms
  A jewel rare;
Never had one so rich and pure
  Engaged my care;
'Twas my own, my precious jewel,
  God gave it me;
'Twas mine, who else could care for it,
  So tenderly?

But the Master came one day
  My gem to take;
"I cannot let it go," I cried,
  "My heart would break":
"Nay, but the Master comes for it,
  To bear above
To deck His royal diadem,
  He comes in love."

"But, Master, it is my treasure,
  My jewel rare,
I'll safely guard and keep it pure,
  And very fair";
"If Thou keep'st my gem," He said,
  "It may be lost;
The threshold of My home, no thief
  Has ever crossed.

"And where the heart's rich treasure is,
    The heart will be;
Thy jewel will be safe above,
    Gone before Thee."
The Master said these words and gazed
    With pitying look,
While in the early hush of morn
    My gem He took.

Close to my heart that morn I held,
    Tears falling fast,
An empty casket—the bright gem
    Was safe at last.
"Yes, Master, Thou may'st keep my own,
    For it is Thine;
Safe in the house not made with hands,
    'Tis Thine and Mine.

There's a land where those who loved when here shall meet to love again.

AUGUST 1 _____

Behold, God exalteth by His power: Who teacheth like Him? (Job 36:22).

The fountains of joy and sorrow are for the most part locked up in ourselves. . . . There come to the great, solitary, and sorely smitten souls moments of clear insight, of assurance of victory, of unspeakable fellowship with truth and life and God, which outweigh years of sorrow and bitterness.

We are but organs mute till a Master touches the keys—
    Verily vessels of earth into which God poureth
    the wine;
Harps are we, silent harps that have hung on the willow
    trees,
    Dumb till our heart-strings swell and break with a pulse
    Divine.

AUGUST 2 _____

Nevertheless afterward (Heb. 12:11).

Most things look different when viewed from different points and in different lights. Events and experiences do not appear the same when we are in the midst of them, and after we have passed through them. The afterview, however, is the truest. This is especially so of life's sorrows: as we endure them they are grievous; but afterward the fruits of peace appear.

In the Canton of Bern, in the Swiss of Oberland, a mountain stream rushes in a torrent toward the valley, as if it would carry destruction to the villages below; but, leaping from the sheer precipice of nearly nine hundred feet, it is caught in the clutch of the winds, and sifted down in fine soft spray, whose benignant showering covers the fields with perpetual green. So sorrow comes, a dashing torrent, threatening to destroy us; but by the breath of God's Spirit it is changed as it falls, and pours its soft gentle showers upon our hearts, bedewing our withering graces, and leaving rich blessings upon our whole life.

We should learn to trust God, even when the hour is darkest. The morning will surely come, and in its light the things that alarm us now will appear in a friendly aspect. The black clouds that appear so portentous of evil pass by, leaving only gentle rain, which renews all the life, and changes desert to garden.

> We pray for growth and strength; grief's dreaded showers
> May be in God's wide purpose, ripening rain:
> He only knows how all our highest powers
> Are perfected in pain.

AUGUST 3

When the Lord saw her, He had compassion on her, and said unto her, "Weep not." (Luke 7:13).

Even now Jesus is saying to those who have lost their beloved ones, "Weep not." Christ will give back to you the dear one you have lost. Wait patiently on Him. The resurrection morning is sure to come!

I SHALL SEE THEM AGAIN

> I shall see them again in the light of the morning,
> When the night has passed by with its tears and its
>   mourning:

When the light of God's love is the sun ever shining
In the Land where the weary ones rest.

I shall know them again, though ten thousand surround
them;
I shall hear their dear voice 'midst the blessed ones round
them;
And the love that was theirs on the earth shall detect
them
In the Land where the weary ones rest.

'Twas their lives in the past helped to fill me with
gladness;
And the future in heaven, the home without sadness,
Where I see them today clad in bright robes of
whiteness—
In the Land where the weary ones rest.

Would I wish for them back from their bright home in
heaven?
No! in patience I'll wait till the veil shall be riven,
And the Saviour restores me the friends He has given—
In the Land where the weary ones rest.   *Rev. E. Husband.*

AUGUST 4

*Them also which are laid asleep by Jesus will God bring with Him (1
Thess. 4:14; Wickliffe, Cranmer and Rheims version).*

This suggests a comforting thought. *That the hour of our death
and the deaths of those we love—is the appointment of
God. We are laid asleep by Him.*

Oh, as not the hours of existence, so not the hour of death is left
an "open question," haphazard, indeterminate. Just as the mother
knows the best hour to lay her little one in its couch or cradle;
undresses it, composes it to rest, sings its lullaby, and the cherub
face, lately all smiles, is now locked in quiet repose; so Christ
comes to His people at His own *selected season,* and says, "Your
hour of rest has arrived. I am to take off the garments of mortality.
Come! I will robe you in the vestments of the tomb."

He smooths the narrow bed, composes the pillow, and sings His
own lullaby of love, "Fear not, my child, for I am with you, sleep
on now and take your rest!"

Be comforted with this blessed truth, that the hour of death cannot come sooner than Jesus appoints. He knows the best time to bid you and yours the long "good-night."

It as HE who gave the final summons to Israel's leader. It was HE who selected the rocky cleft in Mount Nebo for His place of sepulchre, and, under the desert's starry sky, composed His servant's limbs for their final rest.

"David, by the will (or, as that means, by the *appointment*) of God, fell asleep and was laid to his fathers." Interesting it is (and a Bible truth too) to think of troops of angels hovering over the death-pillow, and watching with guardian care the sleeping dust. But more comforting still, surely, is it to think of the Lord of angels closing the eyes and hushing to slumber—Christ Himself leading to the grave—the robing room of immortality—"unclothing," that His people may be "clothed upon," and that "mortality may be swallowed up of life."

You who have nameless treasures in the tomb, rejoice in the assurance that these earthly tabernacles are in the custody of Him who has the keys of the grave and death. The loving hand of Divine parental love was the last to close their eyes; and in the prospect of waking on an eternal morrow, you can go to their graves, and thinking of them as having migrated to the Better Land, away forever from the harsh jarrings and discords and tumults of the present, can write the epitaph:

So giveth HE His beloved SLEEP.   *J. R. Macduff.*

> Angels of Life and Death alike are His;
>   Without His leave they pass no threshold o'er,
> Who, then, would wish or dare, believing this,
>   Against His messengers to shut the door?
>   *H. W. Longfellow.*

"For if we believe that Jesus died and rose again, even so, them also which sleep in Jesus will God bring with Him. . . . Wherefore comfort one another with THESE words" (1 Thess. 4:14, 18).

AUGUST 5

Even so, Father (Luke 10:21).

There are two kinds of sorrow—the sorrow which misses its companion at every turn, and at each fresh sense of loss weeps bitter tears under a keen sense of pain; and there is the hard, bitter, unresigned, and unsubmissive sorrow, which will not forgive God. It is only the latter of these which is wrong. The first is natural, and there is no cause in it for self-rebuke.

When grief is fresh do not try to *feel* resignation, but *will* it. Look up to God, in the first stab of pain, and in all the long weary hours of suffering which follow, and say, "Father, I choose Thy will; I know it is the tenderest and best for my loved one, and for me. Even so, my Father, for so it seemed good in Thy sight; not my will, but Thine be done." And as these words are repeated, and the will offers itself to God, and lays its sacrifice upon the altar, though the hand trembles and the eyes brim with tears, the inward tumult will subside and die down, and the sufferer will come to DELIGHT (not in the sorrow) but in the Father's appointment, which at first it could only *choose* .

We never know from what lingering suffering, from what bitter grief, from what impending disaster, spiritual or temporal, God has taken our dear ones. He knows best and has sufficient reason, which He will clearly explain to us some day. Meanwhile, He who wounds can heal. He who takes will himself fill the vacant place. And He will keep that which we have committed to Him, and give it back restored to perfect health and beauty.   *Selected.*

> One sad day, when the sun's gold crown
>   Jeweled the desolate, dreamy west,
> I came with a burden, and laid it down
>   Under the lilies and leaves to rest;
> And weeping, I left it, and went my way,
>   With the twilight whispering, "God knows best!"
>
> One sweet day—it was long ago—
>   And thorny the paths my feet have pressed,
> Since, with tears and kisses, I laid it low—
>   Soul of my soul and life of my breast!
> But kneeling now in the dark to pray,
>   There comes, with a song from the sunless west,
> The same sweet voice that I heard that day—
>   The twilight whispering, "God knows best!"

He bringeth them unto their desired haven (Psalm 107:30).

Wrecked! That one word tells a tale of storms, gales, high seas, perils, losses. Wrecked! Ship gone, possessions gone, friends gone, home gone, everything gone—life itself, almost gone. What a picture of complete helplessness; could anything be more pitiable?

Watch that man as he drifts on that raft—a broken fragment of the vessel which once bore him proudly over the sparkling waters. ALONE—with an "aloneness" which is oppressive in its intensity; hungry and thirsty—his soul faints within him; for where is he to find bread to satify his hunger, or water to quench his thirst? Exhausted, with the exposure and the mental agony, and almost at the point of death. But, watch! his raft is unconsciously drifting towards a haven of refuge; he will presently find himself wrecked on a hospitable shore in the land of plenty.

Can we read in this a parable of human experience? Ah! yes, indeed; but it is only when the storm-tossed, hurricane-driven, helpless, lonely mariner finds himself wrecked upon God Himself that the experience proves to be a blessing in disguise.

Observation teaches one that it is generally the untoward happenings of life, its limitations, deprivations, and extremities which drive the soul on to GOD.

Have you ever known what it is to find yourself in such circumstances that you are literally at your wit's end? All human helpers have failed, or, possibly, you are cut off from communication with any living being to whom you feel you could open your heart. Troubles gather like storm-clouds, thick and fast, and the winds of adversity blow with relentless fury as you struggle to hold on your way. At length you find yourself *wrecked;* everything is broken up; all your props and stays are gone to pieces; all hope is gone; there is nothing left *but* GOD.

Wrecked *upon* God. What does that mean? Well, it means to find IN GOD HIMSELF at last, a haven of refuge, a safe retreat, sure protection, ample provision, boundless love, limitless resource; in fact, everything and more than everything that the soul has lost. It means to be wrecked upon ALL-SUFFICIENCY—to find out in actual personal experience that God Himself is *enough.*

221

God never fails the soul who is utterly abandoned to Him: He employs all His omnipotence and His omniscience on his behalf.

The one who is thus wrecked upon God *proves* that His "hand is not shortened that it cannot save: neither His ear heavy that it cannot hear," and he is prepared to testify with God's servant of old, "Thou hast been . . . a strength to the needy in his distress, a refuge from the storm, a shadow from the heat" . . . "an hiding place from the wind and a covert from the tempest." See Isa. 25:4 and 32:2.   *A. C. L.*

SHIPWRECKED ON GOD

Shipwrecked on God! Of all else forsaken!
All hope of help from every source has fled.
'Tis then, and only then, we find the Rock beneath us
That wrecked our keel and stranded us on God.
Shipwrecked on God! 'Tis not till then we know Him,
'Tis not till then we trust Him to the uttermost;
'Tis not till then we prove Him all sufficient
And feed upon His breast alone.
Release thy hold of all that binds thee to another;
Let shore-lines go and dare the swelling tide—
It will but bear thee safely into haven,
And land thee safe upon the Rock, shipwrecked on God.
Shipwrecked on God! O Blessed place of safety,
Shipwrecked on God! No greater place of rest,
Shipwrecked on God! All shore-lines broke asunder,
With NOTHING LEFT in all the universe but God.
Shipwrecked on God! Then face to face we see Him,
With naught between to dim the vision of His Love.
'Tis then we learn the secret of Redemption,
When we have NOTHING left in earth or heaven—
      but GOD.
Shipwrecked on God! 'Tis then we learn to know Him,
As heart beats to heart in unison of love.
Then no more twain, but married to another—
He whom God gave from out the bosom of His Love.
Shipwrecked on God! 'Tis not till then we vanish;
'Tis not till then we find we're hid with Christ in God,
And cease from all our trying and our struggling,
To find at last that Christ is ALL IN ALL.
Shipwrecked on God! No land in sight to flee to;
Where height and depth cannot be reached,
Or length or breadth be spanned;
We sink into the might sea of God's own fullness,

To find that NOTHING ELSE REMAINS—but HIM,
   the Christ of God.

Shipwrecked on God! With naught but Christ remaining,
I find Him Life and Breath, Environment—yea ALL!
I've ceased from all my trying and my toiling,
I've entered into rest to toil no more;
He lives His life while I abide within Him.
And now for me to live is Christ for evermore.   *C. M. B.*

AUGUST 7

Blessed be the God and Father of our Lord Jesus Christ, the Father of mercies and God of all comfort; who comforteth us in all our affliction, that we may be able to comfort them that are in affliction, through the comfort wherewith we ourselves are comforted of God (2 Cor. 1:3, 4).

I stood a short time ago in a room which was furnished with wealthy pictures, and I fixed my gaze upon a Highland scene of great strenth and glory. The owner of the picture found me gazing at this particular work, and he immediately said, "I am afraid you won't get the light on the hill." And, sure enough, he was right. From my point of view I was contemplating a dark and storm-swept landscape, and I did not get the light on the hill. He moved me to another part of the room, and, standing there, I found that the scene was lit up with wonderful lights from above.

Everything depends upon our point of view. If you are going to look upon your trouble and sorrow, the primary question will be, "Where do you stand?" See where the Apostle Paul plants his feet. *"Blessed be God."* That is the view-point in the life of faith. Standing there, we shall get the lights on the hill. You see to what elevation he traces his comfort; away up to God! And so his resource is no mere trickle, to be dried up in the day of drought, or swiftly congealed in the nip of the first wintry day. The Apostle loved to proclaim the infinitude of his supply, and no wonder, when he found it upon the everlasting hills.

"Take long looks, away to the hills, every day!" a physician said to one who came to him for advice in the day his sight was failing.

The far look is what we need to give us right views of God and His dealings with us. A little while up there with Him will fit us to come down, heartened, and cheered, and ready once more for life's battles.

Always finish on a mountain-top.

AUGUST 8 ─────────────────────────────────

Thou rulest the raging of the sea; when the waves thereof arise, Thou stillest them (Psalm 89:9).

What else can rock the waves of the soul to rest but the Voice of Him, Who, at the fourth watch of the night, when the darkness is deepest, comes saying: "Fear not, it is I—be not afraid!"

> Fierce was the wild billow, dark was the night,
> Oars labored heavily, foam glimmered white;
> Mariners trembled, peril was nigh:
> Then said the Son of God, "Peace, it is I!"
>
> Jesus, Deliverer! come Thou to me;
> Soothe Thou my voyaging over life's sea:
> Thou, when the storm of death roars sweeping by,
> Whisper, O Truth of Truth, "Peace, it is I!"

The sea is mighty, but a MIGHTIER sways His restless billows.

W. C. Bryant.

ALL THROUGH THE NIGHT

> All through the night,
> Dear Father, when our trembling eyes explore
> In vain Thy heavens, bereft of warmth and light,
> When birds are mute, and roses glow no more,
> And this fair world sinks rayless from our sight,
> O Father, keep us then!
>
> All through the night,
> When no lips smile, nor dear eyes answer ours,
> Nor well-known voices through the shadows come;
> When love and friends seem dreams of vanished hours,
> And darkness holds us pitiless and dumb,
> O Father, keep us then!
>
> All through the night,
> When lone despairs beset our happy hearts,

And drear forebodings will not let us sleep;
When every smothered sorrow freshly starts
And pleads for pity till we fain would weep,
O Father, keep us then!

All through the night,
When slumbers deep our weary senses fold,
Protect us in the hollow of Thy hand;
And when the morn, with glances bright and bold,
Thrills the glad heavens and wakes the smiling land,
O Father, keep us then!   *Selected.*

AUGUST 9

Awake, O north wind; and come, thou south; blow upon my garden, that the spices thereof may flow out (Song of Sol. 4:16).

The garden of the heart is like one of those old-fashioned gardens, surrounded by high brick walls, prepared for fruit trees. The garden is filled with all manner of spices. Sometimes, however, the spices hang heavily upon the air. They are present, but hardly discernible to the quickest sense. Then the wind is needed to blow through the garden path, that the spices may flow out and pass beyond the barriers to the passers-by. How often it has happened in the history of the children of God, that those who have known them have never realized the intrinsic excellence and loveliness of their characters until the north wind of sorrow and pain has broken with blustering force upon them. Then suddenly, spices like rare odors have exhaled and been carried afar. How the delicate trees dread the north wind! What a tremor goes through the crowded garden walks when they hear the husbandman calling to the north wind to awake! We all choose the south wind. But remember that the Euroclydon that swept down the ravines of Crete, upon the Alexandrian corn-ship, brought out the spices which had slumbered unknown in the heart of the great apostle! His courage! His patience! His power of inspiring hope amid despair, and breaking bread with thanksgiving! As, north wind, thy ministry has been of incalculable worth to all of us. We shiver before thy searching power, but the spices will repay. *F. B. Meyer.*

225

There are souls like the "alabaster vase of ointment, very precious," which shed no perfume of devotion, because a great sorrow has never broken them.   *Harriet Beecher Stowe.*

AUGUST 10 ───────────────────────────────

Seeing we are compassed about with so great a cloud of witnesses . . . let us run with patience the race that is set before us (Heb. 12:1).

I believe that I have a right to accept the interpretation of death as given in the New Testament, confirming my own hopes and desires, and to believe that the cloud of witnesses to which the apostle refers, are looking on to see how we run our race, fight our battles, bear our burdens here; and I have wished so to live and so to carry myself in my sorrow as not to minister any element of sorrow to her whom I still regard as my comrade. I think I can truly say that I am never less lonely than at times when I am alone, and when the choir invisible no longer seems invisible; when it seems to me as though I have only to push open the door and enter into the other room where they are, unseen by me but not unable to see and minister to me.   *Dr. Lyman Abbott.*

Our dear ones are with Thee, and if we keep near Thee we cannot be far from them.

AUGUST 11 ───────────────────────────────

And Jesus called a little child unto Him (Matt. 18:2).

When children die, people talk of a life unfinished, of buds broken off before their bloom. But how do we know that it was not the bud God wanted? We never gather a bouquet but we think the buds the finest part. A bud is just as perfect as a flower, only it is not a flower. But shall not God be permitted to have buds in His bouquet, whose fragrance is to perfume the altar in the temple above?

An acorn is just as finished as an oak. A cherub is as perfect as an archangel.

What mother thinks the cooing babe, or laughing boy of three, any less perfect or beautiful than grown-up men and women? Is there not about them, rather, a grace that is peculiarly their own? And how dark our life would be without them! And shall God have no babes, no children, in His beautiful house on high? Must all wait till they be grey, and then go tottering over the threshold of that upper Home? Or shall not, rather, the glad, gleesome children, with flowing hair, and merry, laughing eyes, go smiling through the doorways to meet "their angels" who "do always behold the face of their Father in heaven"? Cannot God be as kind to them as we can, and watch them as tenderly?

> Do you know
>   Where the dear swallows go,
> When winter is near and chill winds blow?
>   Afar they fly
>   In blue ether, so high
> That we cannot follow their course through the sky;
> Yet, in unknown lands of warmth and light,
> They live and forget our winter's night.
>
>   Do you know
>   Where the dear children go,
> When summer fades and chill Death waits?
>   They soar beyond
>   Thoughts tender and fond,
> And watch for our coming at Heaven's gate.
> And happily in worlds outside our ken,
> They pity the earthly sorrows of men.

AUGUST 12

He hath torn, and He will heal us; He hath smitten, and He will bind us up (Hosea 6:1).

Several years ago, I was walking, one autumn afternoon, through a lovely Scottish glen, the Pass of Killiecrankie. To my sorrow, its charms at the time seemed irretrievably spoiled by the formation of a railway. Many of its graceful trees had already fallen. The engineers where blasting its rocks, gashes were being made in the wilderness of wild bracken; the bare, naked piers of a viaduct were half erected. Trails of ivy had been torn from their holdings. Formal embankments were being raised, and artificial bridges were in the course of being built, which appeared fatally to mar all natural grace. There was nothing but havoc on every side. The glory had departed.

This last autumn, I happened again to visit the same part of the country, including this, what I thought hopelessly desecrated ground. To my astonishment the old vanished beauty was singularly restored. The gaps, so disfiguring a few years previously, were refilled. The banks were already clothed with broom and gorse, and the white-stemmed birches were afresh waving their green or golden tresses. The rocks which had been scarred, were tapestried with lichen, the grassy slopes and knolls, so denuded and bare, were again dotted with clumps of native heather and groupings of fern. The very bridges spanning the hollows, which seemed on the former occasion the most glaring offenders, were festooned with ivy. It was altogether a unique and unexpected vision—a resurrection of loveliness. The scene indeed had been altered. Nature had wonderfully reasserted her power of restoration.

Sorrow comes to the heart, and life is shorn of its joy and comfort and peace: it is left, like that valley, a wreck of what it was; but God's solaces are at work. The angels of designation and consolation are commissioned to weave a garment for "the spirit of heaviness" and to "give beauty for ashes." There will be the green pastures once more. The valleys of life will again invite summer tint, and music of stream, and gush of sunshine. O trust thy God! He will gradually, it may be, but surely, put forth His healing touch; bringing calm out of the storm, hope out of dejection and despair. "Trust also in Him and He shall bring it to pass."   *J. R. Macduff.*

A great anguish may do the work of years, and we may come out from the baptism of fire with a soul full of new awe and new pity.   *George Eliot.*

AUGUST 13 _____

Blessed is he, whosoever shall not be offended in Me (Matt. 11:6).

PERFECTION

The Master was painting a picture and we children were
    ranged all about,

228

Entranced by the charm of his colors and the way he
was working it out;
And we'd run every morn to discover some beautiful touch
which was new,
And we'd talk and we'd dream and we'd wonder just
what he intended to do.

The Master spake little while working, but oft as he heard
us he'd smile,
Though we begged him to tell all about it, he'd
answer: "You'll know in a while."
But one morning he put down his brushes, and then with
a turn of his head
To our grief and our great consternation: "The picture
is finished," he said.

"Oh, Master," we begged and implored him, "don't put all
your brushes away:
Please paint something more on the canvas, paint on
to the end of the day.
Paint more, for we're eager to watch you, paint on for we
love it so much."
"It is perfect, my dears," said the Master. "I should
spoil it by adding one touch.

So with us God is painting a picture, and little we know
of His plan—
We look at the lad whom we cherish and are eager to
see him a man;
But God knows the soul He is shaping, and though for
more time He's beseeched,
He hurts us beyond understanding, but He stops when
perfection is reached.   *Edgar Guest.*

AUGUST 14

*For this our light and transitory burden of suffering is achieving for us a
weight of glory; a preponderating weight of glory (2 Cor. 4:17—Weymouth).*

W hy should you carry troubles and sorrows unhealed? There
is no bodily wound for which some herb doth not grow, and
heavenly plants are more medicinal. Bind up your hearts in them,
and they shall give you not only healing, but leave with you the

perfume of the blessed gardens where they grew. Thus it may be that sorrows shall turn to riches; for heart troubles, in God's husbandry, are not wounds, but the putting in of the spade before the planting of seeds. *Life Thoughts.*

Remember: Grief may be joy misunderstood;

> Perhaps the cup was broken here,
> That Heaven's new wine might show more clear.
> *E. B. Browning.*

AUGUST 15

Fallen asleep (1 Cor. 15:6).

MOTHER HAS FALLEN ASLEEP

Mother was tired and weary,
    Weary with toil and with pain;
Put by her glasses and rocker,
    She will not need them again.
Into Heaven's mansions she's entered
    Never to sigh or to weep;
After long years with life's struggles,
    Mother has fallen asleep.

Near other loved ones we laid her,
    Low in the church yard to lie;
And though our hearts are near broken,
    Yet we would not question "Why?"
She does not rest 'neath the grasses,
    Tho' o'er her dear grave they creep;
She has gone into the Kingdom,
    Mother has fallen asleep.

Rest the tired feet now forever,
    Dear wrinkled hands are so still;
Blast of the earth shall no longer
    Throw o'er our loved one a chill.
Angels through heaven will guide her,
    Jesus will still bless and keep;
Not for the world would we wake her,
    Mother has fallen asleep.

Beautiful rest for the weary,
    Well deserved rest for the true;

When our life's journey is ended
  We shall again be with you.
This helps to quiet our weeping—
  Hark! Angel music so sweet!
He giveth to His beloved,
  Beautiful, beautiful sleep.

They had finished *her crown* in glory, and she couldn't stay away from the coronation.

THERE

Not 'neath the sod, in yon green acre, lies
  The one ye so much miss;
The Father's House, beyond the bright, blue skies,
  Is now the place of bliss.

There—shadows come not; grief and tears are past
  And every sense of pain,
And joys are there, which evermore shall last,
  For—night comes ne'er again.

Weep not, beloved—save to give relief;
  With those THERE all is well!
And smiles of peace will radiate through thy grief
  As thou on Heaven dost dwell.

A little while—perchance but weeks, or days—
  Till HE again shall come;
Yea, any hour He may the glad shout raise—
  One moment—and then—HOME!

Reunion then! but richer than below!
  A fuller life than ours!
A perfect "touch"—beyond all we did know
  In earth's sublimest hours.   *J. Danson Smith.*

AUGUST 16

It came to pass, when the Lord would take up Elijah by a whirlwind into heaven (2 Kings 2:1).

When a good man leaves the world he does not cease to live. The Lord took Elijah to live in another country. We are actually to verify this statement. We have but to turn over to the

Gospels to see him again, nine hundred years later, alive, and active still in God's work.

It is just as true of the Christians who die in our homes as it was of this old prophet, that the Lord takes them up into heaven, and that they live on in blessedness forever.

One cold autumn day I saw an empty bird's-nest on a tree. It looked desolate and forsaken. But I knew the birds that once were there were living yet—living now in the warm South, beyond the reach of winter's storms, and singing there their sweet songs. There is an empty love-nest in many a home, in many a heart, but we know that the dear one who is gone is living with God in heaven. There is comfort in this!

THE LOST VOICES

Northward again the happy birds returning
    Shall sing for us the songs we thought were lost,
They were but waiting in a fairer country
    Untouched by storm and frost.

And when the lonely winter of our sorrow
    Has rounded out for us Earth's changing year,
Oh, on some radiant morn what long-hushed voices
    Shall greet our listening ear!   *Annie Johnson Flint.*

In the night of death Hope sees a star, and listening Love can hear the rustling of a wing.

AUGUST 17 ─────────────────────────────────

I will uphold thee (Isa. 41:10).

Take the very hardest thing in your life—the place of difficulty, outward or inward, and expect God to triumph gloriously in that very spot. Just there He can bring your soul into blossom.
                                                    L. Lilias Trotter.

I am leading my child to the heavenly land;
I am leading her day by day,
And am asking her now, while I hold her hand,
To come Home by a rugged way.

By a way that she never herself would choose,
For its beauties she doth not see;

And she knows not yet what her soul would lose
If she trod not this path with Me.

I will walk by her side when the road is wild,
I will ever My succor lend:
She shall lean on My strength, I will shield My child,
As the shadows of night descend.

AUGUST 18

The damsel is not dead, but sleepeth (Mark 5:40).

In these words we discover our Lord's outlook upon death. There was no doubt whatever that the maiden was dead as to her bodily being, her earthly consciousness. Christ's outlook on personality was such that He took in the whole fact. Death of the body was not cessation of being. The child was not dead. She was alive. As to her consciousness of earthly things, she was asleep. Perchance her father and mother had often looked upon her in her sleep in days of health. While she was asleep, she was quite unconscious that they were near her; and they could not communicate with her, save by ending the condition of sleep. Jesus told them that this was so now. From ordinary sleep they could have wakened her. From this deeper slumber, they could not. But He could; and that is what He presently did. He used the same words to describe actual bodily death in the case of Lazarus, until the dullness of His disciples compelled Him to say plainly, "Lazarus is dead."

This outlook upon death is full of comfort. Our Lord always stands by our dead and says to us: "Not dead but sleeping." He does not always waken them. Indeed He rarely did so in His earthly ministry. Such waking would mean for them return to all life's fitful feverishness. Still they are not dead, and one glad day He will waken them again to bodily consciousness in a new and better order. Then we shall gain them, and with them be forever with Him. *Dr. Morgan.*

HIS ANSWER

(Written by Bishop Gilbert Haven after his wife's death)

Beside the dead I knelt for prayer,
And felt a Presence as I prayed.

Lo, it was Jesus standing there!
  He smiled, "Be not afraid."

"Lord, Thou has conquered death, we know;
  Restore again to life," I said,
"This one who died an hour ago."
  He smiled, "She is not dead,"

"Asleep, then, as Thyself did say;
  Yet Thou canst lift the lids that keep
Her prisoned eyes from ours away."
  He smiled, "She doth not sleep."

"Yet our beloved seem so far
  The while we yearn to feel them near,
Albeit with Thee we trust they are."
  He smiled, "And I am here."

"Dear Lord, how shall we know that they
  Still walk unseen with us and Thee,
Nor sleep, nor wander far away?"
  He smiled, "Abide with Me."

AUGUST 19

As an eagle stirreth up her nest, fluttereth over her young, spreadeth abroad her wings, taketh them, beareth them on her wings: so the Lord alone did lead him (Deut. 32: 11, 12).

A fter my beautiful home nest had been despoiled—broken up—I read an article in *Nature Studies,* that greatly encouraged and helped me," wrote a friend.

"This author watched an eagle as she built her nest, and when the eggs were laid and hatched, he watched her as she fed the nestlings, and continued to watch until they were sufficiently developed to try their wings; and he saw the mother bird trust them from the nest, and teach them to fly. He said:

" 'Presently the mother eagle came swiftly up from the valley, and there was food in her talons. She came to the edge of the nest, hovered over it a moment, so as to give the hungry eaglet a sight and smell of food, then went slowly down the valley taking the food with her, telling the little one in her own way to come and he should have it.

" 'He called after her loudly from the edge of the nest, and

234

spread his wings a dozen time to follow; but the plunge was too awful; his heart failed him, and he settled back in the nest. In a little while she came back again, this time without food, and hovered over the nest, trying every way to induce the little one to leave it.

" 'She succeeded at last, when with a desperate effort he sprang upward and flapped to the ledge above. Then after surveying the world gravely from his new place he flapped back to the nest, suddenly, as if discouraged. The mother eagle rose well above him. The little fellow then stood on the edge of the nest looking down at the plunge he dared not take. There was a sharp cry from behind, and the next instant the mother eagle had swooped, striking the nest at his feet, sending his support of twigs and himself with them out into the air together.

" 'He was afloat now, and flapping lustily for life. Over him, under him, beside him, hovered the mother on tireless wings, calling softly that she was there. But the awful fear of the depths was upon the little one. His flapping grew more wild, he fell faster, and soon he folded his wings as if expecting to be dashed to pieces among the lance tops of the spruces.

" 'Then like a flash the old mother eagle shot under him; his despairing feet touched her broad shoulders between her wings. He righted himself, rested for a moment, found his head, then she dropped like a shot from under him, leaving him to come down on his wings. A handful of feathers torn out by his claws hovered slowly down after them. In an instant I lost them among the trees, but when I found them again with my glass the eaglet was in the top of a great pine, and the mother was feeding him.'

"And then standing there alone in the great wilderness, it flashed upon me for the first time just what a wise old prophet meant when he wrote: 'As an eagle stirreth up her nest, fluttereth over her young, spreadeth abroad her wings, taketh them, beareth them on her wings; so the Lord alone did lead him.'

"So I saw that my dear one had plumed her wings for a higher flight; and what seemed a plunge into death and despair was only God stirring up the nest to teach us to mount nearer to Him: and then I saw as never before the true meaning of my darling's last words to me: 'Underneath are the everlasting arms.' "

Come up hither (Rev. 4:1).

As they who navigate the sea know that the land is near by the odors which come to them upon the air, so we at times have a revelation of the kingdom of God. We are carried toward it. Something in us is like it. Some strange thoughts and feelings betoken it. It is coming. Into it have gone, oh, how many! We have sent our dear and precious children there. We have sent brothers and sisters. We have sent there the companions of our life, whose going was as the desolating and the breaking of our hearts. But we have not lost them. They are but just before us, hidden by the brightness in which they dwell. And we are following after, mutely calling for our children and for our friends; and we are drawing near to them as we call

THE VANISHERS

Sweetest of all childlike dreams
　In the simple Indian lore
Still to me the legend seems
　Of the shapes who flit before.

Flitting, passing, seen and gone,
　Never reached nor found at rest,
Baffling search, but beckoning on
　To the Sunset of the Blest. . . .

Doubt who may, O friend of mine!
　Thou and I have seen them too;
On before with beck and sign
　Still they glide, and we pursue . . .

Glimpses of immortal youth,
　Gleams and glories seen and flown,
Far-heard voices sweet with truth,
　Airs from viewless Eden blown;

Beauty that eludes our grasp,
　Sweetness that transcends our taste,
Loving hands we may not clasp,
　Shining feet that mock our haste;

Gentle eyes we closed below,
　Tender voices heard once more,

Smile and call us, as they go
   On and onward, still before . . .

Chase we still, with baffled feet,
   Smiling eye and waving hand,
Sought and seeker soon shall meet,
   Lost and found, in Sunset Land!   *J. G. Whittier.*

AUGUST 21

She shall sing there as in the days of her youth (Hosea 2:15).

You say that you can never sing again, that the spring and
gladness of your life are gone forever; you insist upon it that
you must go mourning to the end of your days, and that life can
only bring added grief. But God says you shall sing. Though the
summer seems gone there will be an Indian, a second, summer,
even mellower than the first. In the days of Israel's youth she sang
glad songs on the banks of the Red Sea. Those notes still hover
over those outspread waters and among those echoing hills. If
God can do this for His people, cannot He do it for you? He will
give you a fresh revelation of His love; He will bind you to Himself
with bonds you shall not wish to break; He will reveal to you such
aspects of His character as to attract you into the tenderest
fellowship and friendship; He will show you mercy with a new and
more delicate flavor than ever before. And when all these things
shall come to pass, that sad heart of yours that had abjured its
song shall break out again into music, and with the Psalmist you
will say: "He hath put a new song in my mouth."

GOD'S PREPARING TIME

Perhaps you have heard of the method strange,
Of violin makers in distant lands,
Who, by breaking and mending with skillful hands,
Make instruments having a wider range
Than ever was possible for them, so long
As they were new, unshattered, and strong,

Have you ever thought when the heart was sad,
When the days seem dark and the nights unending,
That the broken heart, by the Father's mending,
Was made through sorrow a helper glad,

Whose service should lighten more and more
The weary one's burdens as never before?

Then take this simple lesson to heart
When sorrows crowd and you cannot sing:
To the truth of the Father's goodness cling;
Of the wondrous plan that gives through pain
The power to sing a more glad refrain.

AUGUST 22

He shall deliver the needy when he crieth (Psalm 72:12).

Bending down to us in infinite love God says: "My child, how needy are you? What heavy burden is upon you? What grievous sorrow is darkening your faith? What fear of future ill is shadowing your pathway? What spiritual thirst do you want slaked? What barrenness of soul enriched? How hungry, how helpless, how faint, how hopeless are you? What do you need this hour? For I will deliver the needy." And so the very need that burdens, dispirits and perplexes us is at once the condition and pledge of His blessing. . . . You are just the man God is looking for—just the one who is ripe for deliverance—just the special individual to whom His promise is made. "For he shall deliver the needy, and him that hath no helper." Do not be too afraid of getting into the spot where you have no helper, for that is the spot where, like Jacob, you will meet a delivering God. Do not be too anxious to be free from needs, unless you want to be free from prayer-power. Accept them just as God sends them or permits them. The moment you come to a need, remember also that you have come to a promise. "He shall deliver the needy." To miss a need may be to miss a miracle. As soon as one appears in your life, do not begin to worry because it is there, but praise God because it is to be supplied. "For he shall deliver the needy when he crieth."   *James H. McConkey.*

> The day is long, and the day is hard,
> We are tired of the march and keeping guard;
> Tired of the sense of a fight to be won,
> Of days to live through, and of work to be done;
> Tired of ourselves and of being alone.

238

And all the while, did we only see,
We walk in the Lord's own company;
We fight, but 'tis He who nerves our arm,
He turns the arrows which else might harm,
And out of the storm He brings a calm.

The work which we count so hard to do,
He makes it easy, for He works too;
The days that are long to live are His—
A bit of His bright eternities—
And close to our need His helping is.   *Susan Coolidge.*

AUGUST 23

Now our Lord Jesus Christ Himself, and God, even our Father, which hath loved us, and hath given us everlasting consolation . . . comfort your hearts (2 Thess. 2:16, 17).

It is a very pertinent question which any man can put to himself: "Will my present comfort last?" It all depends where he gets it from. Does he get it from friendships, from books, from Nature? We cannot depend upon these ministries. I have known a June day deepen a sorrow! I have known a moonlight night throw a heavy soul into a denser gloom! I have known a little flower to open an old wound! We cannot depend upon the comforting ministries of Nature.

Let us get away to our God, let us bare our souls to Him, and let us receive *His* marvelous gifts of comfort and mercy. *And* then let us use our glorious wealth in enriching other people and by our ministry bring them to the heights.   *Dr. Jowett.*

A PRAYER

O our God, be our soul's sky, into which tall pine-trees grow and where fly the soaring and the singing-birds; where clouds float with water for the thirsty ground; where the stars and the shadows fall for sleep; where walk the ruddy dawns, and where the sunsets glow—be our sky.

Be our sky, whose dawns and whose spaces are invitations, and whose silences make for prayer, and where Thou makest the goings forth of the morning to sing.

Be our sky of hope, of morning, when it is black night—starless, void; be room for our growth and sun for making our broad daylight, so that though we run, we shall not stumble, and so that at eventide it shall be light. Amen!

AUGUST 24

For thus saith the high and lofty One that inhabiteth eternity, whose name is Holy; I dwell in the high and holy place, with him also that is of a contrite and humble spirit, to revive the spirit of the humble, and to revive the heart of the contrite ones (Isa. 57:15).

Does it seem as if your strength of body, mind, and spirit had been dealt a death-blow through your sudden bereavement? You used to grasp your daily tasks with the strength of an athlete, but now, you push them aside with a very feeble touch. The loving Lord, Who created you, can mend that which He has made. Nobody else can help you very much, but He will revitalize your very being and warm your heart if you will draw nigh to Him.

> Why should I repine,
> That Jesus in His bosom wears
> A flower that once was mine?

AUGUST 25

Taken away from the evil to come (Isa. 57:1).

If the life that has gone has been like music, full of concords, full of sweetness, richness, delicacy, truth, then there are two ways to look at it. One is to say, "I have not lost it." Another is to say, "Blessed by God that I have had it so long."   *Beecher.*

(IN LOVING MEMORY OF "JACK" RODEHEAVER)

His sun went down while it was yet day; it went not down behind a cloud, but melted into the pure light of Heaven.

> His sun went down in the morning,
> While all was fair and bright;
> But 'twas not an eclipse of darkness
> That hid him from our sight:
>
> For the valley of death was brighter
> Than the hills of life he trod,

And the peace that fell on his spirit
  Was the calm, deep peace of God.

He knew in Whom he trusted,
  He counted all things loss,
And clung with the arms of faith and love
  To the Christ and to His Cross.

And from that Cross a radiance
  Fell with a softening beam,
That shone through the depths of the shadowy vale,
  And brightened death's narrow stream.

His sun went down in the morning,
  While all was fair and bright;
But it shines to-day on the far-away hills,
  In the land that knows no night.

Life is to be reckoned not only extensively, but also intensively: not merely by the number of its days, but also by the amount of thought and energy which we infuse into them.

Existence is not to be measured by mere duration. An oak lives for centuries, generation after generation of mortals the meanwhile passing away; but who would exchange for the life of a plant, though protracted for ages, a single day of the existence of a living, conscious, thinking man?

It is possible for the longest life to be really briefer than the shortest; and the child or youth may die older, with more life crowded into his brief existence, than he whose dull and stagnant being drags on to an inglorious old age.   *Caird.*

AUGUST 26

My presence shall go with thee (Ex. 33:14).

There is a loneliness in unshared sorrow. Sorrow which has an audience can frequently find relief in telling and retelling its story. The heart eases itself in such shared remembrances. But when sorrow has no companionable presence with which to commune, the grief becomes a withering and desolating ministry. There are multitudes of people who know no friendly ear into which they can pour the story of their woes. What then? Is the desolation hopeless? "*My* Presence shall go with Thee." The story can be whispered into the ear of the Highest. The Companionship is from above.

When some beloved voice that was to you
Both sound and sweetness, faileth suddenly,
And silence, against which you dare not cry,
Aches round you like a strong disease and new—
What hope? what help? what music will undo
That silence to your sense? Not friendship's sigh,
Not reason's subtle count . . . Nay, none of these!
Speak Thou! availing Christ—and fill this pause.
E. B. Browning.

There are burdens we can share with none,
    Save God;
And paths remote where we must walk alone,
    With God.
For lonely burden and for paths apart—
    Thank God!
If these but serve to bring the burdened heart
    To God.
John Oxenham.

AUGUST 27

I will fear no evil, for Thou art with me (Psalm 23:4).

We have a Leader, so gentle, that we can go, as it were, to His tent at night, and tell Him we are afraid of tomorrow's warfare; that the hard battle has weakened our nerves. Tender Saviour, wounded unto death. . . . Thou shalt lead us forth conquering and to conquer! *Bishop Wilkinson.*

When the wild tempest falls with sudden power,
And beats with restless fury in my face,
I cannot raise my eyes to trace His form,
The roaring wind shuts out His loving Voice;
But I can feel the clasping of His Hand,
I know no fear, for still He leadeth me.
And when the storm-cloud lifts its sullen brow
He points to where 'mid wavy lines of gold,
The Father's house and Father's welcome wait.
I know they wait for me—this precious Guide
Was sent to bring the straying children Home,

So I can fully trust His loving Hand,
Nor fear to follow whereso'er He leads.

AUGUST 28

Only believe (Mark 5:36).

The great temptation is to doubt God's love. "He could help, but He will not; He loves not, He cares not." What a dark and cruel insinuation is this! Child of God, flee from the tempter and hide in thy Father's bosom.

FAITH

I will not doubt, though all my ships at sea
   Come drifting home with broken masts and sails;
   I will believe the Hand which never fails,
From seeming evil worketh good for me.
     And though I weep because those sails are tattered,
     Still will I cry, while my best hopes lie shattered:
       "I trust in Thee."

I will not doubt, though all my prayers return
   Unanswered from the still, white realm above;
   I will believe it is an all-wise love
Which has refused these things for which I yearn;
     And though at times I cannot keep from grieving,
     Yet the pure ardor of my fixed believing
       Undimmed shall burn.

I will not doubt, though sorrows fall like rain,
   And troubles swarm like bees about a hive;
   I will believe the heights for which I strive
Are only reached by anguish and by pain;
     And though I groan and writhe beneath my crosses,
     I yet shall see through my severest losses
       The greater gain.

I will not doubt. Well anchored is this faith,
   Like some staunch ship, my soul braves every gale;
   So strong its courage that it will not quail
To breast the mighty unknown sea of death.
     O, may I cry, though body parts with spirit,
     "I do not doubt," so listening worlds may hear it,
       With my last breath.   *Selected.*

Being confident of this very thing, that He which hath begun a good work in you, will finish it (Phil. 1:6 margin).

We do know that God's servants serve Him beyond this life, though it has been thought best to curtain the nature of their work from our curious gaze. Faith says, It is all right. Let God call His workmen Home when it pleases Him; and pray that He may raise up many more to reap what they have sown.

THE COMPLETING GOD

God brings them home, His children of the light;
They live the life abundant in His sight.
There is a break; their works do follow them
Still are they builders of Jerusalem.
In earth's unfinished task is no defeat;
What God began, He will in Heaven complete.
Low, here the Valley of the Shadow ends,
The shining uplands of God's great amends!

God brings them home: now they behold His face,
Receiving, as they serve Him, grace for grace.
The lowliest in the ranks of the redeemed
Have great possessions—above all they dreamed.
The Prince of Suffering leads the beauteous throng,
Each singer master of the perfect song.
Time can no more the worker's hand arrest,
All that on earth was good, grows there the best.
The seeker now holds fast the truth he sought;
The prophet's dream is into glory wrought.
The harpers, bending o'er their harps of gold,
New harmonies of Sovereign Love unfold.

They all are perfected; but not apart;
Wing touches snow-white wing, heart joins to heart.
Complete are they, and theirs, in God alone;
Whole as the rainbow round about the Throne.
God brings them home. He has their place for them,
The singing builders of Jerusalem

Work on, still work—till light of Time grows dim;
Then, to the mornings of the seraphim!
Weep not, but sing; sing, past the broken dream.
Sing on to heaven's Doxology Supreme!   *H. Elvert Lewis.*

244

Not now . . . but hereafter (John 13:7).

It is my comfort to know that the darkest cloud is fringed with covenant love. I can repose on the blessed assurance that present discipline is needed discipline, and that all which is mystery now, will be cleared up hereafter. May it be mine cheerfully to follow the footsteps of the guiding Shepherd through the darkest, loneliest road; and amidst thickening sorrows may I have grace to trust Him fully. In the midst of mysterious providences I will be still—hushing every murmur, and breathing in lowly resignation, "Thy will be done."

HOPE EVER!

The sun will shine and the clouds will lift,
The snow will melt though high it drift;
Across the ocean there is a shore,
Must we learn the lesson o'er and o'er?
To know there is sun when the clouds droop low,
To believe in the violets under the snow,
To watch at the bows for the land that shall rise—
This is victory in disguise.

For we through the Spirit by faith wait for the hope of righteousness (Gal. 5:5, R. V.).

There are times when things look very dark to me—so dark that I have to wait even for hope. It is bad enough to wait *in* hope. A long-deferred fulfillment carries its own pain, but to wait *for* hope, to see no glimmer of a prospect and yet refuse to despair; to have nothing but night before the casement and yet to keep the casement open for possible stars; to have a vacant place in my heart and yet to allow that place to be filled by no inferior presence—that is the grandest patience in the universe. It is Job in the tempest; it is Abraham on the road to Moriah; it is Moses in the desert of Midian; it is the Son of Man in the Garden of Gethsemane.

There is no patience so hard as that which endures, "as seeing him who is invisible"; it is the waiting for hope.

Thou hast made waiting beautiful; Thou has made patience divine. Thou hast taught us that the Father's will may be received just because it is His will. Thou hast revealed to us that a soul may see nothing but sorrow in the cup and yet may refuse to let it go, convinced that the eye of the Father sees further than its own.

Give me this Divine power of Thine, the power of Gethsemane. Give me the power to wait for hope itself, to look out from the casement where there are no stars. Give me the power, when the very joy that was set before me is gone, to stand unconquered amid the night, and say, "To the eye of my Father it is perhaps shining still." I shall reach the climax of strength when I have learned to wait for hope.   *George Matheson.*

> Let there be hope today, Lord,
> Hope as I watch and pray, Lord,
> Hope of a sunlit way, Lord,
>   In the dark day give hope!
>
> Hope when the waves roll high, Lord,
> Hope when the winds sweep by, Lord,
> Hope through a storm-rent sky, Lord,
>   Into my heart send hope!
>
> "In hope against hope," I wait, Lord,
> Faced by some fast-barred gate, Lord,
> Hope never says "Too late," Lord,
>   Therefore in Thee I hope!
>
> Hope though the night be long, Lord,
> Hope of a glowing dawn, Lord,
> Morning MUST break in song, Lord,
>   For we are "saved by hope."   *Bessie Porter Head.*

SEPTEMBER 1

I shall go to him (2 Samuel 12:23).

Sweet Baby won us by his love, his little ways, his broken speech, his helplessness. The big boy said, "I'm coming"; Baby said, "Me tumming.'" "I want to kiss you, if you'll come," said I; Baby said, "Me tumming."

246

That was just what Jesus said,
  Jesus the children's Friend—
Said He, "I want to kiss you, dear,"
  And Baby said, "Me tumming."

When Jesus called for Baby
  My heart was filled with sorrow;
But Jesus dried my tears and said,
  "'Tis only for tomorrow."

So I look up and see him there,
  And smile and say, "Me tumming!"

Dr. Joseph H. Parker.

A royal mourner, as he wept over a rosebud prematurely plucked, has left a brief motto-verse for all who have nameless treasures IN the tomb and BEYOND the tomb—"I SHALL GO TO HIM." (2 Sam. 12:23).

There's a Home for little children
Above the bright blue sky.

"A land where children shall walk on cool springy turf, and among myrtle trees, and eat fruits that shall heal while they delight them, and drink the coolest of water, fresh from the River of Life, and have space to stretch themselves, and bathe, and leap, and run, and whichsoever way they look meet Christ's eyes smiling on them. Sir Thomas Moore.

SEPTEMBER 2

I shall go to Him (2 Samuel 12:23).

It is God's own sweet will that we turn away from our sorrow, and go on with reverent earnestness to the new duties that await us. By standing and weeping over the grave where it is buried we cannot bring back that which we have lost. When David's child was dead, he dried his tears and went at once to the house of the Lord and worshipped saying, "Can I bring him back again? I shall go to him, but he shall not return to me." He turned his eyes forward toward the glory in which his child was waiting for him, and began with new ardor to press toward that Home. He turned all the pressure of his grief into the channels of holy living.

This is the way every believer should deal with his sorrows. Weeping inconsolably beside a grave can never give back love's vanished treasure, nor can any blessing come out of such sadness.

NOT DIVIDED

E'en for the dead, I will not bind
    My soul to grief;
Death cannot long divide.
For is it not as though the rose, that
    Climbed my garden wall,
Had blossomed on the other side?
    Death doth hide,
    But not divide!
Thou art but on Christ's other side.
Thou art with Christ and Christ with me,
    In Him united still are we.

SEPTEMBER 3 _____

Jesus . . . the same yesterday, and today and forever (Heb. 13:8).

Autumn time again. The falling leaves remind me today of the joyous remark of a happy child, who, looking up into the face of one who was lamenting the ravages of autumn among the trees, said: "Just think how much more room it gives you to see the beautiful blue sky beyond!" The year has brought its desolation. The hot tears filled and fell from our eyes, and when clear sight came again, a loved form had vanished; comforts that we had thought we could not live without were suddenly snatched away from us; sickness came at a time when it seemed we could least afford to bear its enforced burden; the hope upon which we had laid our plans was shattered, and the shadow of a great disappointment fell upon our lives. It was God's method of clearing the way that we might look up into the face of the Eternal and Unchangeable, and gather supplies for the needs of the soul. O' the comfort of the upward look at such a time! We miss the blessing of heavenly consolation and vigor of spiritual growth if we keep our eyes upon the dead leaves at our feet, or fail to look beyond the stripped branches of the trees just overhead.

W. N. Burr.

We're old folks now, companion,
    Our heads, they are growing gray;
But taking the year, all round, my dear,
    You always will find the May.
We've had our May, my darling,
    And our roses, long ago;
And the time of the year is come, my dear,
    For the silent night and the snow.

And God is God, my darling,
    Of night as well as of day,
And we feel and know that we can go
    Wherever He leads the way.
Aye! God of the night, my darling—
    Of the night of death so grim:
And the gate that from life leads out, good wife,
    Is the gate that leads to Him!

The longest day bends down toward evening.

SEPTEMBER 4 ——————————————————————————

*To give unto them . . . the oil of joy for mourning, the garment of praise
for the spirit of heaviness (Isa. 61:3).*

LEARNING TO SING

Have you ever thought, when the heart was sad,
When the days seem dark, and the nights unending,
That the broken heart, by the Father's mending,
Was made, through sorrow, a helper glad;
Whose service should lighten more and more
The weary one's burdens as never before?

Then take the simple lesson to heart,
When sorrows crowd, and you cannot sing;
To the truth of the Father's goodness cling:
Believe that sorrow is only a part
Of the wondrous plan that gives, through pain
The power to sing a more glad refrain.

Behind that dark sorrow of yours, there may be the anthem of
angels and the peace of God.

Within the veil; whither the forerunner is for us entered, even Jesus (Heb. 6:19, 20).

Those who are gone, you have. Those who departed loving you, love you still; and you love them always. They are not really gone, those dear hearts and true; they are only gone into the next room, and you will presently get up and follow them, and yonder door will close upon *you,* and you will be no more seen.

Thackeray.

JUST IN ANOTHER ROOM

No, not cold beneath the grasses,
  Not close-walled within the tomb;
Rather in my Father's mansion,
  Living in another room.

Living like the one who loves me,
  Like that child with cheeks a-bloom,
Out of sight at desk or school book
  Busy in another room.

Nearer than the youth whom fortune
  Beckons where the strange lands loom;
Just behind the hanging curtain
  Serving in another room.

Shall I doubt my Father's mercy?
  Shall I think of death as doom,
When I know my love is happy,
  Waiting in the other room?   *Robert Freeman.*

Sorrow vanquished, labor ended, Jordan passed.

Only a step removed,
  And that step—into bliss!
Our own, our dearly loved,
  Whom here on earth we miss.

Not shrouded in the dark,
  But veiled in purest light;
Each safely anchored barque
  Now hidden from our sight.

Not hushed the pleasant song
   That used to greet our ears;
But 'mid the angel throng
   Sounding more sweet and clear.

Not passed away the love,
   So rich, so true, so pure;
But perfected above,
And ever to endure.—
   Only a step removed.

SEPTEMBER 6

When He hath tried me I shall come forth as gold (Job 23:10).

The fire of the furnace and the smoke of the flames—these show how God brings deep things out of darkness—rich treasures out of darkness.

Authorities tell us that the potter never sees his clay take on rich shades of silver, or red, or cream, or brown, or yellow, until after the darkness and the burning of the furnace. These colors come—after the burning and darkness. The clay is beautiful—after the burning and the darkness. The vase is made possible—after the burning and darkness.

After the burning and blackness, we have a wisdom that knows God . . . our weakness is coined into strength and we lean upon God, our faith is no longer a flickering flame, but an eye set in the soul through which we behold the Face of God. If the burning hurts and the darkness brings gloom, as it always does, it is only a prophecy of the strength which will be ushered into the life.

When the little girl told her music teacher that it hurt her fingers to practice the piano, the teacher answered, "I know it hurts, but it *strengthens* them, too." Then the child packed the philosophy of the ages in her reply, "Teacher, it seems that everything that strengthens, hurts."

How wide-lying and universal is the law of life! Where did the bravest man and purest woman you know get their whitened characters? Did they not get them as the clay gets its beauty—after the darkness and the burning of the furnace? Where did Savonarola get his eloquence? In the darkness and burning of the furnace wherein God discovered deep things to him. Where did

Stradavari get his violins? Where did Titian get his color? Where did Angelo get his marble? Where did Mozart get his music, and Chatterton his poetry, and Jeremiah his sermon?

They got them where the clay gets its glory and its shimmer—in the darkness and in the burning. Truly they can testify that God kept His promise, who said, "I will give thee the treasure of darkness.   *Robert G. Lee.*

> Measure thy life by loss and not by gain,
> Not by the wine drunk, but by the wine poured forth.
> For love's strength standeth in love's sacrifice,
> And he who suffers most has most to give.

It is the iron plow-share that goes over the field of the heart, . . . until at night time, down in the deep furrows, the angels come and sow.

SEPTEMBER 7

It is good for me that I have been afflicted (Psalm 119:71).

If any of you have ever stood at the foot of an old beach tree and watched a moth or butterfly emerge from the chrysalis, you will have noticed, after the first little opening, with what seemingly pained struggle the young wings are striving to free themselves. In your pity you take up the chrysalis, and end the struggle by carefully cutting open the useless envelope and freeing the living winged creature. It is said that any such kindness simply means an undeveloped wing-power, by which the butterfly will never be able to soar and enjoy life. The struggle is the needful condition of full wing-power. Men who cannot struggle can never soar.

No stroke of the chisel in the hand of the Great Artificer is redundant. The soul, like the facets of the diamond, needs the best and sharpest tools to fashion it into a gem for the Redeemer's crown.

PAIN is in some wise the artist of the world which creates us, fashions us, sculptures us with the fine edge of a pitiless chisel. It limits the overflowing life; and that which remains, stronger and more exquisite, enriched by its very loss, draws thence the gift of a higher being.   *Michilet.*

252

I THANK THEE

I thank Thee, Lord, for cloudy weather,
   We soon would tire of blue;
I thank Thee, Lord, for Pain, our brother,
   Whose rude care holds us true.

I thank Thee for the weary morrow,
   That makes the past more sweet;
I thank Thee for our sister, Sorrow.
   Who leads us to Thy feet.   *F. L. Knowles.*

SEPTEMBER 8

Hope thou in God (Psalm 42:11).

Now I want you to think that in life troubles will come, which seem as if they never would pass away. The night and the storm look as if they would last forever, but the calm and the morning cannot be stayed; the storm in its very nature is transient. The effort of nature, as that of the human heart, ever is to return to its repose, for God is Peace.   *George MacDonald.*

BE HOPEFUL

Fain would I hold my lamp of life aloft
Like yonder tower built high above the reef;
Steadfast, though tempests rave or winds blow soft;
Clear, though the sky dissolve in tears of grief.

For darkness passes; storms shall not abide:
A little patience and the storm is past.
After the sorrow of ebbing tide
The singing flood returns in joy at last.

The night is long and pain weighs heavily;
But God will hold His world above despair.
Look to the east, where up the lucid sky
The morning climbs! The day shall yet be fair
                                        Celia Thaxter.

There are no somber days to a great soul. Hard days? Some of the greatest souls have paths of anguish to travel; storms beat them full in the face; but the lifting tides of God make *every* day great.

He asked life of Thee, and Thou gavest it him, even length of days forever and ever (Psalm 21:4).

Did you ever climb the winding staircase in the interior of some great monument or tower? At intervals, as you ascended, you came to a window which let in a little light, and through which, as you looked out, you had a glimpse of a great expanse of fair and lovely world outside the dark tower. You saw green fields, rich gardens, picturesque landscapes, streams flashing like flowing silver in the sunshine, the blue sea yonder, and far away, on the other hand, the shadowy forms of great mountains. How little, how dark, how poor and cheerless, seemed the close, narrow limits of your staircase as you looked out upon the illimitable view that stretched from your window?

Life in this world is like the ascent of such a column. But while we climb heavily and wearily up its steep, dark stairway, there lies, outside the thick walls, a glorious world reaching away into eternity, beautiful and filled with rarest things of God's love. And thoughts of immortality, when they come to us, are little windows through which we have glimpses of the infinite sweep and stretch of life beyond this hampered, broken fragmentary existence of earth.

The doctrine of the resurrection is one of these windows. It opens up a vista running away beyond the grave. Death is a mere episode, a mere existence, an incident by the way. Even the grave, which seems to quench all the light of life, is but the chamber in which we shall disrobe ourselves of the infirmities, blemishes and imperfections of mortality and be reclothed in the holy, spotless vesture of immortality.

When the truth of immortal existence comes into our personal consciousness, it opens a wonderful vista before us. It gives life a new glory. It furnishes one of the most powerful motives for noble living.

Winter comes, and the leaves fall, the flowers fade, the plants die, and snow wraps the earth in a blanket of death. But spring comes again, and the buds burst out anew, the flowers lift their heads and the grasses shoot up once more. From beneath the great drifts the gentlest and most delicate forms of life come as fresh and fragrant as if they had been nourished in a conservatory.

Nature rises from the grave of winter in new beauty and luxuriance. In place of the sere leaves and faded loveliness and exhausted vigor of the autumn, there is now all the splendor of the new creation. Every leaf is green, every pore is flowing full of vital sap, and every flower pours sweetest fragrance on the air.

The grave is but life's winter, from whose darkness and chill we shall come with unwasted beauty. Then, away beyond this strange experience, as we look out at the window again, we see life going on, expanding, deepening, enriching. *Selected.*

> . . . for death
> Is but the sunrise of another world.

SEPTEMBER 10 _____

And He took them and went aside privately into a desert place (Luke 9:10).

These hours of the soul's communion with truth and God are the precious hours of life. Sacrifice anything rather than these heavenly impulses. Give up anything that interferes with carrying them out into the life. They are the scattered fountains in the desert, at which the fainting traveller revives his strength and courage. Then heavenly voices speak, and happy is he who give heed to the heavenly vision, which is from God and conducts to God. *Ephraim Peabody.*

THE QUIET HOUR

The quiet of a shadow-haunted pool
　Where light breaks through in glorious tenderness,
Where the hushed pilgrim in the shadow cool
　Forgets the way's distress. —

Such is this hour, this silent hour with Thee!
　The trouble of the restless heart is still;
And every swaying wish breathes reverently
　The whisper of Thy will.

Wrapped in the peace that follows prayer,
　I fold my hands in perfect trust,
Forgetful of the cross I bear
　Through noonday heat and dust.

"Steal away to Jesus"—He is not far from thee at this shadow hour.

_____

A city which hath foundations, whose builder and maker is God (Heb. 11:10).

Yes! earth grows the poorer, Heaven seems more desirable, when our loved ones have gone into the shadowy land. Shadowy, did I say? Nay, *here* is the shadowy, *there* the light blots out the radiance of the sun. With excess of brightness that higher world is dark because our eyes are so weak, our faith so dim. In this ever-changing world of phenomena *we* seem but shadows pursuing shadows, like the rest. When we reach *there* we shall know the truth, that love, and life, were the only real things we have ever found.

THERE!

No shadows There! They joyfully behold Him!
 No cloud to dim their vision of His Face!
No jarring note to mar the holy rapture,
 The perfect bliss of that most holy place.

No burdens There! These all are gone forever!
 No weary nights, no long or dragging days;
No sighings There, or secret, silent longings,
 For all is now unutterable praise.

No sorrows There! no sadness and no weeping!
 Tears wiped away—all radiant now each face;
Music and song, in happy holy blending,
 Fills all the courts of that sweet resting-place.

J. Danson Smith.

_____

Suffer little children to come unto Me (Luke 18:16).

Think not, O mother, of your child as lying lonely in the grave, the snow its winding-sheet or the spring flowers its funeral offering. She is not there; she never was there. You have not committed her to the grave; you are not to go there in quest of her. You have given her back to the Father who gave her to you. You have put her in the arms of Christ, that Christ may bless her. The voice of death is but the voice of the Master saying to you, "Suffer the little children to come unto Me, and forbid them not; for of such is the kingdom of heaven."

THE BABY'S JOURNEY

We know that the baby's journey
  Led first through the valley dim,
But the loving Christ was with her,
  And we trusted it all to Him!
And we know that the royal lilies,
  That lean o'er that restless tide,
Forever are bright with the glory
  That's just on the other side!

O little precious traveler!
  We know that your baby feet
Have passed the mystic boundaries
  Where the earthly and heavenly meet!
Forgotten our good-bye kisses,
  Forgotten our passionate tears,
In the beauty and light and glory
  That met you beyond the stars!

No pain for the brow death kisses
  No tears for the bright eyes to weep!
She hath passed from our caresses
  To those far more tender and deep!
But be pitiful, Lord, if in blindness,
  When the fountains of anguish are stirred,
We forget for a moment Thy kindness,
  And sigh for our Paradise Bird!

THE PATTER OF LITTLE FEET

Those dear, little feet that pattered upstairs,
  Each day at the set of sun,
Are pattering now the golden streets
  With life's short journey done.

And the chubby, pink hands that clasped each night
  On the breast of my darling child;
And the dear little lips, that lisped in prayer;
  And the innocent eyes that smiled:

These are my treasures laid up on high—
　　With Christ—in that blest retreat,
How sweet shall sound when I enter heav'n
　　The patter of little feet.　　　　　　　*M. J. Scott.*

SEPTEMBER 13 _____

Now we see through a glass darkly: but then . . . (1 Cor. 13:12).

Does it seem to you, dear sad Heart, that your life, because of the loss of your loved one, has come to an abrupt ending? Is there nothing left for which to live? Have you ever thought that your bereavement may be part of His plan?

You remember the story of the engineer of the Brooklyn bridge. During its building he was injured. For many long months he was shut up in his room. His gifted wife shared his toils, and carried his plans to the workmen. At last the great bridge was completed.

Then the invalid architect asked to see it. They put him upon a cot, and carried him to the bridge. They placed him where he could see the magnificent structure in all its beauty. There he lay, in his helplessness, intently scanning the work of his genius. He marked the great cables, the massive piers, the mighty anchorages which fettered it to the earth. His critical eye ran over every beam, every girder, every chord, every rod. He noted every detail carried out precisely as he had dreamed it in his dreams, and wrought it out in his plans and specifications.

And then as the joy of achievement filled his soul, as he saw and realized that it was finished exactly as he had designed it; in an ecstasy of delight he cried out: "It's just like the plan; *it's just like the plan.*"

Some day we shall stand in the glory and looking up into His face, cry out: "O God, I thank Thee that Thou didst let me gather up one by one, the golden threads of Thy great purpose for my life. I thank Thee, as, like a tiny trail creeping its way up some great mountain side, that pathway of life has gone on in darkness and light, storm and shadow, weakness and tears, failures and falterings, Thou hast at last brought me to its destined end. And now that I see my finished life, no longer "through a glass darkly" but in the face to face splendor of Thine own glory, I thank Thee,

O God, I thank Thee that, it's just like the plan; *it's just like the plan.*"   *James McConkey.*

He will silently plan for thee.

What your Father, God, has planned for you, He will bring to you in His own way and time.

Wait, patiently wait!

IS IT TRUE?

"Is it true that my Saviour is planning for me,
    When the way is rough and long,
And the clouds hang low and friends are few,
    And I have no voice for song?
Is it true He is planning my whole life through,
    Each moment, from day to day?
Does He love and care enough for me
    To listen to all I say?"
"Yes! He's silently planning, dear one, for you,
    When the days are long and drear,
He loves, and He cares so much for you,
    Take courage and banish all fear.
He is planning the very best for you
    Through tedious days of strife,
Just trust and cling close to that Blessed One
    In the ups and downs of life.

There is a divinity that shapes our ends,
Rough-hew them how we will.   *Shakespeare.*

SEPTEMBER 14 _____

As one whom his mother comforteth (Isa. 66:13).

This is God's picture and emblem of His own great loving self, as He weaves by each life-cradle a lullaby of love.

Who, of all her family, does the mother of earth most love and tenderly care for? Is it not her sick and suffering child? The strong shrubs are left to grapple with the storm: it is the weak and fragile one she specially tends, and props, and shelters form biting frost and scorching sun. The ninety and nine are left by the shepherd to roam at will, untended on the mountain-side: but the *one* footsore fleecetorn wanderer—the one sick and wounded—he grudges no length of journey to succour, or to bear back on his shoulder rejoicing to the fold. Sorrowing one! It is *on you* this great God lavishes His deepest, profoundest sympathy. You are the battered flower He loves most to tend. You are the drooping member of the flock whose wounds He loves most to bind up. It is by the cradle of some great life-sorrow He loves to sit, weaving, as a tender mother, His strains of love and comfort!

And *such* a Prop! such a Sustainer! We are strengthened on earth by the consciousness of some strong friend to minister to us in our sorrows. The stronger the arm and the wiser the heart, the greater we feel the sustaining power of offered sympathy, *What must be the support and consolation of an infinite God!*—Perfect power and Perfect wisdom not only giving up the cup, but holding our hands while we drink it!

THE TIRED HEART

Dear Lord, I bear a tired heart tonight
And need that Thou shouldst come and comfort me,
For well I know what rest and peace will come
Upon the weary soul which turns to Thee.

Take Thou my lifted hands within Thine own,
And let me know that prayer will bring Thee near.
And that no cry of pain or sigh for help
Will fail to reach Thine ever-listening ear.

So though I bear a tired heart tonight,
I know that Thou wilt come and comfort me,
And with the morn the heaviness will pass,
And joy will come because of trust in Thee.

SEPTEMBER 15 _____

The ransomed of the Lord shall return, and come to Zion with songs, and everlasting joy upon their heads. They shall obtain joy and gladness, and sorrow and sighing shall flee away (Isa. 35:10).

After the sorrow, the song! God has not left His people floundering in the fogs of unbelief or amid the morasses of hopeless despair. The way may dip down into the valley of the shadow, but beyond the darkness, there is the dawn.

The steps of a good man are ordered by the Lord. They may have to tread the lonely places of darkness, and pass through the valley of the shadow of death, if the Lord tarries; but as surely as day succeeds night, and reaping follows sowing, so surely shall the redeemed of the Lord arrive at the City of Light and the House of the Father.

WHEN ALL IS DONE

Well, all is done and my last word is said,
And ye who love me murmur, "He is dead";
Weep not for me, for fear that I should know,
And sorrow, too, that ye should sorrow so.
When all is done, say not that my day is o'er,
And that, through night, I seek a dimmer shore;
Say, rather, that my day has just begun;
I greet the dawn, and not the setting sun—
    When all is done.   *Paul Laurence Dunbar.*

SEPTEMBER 16

Though He slay me, yet will I trust in Him (Job 13:15).

My Father, behold Thou comest to me in clouds. Life is overcast to me. Men want me to trace Thee. "The cup which my Father has given me to drink, shall I not drink it?" I accept in the darkness the burden Thou hast laid upon me; *I take it unexplained.* I come to Thee in the night; I accept Thee in Thy mean attire, in Thy unattractive raiment, in Thy repulsive dress. I do not seek to comprehend Thee: I take Thee with Thy mystery. Though Thou slay me, yet will I trust.   *George Matheson.*

There is a rainbow in every storm cloud if we are only at the right angle to see it. In order that we may see the rainbow the sun must face the storm, and if we are to see the utility of suffering the whole problem must be radiant with the sunlight of God's will. We have known the deepest truth of life and touched the highest point of privilege when the heart says, "Thy will be done."

    What matter if God wills
    That we should sometimes walk in shady places?

The shadows of the everlasting hills
Are mirrored in the silver-bosomed rills,
  Whereto we stoop to cool our tired faces.

Once, while under great mental depression, a minister was reading a good book, when his eyes fell upon this sentence, quoted by Luther: "I would run into the arms of Christ, though He stood with drawn sword in His Hand." The thought came bolting into his mind, "So will I too"; and those words of Job occurred immediately, "Though He slay me, yet will I trust in Him." His burden slipped away, and his soul was filled with joy and peace in believing.

Bereaved ones! Your clouds of present sorrow have always their silver lining. Look to Him whom one of the old divines calls your "Upmaking Portion." Go, weary soul, sob yourself to rest in the bosom of God and in the Peace of Christ.

SEPTEMBER 17

Which hope we have as an anchor of the soul, both sure and steadfast, and which entereth into that within the veil (Heb. 6:19).

There is a bird of the Thrush family, found in the south of Ireland, called "The Storm Thrush," from its peculiar love of storms. In the wildest storms of rain and wind it betakes itself to the very topmost twig of the highest tree and there pours out its beautiful song—its frail perch swaying in the wind.

THE STORM THRUSH

There's a sweet little bird in a far-off isle—
  The isle where the shamrocks grow;
And of all the birds in that dear old land,
  He's the dearest that I know;
He is dressed in a suit of sober brown,
  And a speckled breast has he;
But his eye is bright and his voice is tuned
  To heaven's own minstrelsy.
He sits and sings when the sun shines fair
  To his mate in her downy nest,
But the topmost twig of the tallest tree
  Is the place where he sings best!
When the rain pours down and the floods are out,

And the wild winds rage and roar,
Then, clear and high, o'er the shrieking gale,
   The storm thrush sings the more.

That frail little bird on the swaying twig,
   As his clear voice pierced the gales,
Dropped a message sweet at my faltering feet,
   Of a Love that never fails:
Though many a storm has crossed my life,
   And many a grief and fear;
Yet with heart and voice did my soul rejoice,
   For my Lord was always near.
So when dark clouds are about YOUR path,
   Like the storm thrush, learn to sing;
For from topmost height of a lofty faith
   You can always see the King!
And with eyes that gaze on His blessed face,
   You never need fear or fail,
The gales may PROVE, but they CANNOT MOVE,
   The anchor "within the vail."   *Mrs. C. L. de Cheney.*

SEPTEMBER 18

He will swallow up death in victory (Isa. 25:8).

Death is not defeat for the soul that on Jesus hath leaned for repose. Was Henry Martin, the scholar of Oxford and Cambridge, who buried himself in the sands of Arabia for Jesus' sake, defeated? He went in territories that no other man had ever been in, and at last lay down on the desert sand; and they buried him in an unmarked grave. Was this great hero defeated?

No—a thousand times. Put a stone at the head of his grave, and let some angel artist carve it with eternal letters. It is victory.

Was the greatest man who ever lived, next to Jesus Christ, defeated when they laid his head on Nero's block and cut it off?

You call it defeat when God Almighty puts a crown on a man's brow? It is victory to the last limit, and earth knows no victory like that.

The mission of Jesus meant life, but it is only found in Him, and without Him there is no victory in death.

Death says: "The stars are out."

Immortality says: "The stars go down to rise upon some fairer shore."

Death says: "I have plucked your fairest flowers."

Immortality says: "They are but transplanted into bliss to adorn eternal bowers.

Death says: "The torch is quenched."

Immortality says: "The torch shall be relit with all the brilliance of the sun."

Death says: "The column is broken."

Immortality says: "The column is transferred to another building and another city to be a pillar in the temple of God!"

Death says: "The strings of the harp are snapped."

Immortality says: "The harp is not broken but handed to a truer minstrel who will bring out the rich compass of its hidden music."

Death is the putting off of a garment—the moving out of a tabernacle.

"For we know that if our earthly house of this tabernacle were dissolved, we have a building of God, an house not made with hands, eternal in the heavens" (2 Cor. 5:2).

Death is gain to the believer.

"For me to live is Christ, to die is gain. . . . For I am in a strait betwixt two, having a desire to depart, and to be with Christ: which is far better" (Phil. 1:21–23).

The resurrection of Christ furnishes the grand, indisputable proof of *our* resurrection from the dead.

Christ's resurrection proves that immortality is a fact, for He has gone beyond the grave and has come back. Eternally can He say, "I am He that *liveth,* and was *dead,* and behold, I am alive *forevermore* ." (Rev. 1:18)

By His resurrection He has hung, for us, for all, a lamp in the tomb—a lamp which has lighted forever its darkness and assuredly banished its gloom. Through the broken tomb of Christ we may look out, as through a window, and see beyond the dark river the bright and happy faces of the redeemed ones we miss from our earthly circles. And, "having the vision of life as immortal, find in the truth of immortality boundless inspiration, comfort for every sorrow, gain for every loss."

264

Accordingly, in glad chorus of confirmation, we all, in agreement with the great Apostle Peter, singing with exceeding great joy, say:

"Blessed be the God and Father of our Lord Jesus Christ, who, according to His abundant mercy hath begotten us again unto a lively hope by the resurrection of Jesus Christ from the dead."

To an inheritance incorruptible, and undefiled, and that fadeth not away, reserved in Heaven for you. Who are kept by the power of God through faith unto salvation ready to be revealed in the last time. Wherein ye greatly rejoice though now for a season, if need be, ye are in heaviness through manifold temptations" (1 Peter 1:3–6).   *From Beds of Pearls, by Robert G. Lee.*

SEPTEMBER 19 _____

I saw and beheld a great multitude which no man could number, out of every nation and of all tribes, and peoples, and tongues, standing before the throne and before the Lamb (Rev. 7:9).

THE GREAT RE-UNION

There are empty chairs in the home; and voices we have loved to hear are silent. We shall find them in Heaven. In the churchyard—do you think they sleep there? No! No! The body to dust, the spirit to God Who gave it. The home-circle will be filled again. We shall meet our friends there.   *G. Vibert.*

GUESTS OF GOD

From the dust of the weary highway,
    From the smart of sorrow's rod,
Into the royal presence,
    They are bidden as guests of God.
The veil from their eyes is taken,
    Sweet mysteries they are shown,
Their doubts and fears are over,
    For they know as they are known.

For them there should be rejoicing
    For them, the festal array,
As for the bride in her beauty
    Whom love hath taken away;
Sweet hours of peaceful waiting,

265

Till the path that we have trod
Shall end at the Father's gateway.
And we are the guests of God.   *Selected.*

SEPTEMBER 20 ─────────────────────────────

As dying and behold we live (2 Cor. 6:9).

I remember how the day died. The sun went down and deepened into darkness and the darkness into the blackness of midnight, and I shuddered in my loneliness and dread; and I said, "This is the end."

I gazed long at the place where the sun had last been; there was no blacker spot in all the heavens than there, and I turned my back upon it, heartsore and desolate. But I remembered that as the sun descended toward the horizon, it lighted up the west with a glory which even the noonday had not known, and I asked myself why the day smiled as it died. And lo! as I pondered, I lifted up my eye to the east, and the light was breaking for a new and fairer morning.

I remember how the year died. The frost came and the flowers wilted where they stood, and bowed their faded blossoms to earth. The leaves fell, and were driven before the wind.

The clouds put on their black robes; the heavens, attired in deep mourning, gathered about the grave, and rained tears upon the dead earth; then wrapped it in its mantle of snow, and left it silent, alone, and dead.

But as I thought of these things, I remembered how the forests, ere they dropped their leaves, put on their most glorious colors, and smiled in the face of the frost; and every leaf, as it fluttered helplessly from its perch, rejoiced in the bud which it had left beneath its stem as the prophecy of another spring.

William E. Burton.

SEPTEMBER 21 ─────────────────────────────

I will come to you (John 14:18).

HIMSELF

O Friend, on whom this night of grief hath fallen,
  Fain would my heart go with you through its gloom,
Though all my broken words of consolation
  Falter and fail before that open tomb.

I would keep pace with you through that drear silence,
  My love an arm beneath your fainting heart;
But I am powerless to reach or aid you
  On the dark path where each must walk apart—

Yet not alone—for there is One beside you
  With words of comfort like a strong, sweet psalm,
Whose face can bring a light into its darkness,
  Whose hand can soothe your pain with healing balm;

Whose mighty arm can be your sure upholding
  Through all the shadows of the lonely way,
That you may know His strength, His peace, His presence,
  This is my heart's deep prayer for you today. *A. F. J.*

  He gives His angels charge of those that sleep,
  But He Himself keeps watch with those that weep.

SEPTEMBER 22 _____

In the place where He was crucified was a garden; and in the garden a new sepulcher (John 19:43).

Many of you, nay, most of you, know full well what it is to have a sepulcher in the garden of your lives. You know the shadow that it sheds over all the pleasant alleys and the bordered paths. You need not be told how it changes the place for you into something other than it was.

But there is another aspect. Not a spot in all the inclosure brought to Joseph of Arimathea so enduring joy as the very place he had builded for sorrow. And the sepulcher in your garden may do the same for you. It may be a resurrection spot for your soul.

Out of this sorrow which wraps you round, you may rise into a purer and serener day. The rolling of a great stone to the door may mark the finishing and hiding away of one portion of your Christian life; and the rolling of that stone away on the third morning may be the commencement of a higher and more consecrated one.

And if this be the case, then the sepulcher spot in your days will be the most blessed of all. Its joy will reach farther, shine clearer, endure longer, than any belonging to the hours when your garden knew no tomb.

Sorrows are too precious to be wasted. That great man of God in a past generation, Alexander MacLaren of Manchester, used to bring out this overlooked truth. He reminded God's people that sorrows will, if we let them, "blow us to His breast, as a strong wind might sweep a man into some refuge from itself." I am sure there are many who can thankfully attest that they were brought nearer to God by some short, sharp sorrow than by long days of prosperity.

Take care that you do not waste your sorrows; that you do not let the precious gifts of disappointment, pain, loss, loneliness, or similar afflictions that come into your daily life mar you instead of mending you. See that they send you nearer to God, and not that they drive you farther from Him.

There is no failure of life so terrible as to have the pain without the lesson, the sorrow without the softening.   *Hugh Black.*

> Hear me, O God!
>   A broken heart
>   Is my best part;
> Use still Thy rod
>   That I may prove
>   Therein Thy love.
>
> If Thou hadst not
>   Been stern to me,
>   But left me free,
> I had forgot
>   Myself and Thee   *Ben Johnson.*

DO NOT LOSE YOUR SORROW.

SEPTEMBER 23 _____

I go to prepare a place for you (John 14:2).

A place." We have pondered much on this. What kind of a place, and where is it? He evidently wanted us to be content with the fact that if He prepared it, that was all that could be desired. Our fettered imagination can only feebly anticipate that "sweet and blessed country, the home of God's elect."

Its glory will surpass the rising of the sun, when the orb comes up with trembling shafts of light, through filmy curtains of clouds, and fills the eastern sky with opalescent splendors.

Its expanses will exceed the wide stretches of prairies with their waving fields of growing grain.

Its grandeur can only be dimly suggested by up-leaping mountains that offer a footpath to the blue skies.

Its loveliness will be as a garden, more appealing than all earth's flowers—from the dogtooth violet that peeps out in the early spring in answer to the blue bird's call to the riot of color that decorates country highways in the late autumn with cloth of gold.

Its harmonies will be more alluring than all the sweet symphonies of earth, from the gurgling laughter of babies to the union of all earth's choirs in one "Hallelujah Chorus."

"And if I go and prepare a place for you, I will come again and receive you unto Myself, that where I am, there ye may be also.

Charles Nelson Page.

SEPTEMBER 24

I will turn their mourning into joy (Jer. 31:13).

THEY MET AND ARE SATISFIED

They met tonight—the one who closed his eyes unto pain
    forever and the woe;
And the one who found the mansions in the skies in all
    their splendor long, long years ago.

What will they say when first their eyes meet? Or will a
    silence take the place of words?
As only saints can know how strangely sweet a rapture
    such as only Heaven affords.

Will he who went before ask first for those left far
    behind—those whom he loved so well?
Or will the other, new to Heaven's repose, question of all
    its meaning? Who can tell?

One went so long ago, and one tonight took the long
    journey, far across the tide.
This only do I know—they met tonight, and meeting—
    both, I know, are satisfied.   *British Weekly.*

At home with the Lord (2 Cor. 5:8—R. V.).

SEPTEMBER 25

*For David, after he had served his own generation by the will of God, fell
on sleep (Acts 13:36).*

Charles E. Cowman's Coronation Day

In giving light to others I myself am burned away.   *The Candle.*

Great heart is dead they say;
But the light shall burn the brighter,
And the night shall be the lighter
For his going;
And a rich, rich harvest for his sowing.   *John Oxenham.*

T hen," said Christian, "I am going to my Father's house and
    though with great difficulty I am got hither, yet now I do not
repent of all the trouble I have been at to arrive where I am.
    "My sword I leave to him that shall succeed me in my
pilgrimage, and my courage and skill to him that can get it. My
marks and scars I carry with me, to be a witness for me that I have
fought His battles, who will now be my rewarder." When the day
that he must go hence was come, many accompanied him to the
river-side, into which as he went down deeper, he said, "Grave,
where is thy victory?" So he passed over and all the trumpets
sounded for him on the other side.   *Pilgrim's Progress.*

What nobler decoration of honor can any godly man seek after
than his scars of service, his losses for the crown, his reproaches
for Christ's sake, his being worn out in his Master's service!

When I am dying how glad I will be
That the lamp of my life has been blazed out for Thee.
I shall not mind in whatever I gave,
Labor or money, one heathen to save.
I shall not mind that the way has been rough!

That Thy dear Feet led the way was enough.
When I am dying how glad I shall be
That the lamp of my life has been blazed out for Thee!

But are they dead? Our hearts may ask.
They lived, performed their glorious task,
Spent and were spent, and now they bask
    In Gloryland.

Fill up the ranks depleted so!
To us from failing hands they throw
The torch; be ours to hold it high—
If we break faith with those who die
On us the shame! For grasses blow
    In heathen lands.
               Cora Mae Turnbull.

SEPTEMBER 26

Behold, we have forsaken all, and followed Thee; what shall we have therefore? (Matt. 19:27).

It is something to be a missionary. The morning stars sang together and all the sons of God shouted for joy when they saw the field which the first missionary was to fill. The great and loving God, before whom the angels veil their faces, had an only Son, and he was sent to earth as Missionary Physician. It is something to be a follower, however feeble, in the wake of the Great Teacher and only Model Missionary that ever appeared among men, and now that He is the Head over all things, King of kings, and Lord of lords, what commission is equal to that which a missionary holds from Him? For my own part, I never cease to rejoice that God has appointed me to such an office!
               David Livingstone.

"And what shall we have, we who have left all to follow Thee?"

WHAT THEN? (Job 31:14).

"What then?" Why, then another pilgrim song;
  And then a hush of rest divinely granted
And then a thristy stage (Ah, me, so long!)
  And then a brook—just where it so was wanted.

What then? The pitching of the evening tent;
   And then, perchance a pillow rough and thorny
And then, some sweet and tender message sent
   To cheer the faint one for the morrow's journey.

What then? The wailing of the midnight wind;
   A feverish sleep; a heart oppressed and aching;
And then, a little water cruise to find
   Close by my pillow, ready for my waking.

What then? I am not careful to enquire,
   I know there will be tears and fears and sorrow,
And then a loving Saviour drawing nigher,
   And saying, "I will answer for the morrow."

What then? A shadowy valley, lone and dim
   And then a deep and darkly rolling river;
And then a flood of light, a seraph hymn,
   And God's own smile forever and forever.

Jane Crewdson.

We ask no other wages
When Thou shalt call us Home,
Than to have shared Thy labors,
That made Thy Kingdom come.

SEPTEMBER 27

Weeping may endure for a night, but joy cometh in the morning (Psalm 30:5).

Sorrow does not control life. The overcoming life is greater than sorrow. Through the gate of sadness, we pass into a richer, sweeter, finer life. After the shadow of night, morning breaketh. Night comes before the unfolding beauty of a dawning day. The overcoming life is triumphant over sadness. It is victorious *in* and *over* sorrow.

Today, "I walk through the valley and shadow of death," but tomorrow, I shall see as in "the light of the morning, when the sun riseth, even after rain." Today my soul is bowed down; but tomorrow, "I take the wings of the morning." Today "my tears have been my meat"; but "in the morning will I direct my prayers and will look up."

All morning would be glaring. There would be no minor keys to soften the tone. Night comes, dew falls, and while the earth lies in darkness, it has been made cooler. After awhile day breaks across the hills—brighter and brighter. Joy cometh.

As we pass beneath the hills which have been shaken by the earthquake and torn by convulsion, we find that periods of perfect repose succeed those of destruction. The pools of calm water lie clear beneath their fallen rocks, the water lilies gleam, and the reeds whisper among the shadows; the village rises again over the forgotten graves, and its church tower, white through the storm twilight, proclaims a renewed appeal to His protection "in whose hands are all the corners of the earth, and the strength of the hills is His also. *Ruskin.*

SEPTEMBER 28 _____

There is no other God that can deliver after this sort (Dan. 3:29).

The ways of life are supremely mysterious and we must not hope to fathom them this side of Paradise.

One thing is certain—God does not permit a burden to come to us without having provided strength sufficient to carry it.

Your life task is to demonstrate what miracles God can work through a man's triumph over the seemingly insurmountable. If your burden is supremely heavy it is evidence that God has superior confidence in you and that He is permitting you to undertake a task of particular significance. He trusts you to win.

God's requirements are met by God's enablings.

SEPTEMBER 29 _____

She goeth unto the grave to weep there (John 11:31).

The Jews thought Mary was going to weep at the sepulchre, and so she did; but she heard that the Master had come, and she went *first to Him* and *He went with her to the grave.* He went with her first to weep and then to turn her mourning into joy with life from the dead. Ah! my friend, whatever we mean to do, let us go to Jesus first.

Mary wept for her brother and she had the sympathy of Him

whom it is our blessed privilege to claim as our Elder Brother; but the widow weeping over the grave of him who was the bosom companion of her life, until it pleased God to receive his spirit sanctified through Christ, may appeal to the Mediator's heart by a yet dearer name; for whom the Lord would show how tenderly and faithfully He "nourisheth and cherisheth His Church." (Eph. 5:29.) He calls Himself her husband, her precious, holy, affectionate "husband." "Thy Maker is thine Husband." (Isa. 54:5.)

So, heart stricken mourner, He knows the grief and anguish you feel; He knows the desolations of your spirit and its yearnings after a solace the world cannot give!

Go to the grave of your beloved one; but as you go let not your tears so blind you, neither so hang down your head that you may not see that Jesus has come to sustain you. Hear His gracious voice from beside the tomb *"I am the Resurrection and the life. "*

Your husband is not dead. His believing soul that lived with Christ here, now lives with Christ in heaven; and his Christian dust is sleeping sweetly until He shall rise, immortal, glorious, and incorruptible at the resurrection of the last day. All your love, and watching, and anxious nursing could not save him from suffering and sickness and the tomb; but the love of Jesus has delivered him from all, and taken him up to that sinless, sorrowless home where there "shall be no more death, neither sorrow or crying, neither shall there be any more pain; for the former things have passed away."

Here you were united in a better than an earthly love, the love of Christ, and in that love you are and shall be united forever. Look, then, beyond the scene of your mortal grief, to the home of your perpetual bliss. Christ has lain in the tomb and sweetened it for the sleep of His beloved and yours; but as you stoop to see within the sepulchre see you not that it is broken, and that the uprising Master has opened a way through it, up through the rent veil, up through the everlasting doors, to the paradise of God! There seek to follow; and when you draw near the celestial band you will find waiting to welcome you one more radiant than an angel, in whose transfigured countenance you will recognize him you have not lost, but who has gone before to our Father's house.

If I should die and leave you here awhile,
Be not like others, sore undone, who keep
Long vigils by the silent dust, and weep:

For my sake turn again to life, and smile,
Nerving thy heart and trembling hand to do
Something to comfort weaker hearts than thine;
Complete these dear unfinished tasks of mine,
And I, perchance, may therein comfort you.

SEPTEMBER 30

Thy brother shall rise again (John 11:23).

Not a stranger, but *her brother,* —the very Lazarus over whose loss she had just uttered her despairing cry. "There is one thing that puzzles me," wrote one, "and worries me too. Will *anything* stay, among all the changes? Will faces be different? And voices strange? And hands lose their touch? Will our friends *be* our friends, or will they be just part of a great crowd with whom we must be acquainted? Will they be the very same, do you think?"

Of course there will be identity. "To every seed his own body." (1 Cor. 15:38.) Remember that no one thing *ever* changes according to any law but its own; so that the oak can never grow into a maple, nor the willow straighten up like the ash; nor the dogwood leaves turn yellow instead of crimson, nor the grass wear any shade of green but its own. Think of this when you fear that hand and face which you have loved, may somehow change into another for which you care nothing.

At the transfiguration, when Moses and Elias appeared with Christ "in glory," they were still Moses and Elias—not two unknown ones.

"Thy brother," could not mean Lazarus in some other form, so that his sisters could not recognize him, some unknown one with whom they must become familiar by degrees, one who did not know them, who did not love them.

THE SAME OLD FACES

God does not send us stronger flowers, every year,
When the soft winds blow o'er the pleasant places;
The same old forms, look out from the same old faces,
The violet is here.

It all comes back—the odor, grace, and hue—
Each fond relation of the life repeated;

Nothing is lost, no looking for is cheated,
It is the thing we knew.

So, after death's winter, it shall be
God will not put strange sights in heavenly places;
The same old love will look from the same sweet faces,
And we shall cry, "Beloved I have thee!"

OCTOBER 1

ALONE (Deut. 32:12).

The hill was steep, but cheered along the way
By converse sweet, I mounted on the thought
That so it might be till the height was reached;
But suddenly a narrow winding path
Appeared, and then the Master said, "My child,
Here thou wilt safest walk with Me alone."

I trembled, yet my heart's deep trust replied,
"So be it, Lord." He took my feeble hand
In His, accepting thus my will to yield Him
All, and to find all in Him.
One long, dark moment,
And no friend I saw, save Jesus only.

But oh! so tenderly he led me on
And up, and spoke to me such words of cheer,
Such secret whisperings of His wondrous love,
That soon I told Him all my grief and fear,
And leaned on His strong arm confidingly.

And then I found my footseteps quickened,
And light ineffable, the rugged way
Illumined, such light as only can be seen
In close companionship with God.

A little while, and we shall meet again—
The loved and lost; but in the rapturous joy
Of greetings, such as here we cannot know,
And happy song, and heavenly embraces,
And tender recollections rushing back
Of pilgrim life, methinks one memory
More dear and sacred than the rest, shall rise.

And we who gather in the golden streets,
Shall oft be stirred to speak with grateful love
Of that dark day when Jesus bade us climb
Some narrow steep, leaning on Him alone.

"They two went on" (2 Kings 2:6).

WE TWO

So far with me, no further now!
Our journey all so brief is done:
Thou goest on thine unseen way,
And I must read my path alone.

"They two went on," and we have been
Through Bethel's plain and Jordan's flood—
Then one went back to serve, and wait—
And one soar'd up to dwell with God.

We two went on, ah, not alone!
And though no car of light I see—
There walks with me the Holy One,
And Christ the living God with thee.

OCTOBER 2

She that is a widow indeed, and desolate, trusteth in God (1 Tim. 5:5).

Art thou desolate indeed, because the light of thine eyes has passed from view, leaving thee immeasurably lonely? Dear soul, do not look down into the grave which has received the precious mortal frame, but up into the face of God.

He lent thee thy beloved. From the time of the first knitting of soul with soul he was but a loan for a specified time; and wouldst thou not rather have had him for so short a time than not at all? Wouldst thou not have said, had God asked thee "I would rather have a year or month of such love as his than none?"

That beloved one is still thine. Thy love has so entered into his heart that it could not be eradicated, though ages should pass. Do not suppose that death is so mighty a magician as to alter the very nature of those who pass for a moment beneath His wand.

And God will care for thee. Trust Him for society, that thou be not lonely; for the provision of what is necessary to thy support;

and for the protecting love which thy shrinking nature calls for.
Thy Maker is thy husband.

> Be ye strong of heart and come
> Bravely onward to your Home
>
> *Edwin Arnold.*

A LITTLE WAY

A little way—I know it is not far
To that dear home where my beloved are;
And yet my faith grows weaker, as I stand
A poor, lone pilgrim in a dreary land,
Where present pain the future bliss obscures;
And still my heart sits like a bird upon
The empty nest, and mourns its treasures gone;
 Plumed for their flight,
 And vanished quite,
Ah me! where is the comfort?—though I say
They have but journeyed on a little way!

A little way!—this sentence I repeat,
Hoping and longing to extract some sweet
To mingle with the bitter. From Thy hand
I take the cup I cannot understand,
And in my weakness give myself to Thee!
Although it seems so very, very far
To that dear home where my beloved are,
 I know, I know,
 It is not so;
Oh! give me faith to feel it when I say
That they are gone—gone but a little way.

OCTOBER 3 _____

So He giveth His beloved sleep (Psalm 127:2).

That is true! And especially illustrated in this Autumn season.
Let thy leaves drop, hawthorn, lilac and rose; let thy foliage
pass in glory out of sight, maple, dogwood and sumac; lift thy
bared branches bravely, oak and elm and ash, for the God who
had joy in making is the God of Summer as also of Winter. He is
God who knows the glory of the coming Spring and as a
preparation for it He now gives in this restful winter season a
fulfilment of the sentence "So He giveth His beloved sleep."

Do you remember how you stood where the shadows length-ened athwart the graves of the cemetery, when the wild winds sadly moaned in the tree tops as you laid away the fairest form in all the world? But it was no mere chance that bereaved thee, nor has any loss o'ertaken the Beloved; no, it was but a tender call that the dear one heard, and gentle was the touch that arrested longer stay in a world of care and pain. "So He giveth His beloved sleep."

But do you know what the Psalmist really said was this: "He giveth His beloved in sleep." Let the earth hear that as the Autumn leaves rustle down and as the autumn winds cry with a true voice—O Earth, thou art not forgotten by God for he knows where the lily bulbs lie sleeping, and He will impart such power to them as shall make them able to bear on their succulent stems the many tinted bells from which Divinest melody and sweetest perfume shall fall and float.

Even so, Pilgrim of the long night march and warrior fight begrimmed, and sailor spray-encircled, ye shall lay down worn bodies on the bosom of the earth and in the repose of the quiet grave, "He will be giving His beloved in sleep," such gracious gifts as shall result in the mystery of the Great Spring of the Resurrection, and of that spiritual body which shall be the Tabernacle fitted by God for the housing of the Soul made majestic as the face of Christ.   *W. B. Hinson.*

SLEEP, IT IS BEST

Sweet as the tender fragrance that survives,
When martyred flowers breathe out their little lives;
Sweet as a song that once consoled our pain,
But never shall be sung again,
Is thy remembrance. Now the hour of rest
Hath come to thee. Sleep, loved one, it is best
                    Henry W. Longfellow.

OCTOBER 4 _____

Return unto thy rest, O my soul; for the Lord hath dealt bountifully with thee (Psalm 116:7).

Yes, thank God! there is rest—many an interval of saddest, sweetest rest—even here, when it seems as if evening breezes from that other land, laden with fragrance, played up on the cheeks, and lulled the heart. There are times, even on the stormy sea, when a gentle whisper breathes softly as of heaven, and sends into the soul a dream of ecstasy which can never again wholly die, even amidst the jar and whirl of daily life. How such whispers make the blood stop and the flesh creep with a sense of mysterious communion! How singularly such moments are the epochs of life—the few points that stand out prominently in the recollection after the flood of years has buried the rest, as all the low shore disappears, leaving only a few rock points visible at high tide.   *F. W. Robertson.*

Listen, O listen, my soul to the voice of God speaking through the melody of music. Be still in the cool of the day and hear Him in the soft breezes ask "Where art thou?" Bend your ear close to the flowers, let them whisper His love and beauty. Open your ears and hear Him through the song of the bird. Look up at the stars and recall His infinity and constancy. Tune your heart to the bubbling brook that brings peace and gladness from His throne. Remember in the storms the Power that can speak, "Peace be still." Open thy window, soul of mine, to the beauty and glory of God. And the most wonderful peace that ever slumbered in the heart of God shall fill your life, even through its darkest hours.

The Life Beautiful.

OCTOBER 5 _____

I am the Resurrection, and the Life; he that believeth in Me, though he were dead, yet shall he live: and whosoever liveth and believeth in Me shall never die (John 11:25, 26).

Death is as sweet as flowers are. It is blessed as bird-singing in spring is. I never hear of the death of any one who is ready to die, that my heart does not sing like a harp. I am sorry for those left behind, but not for those who have gone before.

It is always a sad day to me in Autumn when I see the change that comes over nature. Along in August the birds are all still, and you would think there were not any left; but, if you go out into the field, you find them feeding in the trees, and hedges, and everywhere. By and by September comes, and they begin to gather in groups; and anybody that knows what it means, knows that they are getting ready to go. And then come the later days of October—the sad, the sweet, the melancholy, the deep, days of October. And the birds are less and less. And in November, high up you see the sky streaked with water-fowl going southward; and strange noises in the night, of these pilgrims of the sky, they shall hear whose ears are attuned to natural sound. Birds in flocks, one after another, wing their way to the South. Summer is gone, and I am left behind; but they are happy. And I think I can hear them singing in all these States clear down to the Gulf. They have found where the sun in never cold. With us are frosts, but not with the bird that has migrated.

> The little birds trust God, for they go singing
>   From Northern woods where autumn winds have blown.
> With joyous faith their trackless pathway winging
>   To summer lands of song, afar, unknown.
>
> And if He cares for them through wintry weather,
>   And will not disappoint one little bird,
> Will He not be as true a heavenly Father
>   To every soul who trusts His holy word?
>
> Let us go singing then, and not go sighing
>   Since we are sure our times are in His hand.
> Why should we weep, and fear, and call it dying?—
>   'Tis only flitting to a Summer land!   *Annie Johnson Flint.*

OCTOBER 6

He saw them toiling in rowing (Mark 6:48).

O tempest-tossed soul! Thou too art toiling with the rowing. The sky has gathered blackness! The night is dark, the winds howl and rage around thy frail bark; the sea rises and lashes thy groaning, shivering vessel until every timber quivers, and every joint starts. The laughter of devils seems to mingle with the shriek of the storm.

And thou dost think that thou art alone, fighting alone, struggling alone, and that thy ship *must* go down.

Oh, no, the ship won't go down! Jesus is on the mount of prayer. He sees thee down there in the hollow of the trough of the sea. He sees thee again on the treacherous crest of the wave. He sees thy vain toil and struggle, and forth from Him has come the power of salvation, "saving to the uttermost," and in the gray dawn before the morning breaks, He will come to thee, and thy weary panting heart shall grow reposeful and restful, for He will come into thy shattered bark, and steer it to shore.

THE EYE OF THE STORM

Fear not that the whirlwind shall carry thee hence,
Nor wait for its onslaught in breathless suspense,
Nor shrink from the whips of the terrible hail,
But pass through the edge to the heart of the gale,
For there is a shelter, sunlighted and warm,
And FAITH sees her God through the eye of the storm.

The passionate tempest with rush and wild roar
And threatenings of evil may beat on the shore,
The waves may be mountains, the fields battle plains,
And the earth be immersed in a deluge of rains,
Yet, the soul, stayed on God, may sing bravely its psalm,
For the heart of the storm is the center of clam.

Let hope be not quenched in the blackness of night,
Though the cyclone awhile may have blotted the light,
For behind the great darkness the stars ever shine,
And the light of God's heaven, His love shall make thine,
Let no gloom dim thine eyes, but uplift them on high
To the face of thy God and the blue of His sky.

The storm is thy shelter from danger and sin,
And God Himself takes thee for safety within
The tempest with Him passed into deep calm,
And the roar of the winds is the sound of a psalm,
Be glad and serene when the tempest clouds form;
God smiles on His child in the eye of the storm.

OCTOBER 7 _____

I know, O Lord, that . . . Thou in faithfulness has afflicted me (Psalm 119:75).

Pilgrim of sorrow, recognize your afflictions to be laddersteps to help you in reaching the Gate of the City. It was the beautiful saying of young Prince Otto of Weid, brother to the Queen of

Roumania, who endured with such heroic Christian fortitude: *"More than we can bear is not sent to us; and when we can bear no longer, the end comes, and we are blest in heaven."*

Yes, "more than we can bear is not sent us": Whatever *is* sent, in the way of pain and suffering and bereavement, *is* God's needed discipline—God's best discipline. The gifts and graces of the Christian have been nurtured thereby. To borrow the words of a friend, *"In the garden of sorrow the soul's loveliest passion-flowers reach their ideal perfection."*

The noblest heroes and heroines of the Faith have been braced by "great tribulation." It is often the bruised reeds the Almighty converts into golden arrows for His quiver. Go, then, fellow-pilgrim, through the wilderness leaning on the arm of your Beloved, whispering to Him. "I know that Thy ways are right."

> Child of My love, "lean hard."
> And let Me feel the pressure of thy care.
> I know thy burden, child; I shaped it,
> Poised it in Mine own hand, made no proportion
> In its weight to thine unaided strength;
> For even as I laid it on, I said,
> "I shall be near, and while she leans on Me,
> This burden shall be Mine, not hers:
>
> "So shall I keep My child within the circling arms
> Of Mine own love." Here lay it down, nor fear
> To impose it on a shoulder which upholds
> The govenment of worlds. Yet closer come—
> Thou art not near enough—I would embrace thy care.
> Thou lovest Me? I know it. Doubt not then:
> But, loving Me, lean hard. *Paul Pastnor.*

OCTOBER 8

God is able to make all grace abound toward you (2 Cor. 9:8).

What could we do, in the midst of the thick darkness of trial, but for the sustaining grace of Christ?

Do not misinterpret or misunderstand *the way* in which this promised grace is given. It does not come with a torrent, in rain-floods or water-floods. Submission is evolved gradually. Not all at once, with impetuous rush, is the stranded vessel moved. But as tidal wave after wave comes rolling in, inert mass seems to wake up to the sound of many waters. Gradually the conquest is made; and in due time, with white wings outspread, she is once more buoyant on summer seas.

Thus is it with the tidal wave of God's love in a time of affliction. The agitated, shattered, stranded heart is gradually swayed by an influence above. In this, as in other things, "he that believeth shall not make haste."

Beloved, God, in His infinite wisdom, has seen meet to touch you in your tenderest part. The world is changed to you. You have, indeed, the same old environments. You feel yourself plodding on in the old mechanical way: life and its exacting duties cannot be evaded, but its glory has departed. Yes, true, and yet not true. If your sun has gone down in the darkness of bereavement and death, that is the time for the bright unfoldings of His grace.

But the God of all grace, Who hath called us unto His eternal glory by Christ Jesus, after that ye have suffered awhile, make you perfect, stablish, strengthen, settle you (1 Pet. 5:10).

> Through many dangers, toils and snares,
>   I have already come;
> 'Tis grace that brought me safe thus far,
>   And grace will lead me Home.

OCTOBER 9

Because I live ye shall live also (John 14:19).

Approaching death, Victor Hugo said: "I feel in myself the future life. I am rising, I know, toward the sky. The sunshine is over my head. Heaven lights me with the reflection of unknown worlds.

"You say the soul is nothing but the result of bodily powers; why, then, is my soul the more luminous when my bodily powers begin to fail? Winter is on my head, and eternal spring is in my heart.

"The nearer I approach the end, the plainer I hear around me the immortal symphonies of the worlds which invite me. It is marvelous, yet simple. It is a fairy tale, and it is a history. For half a century I have been writing my thoughts in prose, verse, history, drama, romance, tradition, ode, song—I have tried all. But I feel that I have not said the thousandth part of what is in me. When I go down to the grave I can say, like so many others, 'I have finished my day's work,' but I cannot say, 'I have finished my life.' My day's work will begin the next morning.

"The tomb is not a blind alley; it is a thoroughfare. It closes in the twilight to open with the dawn. I improve every hour because I love this world as my fatherland. My work is only beginning. My work is hardly above its foundation. I would be glad to see it mounting and mounting forever. The thirst for the infinite proves infinity."

O death! dark hour to hopeless unbelief! What art thou to the Christian's assurance? Great hour of answer to life's prayer; great hour that shall break asunder the bond of life's mystery; hour of release from life's burden; hour of reunion with the loved and lost—what mighty hopes hasten to their fulfilment in Thee! What longings, what aspirations—breathed in the still night beneath the silent stars; what dread emotions of curiosity; what deep meditations of joy; what hallowed imaginings of never experienced purity and bliss; what possibilities, shadowing forth unspeakable realities to the soul, all verge to their consummation in thee! O death! the Christian's death! what art thou but the gate of life, the portal of heaven, the threshold of eternity?   *Orville Dewey.*

THE GATE OF LIFE

We say, "Good-bye!" but not for evermore;
The Call but summons to yon farther shore.
    And when we too embark,
    It is not for the dark
Of unknown seas, but for the welcome meeting
With loved ones gone before, who wait our greeting.
Living in Hope and Faith, we fear not death;
    'Tis but the Gate of Life.

What we call life is a journey to death. What we call death is the gateway to life.

OCTOBER 10 _____

And whither I go ye know, and the way ye know (John 14:4).

I am the way (John 14:6).

I s the white tomb of our loved one—who died in our arms, and had to be left behind us there—which rises in the distance like a pale mournfully receding milestone, to tell how many toilsome, uncheered miles we have journeyed on alone—but a pale, spectral illusion? Is the lost friend still here, even as we are here mysteriously, with God? Know of a truth that only the time-shadows have perished, or are perishable; that the real being of whatever *is*, and whatever will be, *is* even now and forever.

Carlyle.

Where are the swallows fled?
    Frozen and dead
Perchance upon some bleak and stormy shore.
    O doubting heart!
    Far over purple seas,
    They wait in sunny ease,
    The balmy southern breeze
To bring them to their northern homes once more.

Why must the flowers die?
    Prisoned they lie
In the cold tomb, heedless of tears or rain.
    O doubting heart!
    They only sleep below
    The soft white ermine snow
    While winter winds shall blow,
To breathe and smile upon you soon again.

Fair hope is dead, and light
    Is quenched in night.
What sound can break the silence of despair?
    O doubting heart!
    The sky is overcast,
    Yet stars shall rise at last,
    Brighter for darkness past,
And angel's silver voices stir the air.   *Adelaide A. Procter.*

OCTOBER 11 ───────────────────────────

At home with the Lord (2 Cor. 5:8—R. V.).

S he is gone! No longer shrinking from the Winter wind, or lifting her calm forehead to the Summer's kiss. No longer gazing with her . . . glorious eyes into a far-off sky. No longer yearning for a holy heart for Heaven. No longer toiling painfully along the path upward and upward, to the Everlasting Rock on which are based the walls of the City of the Most High. No longer here, she is there—gazing, seeing, knowing, loving, as the blessed only see and know and love. Earth has one angel less; and Heaven one more since yesterday.   *Nathaniel Hawthorne.*

> And death itself, to her, was but
>   The wider opening to the door
> That had been opening, more and more,
>   Through all her life, and ne'er was shut—
>
> And never shall be shut. She left
>   The door ajar for you and me;
> And looking after her, we see
>   The glory shining through the cleft.   *John Oxenham.*

SAFE

> From foreign lands they sent the word
> That she is safe from wind and tide,
> And happy on the other side.
> But strange that I who loved her well
> Should weep as if some woe befell—
> Should weep when far from storm and sea
> My friend is safe as safe can be.   *Ruth Sterry.*

OCTOBER 12

The eternal God is thy refuge (Deut. 33:27).

My hiding-place (Psalm 32:7).

A stronghold in the day of trouble (Nah. 1:7).

MY REFUGE—

A refuge from the storm (Isa. 25:4).
A refuge for the oppressed (Psalm 9:9).
A refuge in the day of trouble (Psalm 59:16).

MY HIDING-PLACE—

In the shadow of Thy wings will I rejoice (Psalm 63:7).
Under whose wings thou art come to trust (Ruth 2:12).
I flee unto Thee to hide me (Psalm 143:9).

MY STRONGHOLD—

Thy right hand shall hold me (Psalm 139:10).
Hold Thou me up and I shall be safe (Psalm 119:117).
I said "my foot slippeth"; Thy mercy, O Lord, held me up
(Psalm 94:18).

O God, Thou dost multiply words for my comfort. How often have I desperate need of a refuge, a heart where I am sure of welcome and understanding! How often do I need a hiding-place from life and its puzzles! How often I feel childish, small and frightened, and want a strong hand to take hold of mine! O God, in Thee I find them all!

UNDER HIS WINGS

The wings of God are wide and cast a shadow
    Wider than condor's wings or the albatross;
Their shadow is very dark, as dark as midnight,
    Their shadow is dark as the shadow of the Cross.

Yet under them shalt thou trust. Evil shall go by thee
    Safe in the darkness under thy God's wide wings;
Though thou hear mountains moving and arrows are flying,
    Thou shalt be still as a child whose mother sings.

Far outside in the light are thy joy and sorrow;
    Forget, forget the pleasant things thou hast left,
Out from thy mind anxiety and hunger,
    Hope that was long deferred and love bereft.

Have now no fear of the darkness that enfolds thee,
    God's wings are spread as an eagle's over her nest.
The wings of God are wide and safe for hiding,
    There in the darkness shall thy soul find rest.
                                        Author Unknown.

OCTOBER 13 _____

He healeth the broken in heart, and bindeth up their wounds. He telleth the number of the stars (Psalm 147:3).

O ne woman wrote to another in deep grief: "The shadow of death will not always rest on your home: you will emerge from its obscurity into such light as they who have never sorrowed cannot know. We never know, or begin to know, the great Heart that loves us best, till we throw ourselves upon it in an hour of our despair."

It cannot be but grief and pain will come;
We know not how to strive and never fail;
We know not how to have and not to lose;
There is no way to love and not to fear;
There is no way to love and not to feel
The pangs of parting when seas roll between,
Or when in vain we seek a faithless love,
Or when—less loss—the sky—pits yawn, and friends
Fall out of sight into their blue abyss.
Then the One Lord takes up our weary woes
As He takes up the isles, or steers a star.
So wonderful His laws that He hath ways
He cope with our great pain.

God hath two temples—
The infinite of starry heavens, one
Where shining ranks of servants throng and move
In unimaginable multitudes
At His command: the lovely soul,
The other, where He hath made His mercy-seat.
One Life and Love He is through all the vast,
From star to heart. Swifter than light
Or thought He comes from some great sun convulsed,
To hold a heart that it break not too far.
He weighs it in His hand against a world;
It is as heavy to the Lord as all
His suns if it the more hath need of healing.
Praise! Praise! Thanksgiving! Praise! Amen!   *James Blake*

Be not discouraged. The farther you go the less severe the way.

Jesus has many hidden joys
And comforts for His own.

OCTOBER 14 ───────────────────────

No man having put his hand to the plough and looking back is fit for the kingdom of God (Luke 9:62).

*D*o not shut yourself up with your sorrow. A friend, in the first anguish of bereavement, wrote, saying that he must give up the Christian ministries in which he had delighted; and I replied immediately, urging him not to do so, because there is no solace for heart-pain like ministry. The temptation of great suffering is toward isolation, withdrawal from the life of men, sitting alone, and keeping silence.

Do not yield to it. Break through the icy chains of reserve, if they have already gathered. Arise, anoint your head, and wash your face; go forth to your duty, with willing though chastened steps.

Selfishness, of every kind, in its activities, or its introspection, is a hurtful thing, and shuts out the help and love of God.

Sorrow is apt to be selfish. The soul, occupied with its own griefs, and refusing to be comforted, becomes presently a Dead Sea, full of brine and salt, over which birds do not fly, and beside which no green thing grows. And thus we miss the very lesson that God would teach us.   *F. B. Meyer.*

> Nothing to live for? Soul, that cannot be,
> Though when hearts break, the world seems emptiness;
> But unto thee I bring in thy distress
> A message, born of love and sympathy,
> And it may prove, O soul, the golden key
> To all things beautiful and good, and bless
> Thy life which looks to thee so comfortless!
> This is the word: "Some one hath need of thee."
> *Emma C. Dowd.*

To be needed in other human lives—is there anything greater or more beautiful in this world!   *David Grayson.*

> Keep me from turning back!
> My hand is on the plough, my faltering hand.
> Behold, in front of me is untilled land,
> The wilderness and solitary place,
> The desert with its lonely interspace,
> Keep me from turning back!

OCTOBER 15 ⸺⸺⸺⸺⸺⸺⸺⸺⸺⸺⸺⸺⸺⸺⸺⸺⸺

Because Thou hast been my help, therefore in the shadows of Thy wings will I rejoice (Psalm 63:7).

S hall I bury the past? Oh, no! There are precious memories which make life better.

Oh, how sweet, how painful and sweet, it is to stoop and bend, day after day, with weary care, over the common dust-heap of our past experiences, and humming old tunes to ourselves, and thinking of our lost hopes and buried loves, to pick out the little diamonds of memory and put them into our bosoms!

And we may do this without *living* in the past.

DO YE THINK OF THE DAYS THAT ARE GONE?

Do ye think of the days that are gone, Jeanie,
  As ye sit by your fire at night?
Do ye wish that the morn would bring back the time
  When your heart and your step were so light?
  I think of the days that are gone, Robin,
  And of all that I joyed in then;
But the brightest that ever arose on me
  I have never wished back again!

Do ye think of the hopes that are gone, Jeanie,
  As ye sit by your fire at night?
Do ye gather them up as they faded fast,
  Like buds with an early blight?
  I think of the hopes that are gone, Robin,
  And I mourn not their stay was fleet;
For they fell as the leaves of the red rose fall,
  And were even in falling sweet!

Do ye think of the friends that are gone, Jeanie,
  As ye sit by your fire at night?
Do ye wish they were round you again once more,
  By the hearth that they made so bright?
  I think of the friends that are gone, Robin,
  They are dear to my heart as then;
But the best and the dearest among them all
  I have never wished back again!

OCTOBER 16 _____

When the enemy shall come in like a flood, the Spirit of the Lord shall lift up a standard against him (Isa. 59:19).

Sometimes the flood is in the form of a great *sorrow*, and we are engulfed by it. Billow after billow goes over us, and does tremendous damage. I know that there is a sorrow appointed of the Almighty, but it is never ordained to hurt or destroy. And yet how often this particular flood, rushing into a life, works havoc with spiritual things.

Have we not known many such in our own experiences? "Was not So-and-so at one time a great worker in the Church?" And the answer was, "Yes, but he has never done anything since his child died!" The flood has done its evil work.

But it is in the flood times of sorrow that "The Spirit of the Lord" will engage for us, "lest we be swallowed up with overmuch sorrow." Have I not seen it done a hundred times? Have I not seen sorrow come into a life, and it has been entirely a minister of good and never of evil? The devil has not got hold of it, and used it as a destructive flood. Not one thing has been damaged or destroyed. It has been a minister of irrigation rather than destruction, and in the moist place of tears beautiful ferns have grown, the exquisite graces of compassion and long-suffering and peace.

"The Spirit of the Lord will lift up a standard!" Well, then let Him do it. Let us hand it over to Him. "Undertake Thou for me, O Lord." The life of faith just consists in a quiet, conscious, realizing trust in the all-willing and all-powerful Spirit of God.   *Dr. Jowett.*

This sorrow, which has cut down the root, has come, not as the spoiling of your life, but as a preparation for it. The soul needs sorrow—as a picture needs shadows; music its minor chords; a good harvest, its frosts and storms. *"Faith builds on the ruins of sorrow."*

> We will trust God. The blank interstices
>   Men take for ruins, He will build into
> With pillared marbles rare, or knit across
> With generous arches, till the fane's complete
>   *Elizabeth Barrett Browning.*

THE CAVERNS OF SORROW ARE MINES OF DIAMONDS.

OCTOBER 17 —————————————————————————

As we have borne the image of the earthly, we shall also bear the image of the heavenly (1 Cor. 15:49).

NOT CHANGED, BUT GLORIFIED

Not changed, but glorified! Oh beauteous language
  For those who weep,
Mourning the loss of some dear face departed,
  Fallen asleep,
Hushed into silence, never more to comfort
  The hearts of men,
Gone, like the sunshine of another country,
  Beyond our ken.

Oh dearest dead, we saw thy white soul shining
  Behind the face,
Bright with the beauty of celestial glory
  Of an immortal grace.
What wonder that we stumble, faint and weeping,
  And sick with fears,
Since thou hast left us—all alone with sorrow,
  And blind with tears.

Can it be possible no words shall welcome
  Our coming feet?
How will it look—that face that we have cherished—
  When next we meet?
Will it be changed, so glorified and saintly,
  That we shall know it not?
Will there be nothing that will say, "I love thee,
  And I have not forgot?"

Oh faithless heart, the same loved face transfigured
  Shall meet thee there,
Less sad, less wistful, in immortal beauty,
  Divinely fair,
The mortal veil, washed pure with many weepings,
  Is rent away,
And the great soul that sat within its prison
  Hath found the day.

In the clear morning of that other country,
  In Paradise,
With the same face that we have loved and cherished,
  He shall arise!
Let us be patient, we who mourn, with weeping,
  Some vanished face,
The Lord hath taken, but to add more beauty
  And a diviner grace.

And we shall find once more, beyond earth's sorrows,
 Beyond these skies,
In the fair city of the "sure foundations,"
 Those heavenly eyes,
With the same welcome shining through their sweetness,
 That met us here—
Eyes, from whose beauty God has banished weeping,
 And wiped away the tear.

Think of us, dearest one, while o'er life's waters we seek
 the land,
Missing thy voice, thy touch, and the true helping of
 thy pure hand,
Till, through the storm and tempest, safely anchored just
 on the other side,
We find thy dear face looking through death's shadows,
 not changed, but glorified.   *Selected.*

OCTOBER 18

He hath stripped me (Job 19:9).

A leafless tree—is there anything to compare with it in symmetry and beauty of structure? To the careless observer the outer world in the winter season presents little that is attractive; but to one whose soul is ever open to the influences of nature, the winter landscape is a wonderful teacher. Mark the exquisite architecture of that bare, brown tree, crowning the summit of the wind-swept hilltop! Against the clear, sunset-tinted sky how vividly the delicate outlines are traced, every branch and little twig cut in silhouette sharpness, while the rosy light glorifies the whole.

Does your life seem desolate and bare, O sorrowing one? Do you stand alone, stripped of all that made living a joy and a blessing, on the bleak summit of unutterable grief, where the cold winds of despair beat fiercely upon your unsheltered head? O bear up bravely, bereaved soul! Into your darkened life the blessed Sun of Righteousness is ready to pour His cheering, vivifying rays, irradiating its gloom with a glory indescribable.

Ah! Lord, dear Lord, my life is dry and bare;
 How stript of summer grace, is known to Thee,

294

Shall nights of weariness and days of care
  Be pleasing in Thy sight? Yea, passing fair,
If thus Thy love stream through me, so I be,
  Within Thy gracious light, a naked tree.

OCTOBER 19 ⸻

Jesus said unto her, Thy brother shall rise again (John 11:23).

There is wondrous music in those words as they are spoken in the ears of the sorrowing ones beside the coffin and by the new-made grave. It was a dim teaching in Martha's time, but soon afterward that occurred which made it bright and clear as day. Jesus Himself lay in the grave, and then rose from death, walking forth in the light of radiance of immortal youth.

Christ was the first-fruits of the resurrection; that is, His resurrection was an earnest pledge as well as an example of the coming resurrection of all who believe in Him.

We have a right to lay flowers on the coffins of our Christian dead. They will come forth in the beauty of new life. We open our New Testament and see Jesus, after He had risen, away beyond death. He had not been harmed by dying. No beam of the beauty of his life is quenched. The threads of the earthly life are not severed. He has not forgotten His friends, but takes up again the old companionships and friendships.

So will it be with our beloved ones who sleep in Jesus. They will rise; and they will be the same persons we have known here, only they will be cleansed of their earthliness and their mortality. And they will not have forgotten us. Love never faileth. We shall resume friendship's story on the other side.

"It is sown in corruption; it is raised in incorruption: it is sown in dishonour; it is raised in glory: it is sown in weakness; it is raised in power" (1 Cor. 15:42, 43).

WHY SHOULD WE WEEP?

Why should we weep for those who sleep?
  Our God doth comfort give;
Above the night, in realms of light
  Our dead in Christ still live:
Our God is God not of the dead

Who cease to see and know,
He is the God of saints who live
    Where joys forever flow.

Our dead are blest, from toil they rest,
    Beyond all pain and care;
No tear, no sigh, no wailing cry
    Can touch their spirits there:
In safe retreat, in joy replete,
    They dwell in peace at home;
They always wait, at heaven's gate,
    The hour that we shall come.

Our Lord hath said, "I'll bring your dead
    When I come down the skies";
Then, from the gloom, of dismal tomb,
    Their bodies shall arise:
Up in the air, some place up there
    We'll all be gathered home;
With Christ to dwell, where all is well,
    Where death can never come.   *Dr. R. E. Neighbour.*

Never forget that the "*it*" that was laid to sleep in the dust, is the very "it" that shall be raised again in newness of life.

OCTOBER 20 ————————————————————————

Be thou strong, and very courageous (Joshua 1:7).

Bereavement is common. No family long misses a break in its circle. Let the break be met with courage! Courage and unselfishness are developed by great sorrow or suffering. In times of overwhelming danger and disaster people rise to unusual heroism.

George Kennam tells of the remarkable exhibition of courage and generous characteristics shown by the people of San Francisco during the great fire and earthquake. The behaviour of the population after the disaster impressed those who witnessed it. One thoughtful and undemonstrative man said he was glad he had lived to see the things that happened the first ten days after the catastrophe.

Those days were the best and most inspiring, he said, of all his life. Religious people talked about the things of God and heaven.

"Cowardice, selfishness, greed, and all the baser emotions and impulses of human character practically disappeared in the tremendous strain of that experience, and courage, fortitude, sympathy, and unbounded self-sacrifice took their place."

A like display of the finer and nobler qualities of human nature was witnessed that terrible night on the sea when the Titanic went down. The majority of the passengers and crew behaved with the most remarkable courage, and the most noble unselfishness.

Let God—*through your bereavement*—bring out the finer and nobler qualities *in you.*   *Selected.*

COURAGE

We met by chance—I do not know his name,
Whither he went his way or whence he came again.
He said no word but "Courage": then again
"Courage," he said, and gripped me by the hands.
A moment—he was vanished in the throng
That hurried homeward in the drizzling rain.
I wonder if he knows and understands
How suddenly the world was full of song;
Laughter and hope had burst their prison bars,
And life had lost its loneliness and pain.
My fears were underfoot. I saw the stars
The blinding mists had hid this many a day,
And clear before me gleamed a great highway,
Where yesterday I sought a path in vain.

E. Williams David.

OCTOBER 21

The land whereon thou liest, to thee will I give it (Gen. 28:13).

These words were spoken to the prostrate Jacob on his stone pillow at Bethel, and the promise is the strangest ever conceived. It says, "There is a time coming in which your glory shall consist in the very thing which now constitutes your pain." Nothing could be more sad to Jacob than the ground on which he was lying. It was the season of his night. It was the seeming absence of his God. His deepest thought at the time was that God had forgotten him. And yet the dream declares that this rejected moment is to be the scene of his glory—"The land whereon thou liest will I give thee, the place of thy prostration will be thy paradise."

There is no promise in the world so sweet to the distressed soul as this. The promise of deliverance is dear, but it is not the dearest. It is not mere Easter morning; it is the Easter of Calvary. The day of my trial has been the dawn of my triumph.

My soul, reject not the place of thy prostration! It has ever been the robing-room for royalty. Ask the great ones of the past what has been the spot of their prosperity; they will say, "It was the cold ground on which I was lying." Ask Abraham; he will point you to the sacrifice on Moriah. Ask Joseph; he will direct you to his dungeon. Ask David; he will tell you that his songs came from the night. Ask Job; he will remind you that God answered him out of the whirlwind. Ask John; he will give the palm to Patmos. Ask Paul; he will attribute his inspiration to the light which struck him blind. Ask one more—the Son of Man. Ask Him whence has come His rule over the world. He will answer, "From the cold ground on which I was lying—the Gethsemane ground; I received My sceptre there."

Thou, too, my soul, shalt be garlanded by Gethsemane. The cup thou fain wouldst pass from thee will be thy coronets in the sweet by-and-by. The hour of thy loneliness will crown thee. The day of thy depression will regale thee. It is thy *desert* that will break into singing; it is the trees of thy *silent forest* that will clap their hands. The last things will be first in the sweet by-and-by. The thorns will be roses; the vales will be hills; the crooks will be straight lines; the ruts will be level; the mist will be heat; the shadows will be shining; the losses will be promotions; the tears will be tracks of gold. The voice of God to thine evening will be this, "Thy treasure is hid in the ground where thou are lying."

George Matheson.

OCTOBER 22 _____

O thou afflicted, tossed with tempest, and not comforted, behold, I will lay thy stones with fair colors, and lay thy foundations with sapphires (Isa. 54:11).

From His standpoint of vision on the hilltops of Glory, He sees the tossing of thy craft. Every billow, every lurch, every rebuff, is discerned and felt by Him. He, too has sailed through stormy seas, acquainted with grief. Not comforted by man, thou shalt be consoled by the divine Comforter.

When the man born blind was cast out of the synagogue, Jesus found him; and He will find thee. Deep down in the tossing waves, He will lay thy foundations in fair colors, and will spare no stones, however precious, in the elaboration of thy character. Sapphires, rubies, and carbuncles are very resplendent and beautiful; but they are all the children of fire. These jewels are produced of very ordinary ingredients, which have been subjected to tremendous pressure and terrific heat.

When next your heart misgives you amid fiery trials, remember that God is at work making the rubies and carbuncles of your eternal array. You will be well compensated.

Daily Devotional Commentary.

> The road of life is rough
> But then, there is the glory of the sky.

OCTOBER 23 ─────────────────────────

I called him alone, and blessed him and increased him (Isa 51:2).

No great book, or statue, or painting was ever conceived, no great decision ever made, no great plan ever perfected, save in the depths of what we call human loneliness, with all bonds for the time severed. God seems to have need of all there is of us when He has a thing of any considerable proportions to be done; and sometimes He must cut away everything else in what may seem like a cruelty to get us at it.

Let us, then welcome loneliness; let us use it as a sanctuary. If we get from it only the understanding that all the world is lonely at time, we have come that much closer to the human heart, and that is well; but it may bring us peace in our lives, it may bring us easement, it may bring light; and always, if we will but let it, it will be as a dip in the cool, deep places of the spirit.

We are but migrants—here for a little—soon to be gone. We came alone. We go alone. Can we not bide with God alone for a little while?   *Anne Monroe Morrow, "Singing in the Rain."*

THE LONELY WAY

I'll hide my heart where the white stars burn
    And the clean winds sweep the sky,
That none may seek it out or learn
    Of the dreams that whisper by.

For the great souls choose the lonely way,
    Though tears are dew mist there,
And the fierce white light of the searching day
    Lays the scars of the seared heart bare.

Oh, lone and stark the white way streams
    Like the lash of a scourging rod;
But the stars are there, and those whispering dreams—
    Aye, and the heart of God.   *Selected.*

Not only love but also loneliness:
Yea, ever so.
What though thy dearest may not ever know
All that in this must be,
That being a secret between Thee and me,
Thou knowest; and it cannot work me ill
Being Thy will;
And by and by
Thou'lt satisfy.

But unknown years stand up and stare at me,
The sun beats hot;
I look around for shelter, find it not:
Companion me,
Be shelter, Lord to me!
O let Thy shadow be
As the cool star-lit night in noonday, unto me!

OCTOBER 24

Even so, Father; for so it seemed good in Thy sight (Luke 10:21).

Purge your heart of charges of unfairness against God. Stop
thinking "Because my dearest one was so brave and good it
was not fair that he should suffer so!"

To a degree beyond our analysis the qualities he manifested
were the outcome of his courageous endurance of his heavy
burden. "Why" this is so, man does not know, but it is obvious

that man does not develop such a personality when the strain of suffering is absent.

The hard days are behind him now, and he has entered into his joyous reward. Only God can measure the service he has rendered, but He would not have permitted it apart from some mighty purpose of eternal significance. *Selected.*

> What was the answer of God's love
> Of old, when in the olive-grove
> In anguish-sweat His own Son lay,
> And prayed "O God, take this cup away?"
> Did God take from Him then the cup?
> No, child, His Son must drink it up. *Ibsen, Brand.*

There is not one drop of wrath in the cup you are drinking. He took all that was bitter out of it, and left it *a cup of love.*

OCTOBER 25

Now abideth faith, hope, love, these three; but the greatest of these is love (1 Cor. 13:13).

L ove never dies. Our partial *knowledge* dies amid the revelations of perfect vision. *Faith* will be needed no more where we know as we are know. *Hope* fades in fruition. But *Love* abides forever. It never fails. Death may cut off the interchange of words and acts of love, but its cold hand cannot touch that which is Divine in origin, eternal in nature, and everlasting in duration.

That is what we pine to know. It is not the distance that makes our souls faint and fear; we could bear that; but the feeling that perhaps we have lost forever the love which was the light of our existence, the fire at which we were wont to warm ourselves.

Let us know that this is preserved to us still; that they love us still who have left us; that their thoughts still enfold us in tender embracements, and follow us in our wanderings, and hover over us like ministering angels—then we can afford to be without their presence; nay, we gladly resign them, because they are happier where they are than we could ever have made them.

Oh, press this thought to your innermost soul—that those whom you have "loved long since and lost awhile," love you still, care for you still, with a warmth of affection which kindles into an intenser brilliance, as they come nearer to the heart of the Eternal Father, the Source and Sun of Love. And in this love they wait for us. They cannot attain their full consummation and bliss until we, too, emerge from the shadows of death into the perfect light of eternity. So only shall love be satisfied.   *Selected.*

O Death, thou angel of God, thou dost seem to rob us of our treasures, but thou dost really make them ours forever in the dew of immortal youth; transfiguring them with a light that can never fade from their faces or our lives; blotting out only what we are glad to forget; preserving what we loved in imperishable beauty.
                                                        Selected.

OUR OWN FOREVER

Our own are our own forever, God taketh not back
      His gift:
They may pass beyond our vision, but our souls shall find
      them out,
When the waiting is all accomplished, and the deathly
      shadows lift,
And glory is given for grieving, and the surety of God
      for doubt.

We may find the waiting bitter and count the silence long;
God knoweth we are dust, and He pitieth our pain;
And when faith hath grown to fullness and the silence
      changed song,
We shall eat the fruit of patience and shall hunger not
      again.

So, sorrowing hearts, who wait in the darkness and all
      alone,
Missing a dear lost presence and the joy of a vanished
      day,
Be comforted with this message, that our own are forever
      our own,
And God, who gave the precious gift, He takes it never
      away.   *Susan Coolidge.*

OCTOBER 26 ————————————————————————

As dying and behold we live (2 Cor. 6:9).

I had a bed of asters last summer, that reached clear across my garden in the country. Oh, how gaily they bloomed. They were planted late. On the sides were yet fresh blossoming flowers, while the tops had gone to seed. Early frosts came, and I found one day that that long line of radiant beauty was seared, and I said, "Ah! the season is too much for them; they have perished;" and I bade them farewell.

I disliked to go and look at the bed, it looked so like a graveyard of flowers. But, four or five weeks ago one of my men called my attention to the fact that along the whole line of that bed there were asters coming up in the greatest abundance; and I looked, and behold, for every plant that I thought the winter had destroyed there were fifty plants that it had planted. What did those frosts and surly winds do?

They caught my flowers, they slew them, they cast them to the ground, they trod with snowy feet upon them, and they said, leaving their work, " *This is the end of you.* " And the next spring there were for every root, fifty witnesses to rise up and say, " *By death we live.* "

And as it is in the floral tribe, so it is in God's kingdom. By death came everlasting life. By crucifixion and the sepulchre came the throne and the palace of the eternal God. By overthrow came victory.

Do not be afraid to suffer. Do not be afraid to be overthrown.

It is by being cast down and not destroyed; it is by being shaken to pieces, and the pieces torn to shreds, that men become men of might, and that one a host; whereas men that yield to the appearance of things, and go with the world, have their quick blossoming, their momentary prosperity and then their end, which is an end forever. *H. W. Beecher.*

> Die to thy root, sweet flowers!
> If God so wills, die, even to thy root.
> Live there awhile, an uncomplaining, mute,
> Blank life, with darkness wrapt about thy head.
> And fear not for the silence round thee spread,
> This is no grave, though thou among the dead
> Art counted—but the Hiding-place of Power.
> Die to thy root, sweet flower.
>
> Spring from thy root, sweet flower!
> When so God wills, spring even from thy root.

Send through the earth's warm breast a quickened shoot
And lift into the sunny air thy dower
Of bloom and odor; life is on the plains,
And in the winds a sound of birds and rains
That sing together; lo! the winter cold
Is past; sweet scents revive, thick buds unfold;
Be thou, too, willing in the day of Power.
    Spring from thy root, sweet flower.   *Dora Greenwell.*

OCTOBER 27

Why art thou cast down, O my soul? Hope thou in God: for I shall yet praise Him (Psalm 42:5).

He cannot rightly carry out any true or noble object in life in a spirit of despondency. A depressed life—a life which has ceased to believe in its own sacredness, its own mission—a life which contentedly sinks into querulous egotism or vegetating aimlessness—has become, so far as the world is concerned, a maimed and useless life.

All our lives are in some sense a "might have been"; the very best of us must feel, I suppose, in sad and thoughtful moments, that he might have been transcendently nobler, and greater, and loftier than he is; but while life lasts every "might have been" should lead, not to vain regrets, but to manly resolutions; it should be but the dark background to a "may be" and "will be yet."
    Canon Farrar.

I entreat you, give no place to despondency. This is a dangerous temptation—a refined, not a gross temptation of the adversary. Melancholy contracts and withers the heart, and renders it unfit to receive the impressions of grace. It magnifies and gives a false coloring to objects, and thus renders your burdens too heavy to bear. God's designs regarding you, and His methods of bringing about these designs, are infinitely wise.   *Madame Guyon.*

There are noble and beautiful souls who have walked much in gloom—Thomas called Didymus, William Cowper, Ameil of Geneva, Gilmour of Mongolia: often their life seemed to them "but as an arrow flying in the dark." But, because I have such a

God, and because He is my own, let me put sadness away and array myself in joy.

> Dark! Well what of that?
> Didst fondly dream the sun would never set?
> Dost fear to lose thy way? take courage yet!
> Learn thou to walk by faith and not by sight
> Thy steps will guided be, and guided right.
>
> Lonely! And what of that?
> Some must be lonely. 'tis not given to all
> To feel a heart responsive rise and fall,
> To blend another life into his own;
> Work may be done in loneliness; work on!
>
> No help! Nay, it's not so!
> Though human help be far, thy God is nigh;
> Who feeds the ravens, hears His children's cry;
> He's near thee, whereso'er the footsteps roam,
> And He will guide thee, light thee, help thee home.

I love better to count time from spring to spring; it seems to me far more cheerful to recken the year by blossoms than by blight.

Chas. E. Cowman.

OCTOBER 28

Her sun is gone while it was yet day (Jer. 15:9).

Taken away from the evil to come (Isa. 57:1).

There are few trials among the varied phases of affliction more mysterious and overwhelming than that of *early death*. We can understand the autumn foliage—leaves golden with age dropping to the ground. They have been nurtured in spring, fanned by its balmy zephyrs; they had been matured by summer's suns. And now that the waning year asserts it right, they have only fulfilled their appointed destiny, and fall as they are touched by the poet's "fiery finger."

But what of the tender sapling that has hardly taken on the verdant mantle of the opening season, when it is snapped in twain by the tempest, its leaves strewing the sward or swept down the brook? All the stranger when other trees, its compeers, are spared, bursting in resurrection foliage, or made perches for a chorus of summer song? It is the sweep of the scythe amid the early dews of life.

We can understand the pathetic twilight followed by the sun sinking in bars of gold in the western sky, but what of eclipse before reaching the meridian? If the Earth-bower of our earthly happiness has thus been stripped "ere the sun has risen," can we, dare we, look for any possible dewdrops of comfort lingering on the prostrate leaves?

Yes, in the midst of these blighted hopes, shattered wrecks, vanished suns, life's fondest ideals unfulfilled, there are, O suffering one! when the healing hand of time will permit you calmly to ponder the dealings of God, gracious *mitigations* at all events in your trial, if you fail to accord to them the more pronounced epithet of consolations. Your future may truly be spoken of as "night"—night in the desert, night with its dearest star, its "morning-star," expunged from the sky. But HE who has alike brought you into the night and the wilderness has some gracious gleams from His pillar-cloud.

Your loved one is *"taken away from the evil to come." You* are unable to anticipate the future. *You* have eyes only to see a life of rare promise terminated, and a future of noble fulfilment shrouded in death. *You* have eyes only to see the skiff gliding amid gentle ripples, sure at last to sleep quietly in the distant lake; all its course a "melody of Song."

God, the Omniscient One, the Loving One, knows otherwise. He foresees the jagged rocks and foaming eddies and rush of cataracts that would have beset the long voyage: or leaving out figures—the trials of sorrows, the buffeting temptations—it may be even the sad sins, that would make shipwreck of a loving life. He ordains in infinite wisdom that it is better to elude the suffering and peril by giving an early summons to an early crown. He takes the lamb, before the fleece is stained—away from the possibilities of evil.

The young warrior falls, *we* may think prematurely in the fray— the laurel not having time even to be green on his brows; but the All-Wise knew of hazard and peril and environing evils hidden from our sight. He deemed it better, kinder, to give, all at once, "Peace beyond the strife," to add all at once a name to the better roll-call; to usher all at once ere the heart could grieve, or the eye be dimmed, or the will falter, or the tempter triumph, amid the unceasing ministries of the glorified. Oh for faith in such an hour to day, "He hath done all things well!" satified that our prayers are best answered and our longings best fulfilled, not in our way but His. He willed it.

Bereaved one! Do not dwell on the mysterious muffling of the morning bells. In your *better* moments you will only be glad at the thought of your dear one being taken away from the hurricane and storm. *"From the evil to come."*

OCTOBER 29 _____

And the peace of God, which transcends all our powers of thought, will be a garrison to guard your hearts and minds in Christ Jesus (Phil. 4:7—Weymouth).

When you look at the Believer's busy life, you may see no trace of his inward peace of soul. But you know that the ocean under the hurricane is lashed into those huge waves and that wild foam only upon the surface. Not very far down, the waters are as still as an autumn noon; there is not a ripple or breath or motion, and so, my friends, if we had the faith we ought, though there might be ruffles upon the surface of our lot, we should have the inward peace of perfect faith in God.

Amid the dreary noises of this world, amid its cares and tears, amid its sorrows, heart-breaks and disappointments, we should have an inner calm like the ocean depths, to which the influence of the wild winds and waves above can never come.

PEACE

Winds and wild waves in headlong huge commotion
    Scud, dark with tempest, o'er the Atlantic's breast;
While undernearth, few fathoms deep in Ocean,
    Lie peace and rest.

Storms in mid-air, the rack before them sweeping,
    Hurry and hiss, like furies hate-possessed;
While over all white cloudlets pure are sleeping
    In peace, in rest.

Heart, O wild heart! why in the storm-world ranging
    Flitt'st thou thus midway, passion's slave and jest,
When all so near above, below, unchanging
    Are Heaven and rest?   *A. G. B.: London Spectator.*

Surely goodness and mercy shall follow me all the days of my life and I will dwell in the house of the Lord forever (Psalm 23:6).

There is always To-morrow, with its promise of better things. Let us think of Death as but one more To-morrow, filled with infinite promise and fulfilment.

FARTHER ON

As up life's mountain side I stray,
Thinking how wearisome the way,
I hear a sweet voice softly say,
   "'Tis better farther on."

What! though the way be rough and dreary,
What though thy footsteps be aweary,
Look up, faint heart! and be more cheery,
   'Tis better farther on.

Though thickest mist thy path doth veil,
And storms and thunder-clouds prevail,
No heart that trusts in God should quail,
   'Tis better farther on.

When up the last steep hill we go,
And see the valley all below,
'Tis then we fell and see and know
   'Tis better farther on.

Behind are all the mists and tears,
Behind are all the cares and fears,
And Heaven's pearly gate appears,
   A little farther on.

Dear tired heart, look up and see the dawn—'tis God's tomorrow!

Woman why weepest thou? (John 20:13).

TRY PRAISING

There is no use in yielding to *sadness;* for it leaves the soul very much like an instrument out of tune; and *Satan,* unlike all other *musicians,* has a great fancy for playing on an untuned instrument. *Gladness!* I like to cultivate the spirit of gladness! It puts the soul in tune again, and keeps it in tune, so that Satan is shy of touching it!—The chords of the soul become too warm, or too full of electricity, for his infernal fingers, and he goes off somewhere else. Satan is always very shy of meddling with me when my heart is full of gladness and joy in the Holy Ghost. Sadness discolors everything; it leaves all objects *charmless;* it involves future prospects in darkness; it deprives the soul of all its aspirations, enchains all its powers, and produces mental paralysis. Melancholy clips our wings, takes off our chariot wheels, and makes them, like those of the Egyptians, to drag heavily. Let us shun the spirit of sadness as we would shun Satan.

Why should we weep when 'tis so well with him?

'Twas but a step from out our muddy street
Of earth, on to the pavement all of pearl!
Why should we weep?   *Gerald Massey.*

GOD'S SKY IS OVER US YET!

A mother, after a sore bereavement, which changed all her life, was grieving at having to leave the old home where everything had grown sacred. Tears filled her eyes as she took the last look at the familiar scene—home, grounds, trees and hill. Her little boy tried to comfort her and as he looked out of the window of the car, he said, *"Why, mother, God's sky is over us yet! It's going right along with us!"*

We can never get beyond the blue of heaven. We can never get out from under the shadow of the Almighty. Wherever we may have to go we shall always have the love of God over us.

BE STILL MY HEART

I will commit my way, O Lord, to Thee,
Nor doubt Thy love, though dark the way may be,
Nor murmur, for the sorrow is from God,
And there is comfort also in Thy rod.

I will not seek to know the future years,
Nor cloud today with dark tomorrow's fears;
I will but ask a light from heaven, to show
How, step by step, my pilgrimage should go.

And if the distant perils seem to make
The path impossible that I must take,
Yet as the river winds through mountains lone,
The way will open up—as I go on.

Be still, my heart; for faithful is thy Lord,
And pure and true and tried His Holy Word;
Through stormy flood that rageth as the sea,
His promises thy stepping-stones shall be.

NOVEMBER 1

They looked . . . and behold, the glory of the Lord appeared in the cloud (Ex. 16:10).

The bereavement which looks into the grave is leaden; the bereavement which dares to look toward the stars with hope is golden. If the heart says, "Finis," it is wounded beyond all surgery. If it says, "to be continued," it is like a Toledo blade which bends but cannot snap. *Selected.*

There is a picture of a woman seated on the low rocks, looking out upon a wild sea down into which the treasures of her heart have gone. Her face is stony with hopeless, despairing grief. Almost touching the black robe of the mourner, hovering over her shoulder, is the shadowy form of an angel softly touching the strings of a harp. But she is unaware of the angel's nearness, nor does she hear a note of the celestial music. She bows in dumb unconsciousness, with breaking heart and unsoothed sorrow, while the heavenly consolation is so close.

Thus many of God's dear children sit in darkness, crushed by their sorrows, yearning for comfort and for an assurance of the divine love and sympathy, hearing no soft beautiful music, no whisper of consolation, while close beside them the Master Himself stands unperceived, and heaven's sweetest songs float unheard in the very air they breathe. It is a simpler faith we need to take the consolation our Father sends when our hearts are breaking.

NOVEMBER 2

In the wilderness shall waters break out, and streams in the desert (Isa. 35:6).

Our sorrows often appear to us as a desert. We pass into experiences that are dark and cold and lonely, and over which there blows a bitter wind. Surely sorrow is a Black Country to untold multitudes of souls! "Can God furnish a table in the wilderness?" Can He feed us in the season of sorrow? Let us remember it was in the desert that the miracle of the loaves was wrought; and in the desert of our sorrow a harvest miracle may be wrought today. At His Word our desert can abound with lilies and violets and forget-me-nots. "He will also feed thee with the finest of the wheat." Your sorrow shall be turned into joy. Oh, thou troubled soul, turn to the great Wonder Worker, and thy desert shall blossom as the rose!

From the desert of loneliness and despair came Hagar's, "Thou God, seest me!"

From a heart tested and tried came Job's, "I know that my Redeemer liveth."

From a broken and contrite heart was David's, "Wash me and I shall be whiter than snow." Out of lonely Gethsemane came perfect submission, "Thy will be done." Through the gates of deepest sorrow, great souls found their way to a more splendid life. At the foot of the cross, the crown was found. The tomb is the gate of the resurrection. Death is the door to life.

NOVEMBER 3

In full assurance of faith (Heb. 10:22).

NATURE AND FAITH

We wept—'twas NATURE wept, but Faith
Can pierce beyond the gloom of death,
And, in yon world so fair and bright,
Behold thee in refulgent light!

We miss thee here, yet FAITH would rather
Know thou art with thy heavenly Father.

NATURE sees the body dead—
FAITH beholds the spirit fled;
NATURE stops at Jordan's tide—
FAITH beholds the other side;
THAT but hears farewell and sighs,
THIS, thy welcome in the skies;

NATURE mourns a cruel blow—
FAITH assures it is not so;
NATURE never sees thee more—
FAITH but sees thee gone before;
NATURE tells a dismal story—
FAITH has visions full of glory;
NATURE views the change with sadness—
FAITH contemplates it with gladness;
NATURE murmurs—FAITH gives meekness.
"Strength is perfected in weakness";
NATURE writhes, and hates the rod—
FAITH looks up and blesses God;
SENSE looks downwards—FAITH above;
THAT—sees harshness—THIS sees love.
Oh! let FAITH victorious be—
Let it reign triumphantly!

But thou art gone! not lost, but flown,
Shall I then ask thee back, my own?
Back—and leave thy spirit's brightness?
Back—and leave thy robes of whiteness?
Back—and leave thine angel mould?
Back—and leave those streets of gold?
Back—and leave the Lamb who feeds thee?
Back—from founts to which He leads thee?
Back—and leave thy Heavenly Father?
Back—to earth and sin?—Nay, rather
Would I live in solitude!
I would not ask thee if I could;
But patient wait the high decree,
That calls my spirit Home to thee!   *Selected.*

NOVEMBER 4 _____

I am the Lord, I change not (Mal. 3:6).

With Whom is no variableness, neither shadow of turning (James 1:17).

TODAY AND TOMORROW

Today's wealth may be tomorrow's poverty, today's health, tomorrow's sickness, today's happy companionship of love, tomorrow's aching solitude of heart; *but today's God will be tomorrow's God, today's Christ will be tomorrow's Christ.*

Other fountains may dry up in heat or freeze in winter, but this knows no change, "in summer and winter it shall be." Other fountains may sink low in their basins after much drawing, but this is ever full; and, after a thousand generations have drawn from its stream, is broad and full as ever.

We can be sure of this, that God will ever be with us in all the days that lie before us. What may be round the next headland we know not; but this we know, that the same sunshine will make a broadening path across the waters right to where we rock on the unknown sea, and the same unmoving mighty star will burn for our guidance.

So we may let the waves and currents roll as they list—or rather as He will, and be little concerned about the incidents or the companions of our voyage, since He is with us.

Alexander Maclaren.

> God will not change; the restless years may bring
> Sunlight and shade—the glories of the Spring,
> And silent gloom of sunless winter hours,
> Joy mixed with grief—sharp thorns with fragrant flowers;
> Earth-lights may shine a while, and then grow dim,
> But God is true; there is no change in Him.

NOVEMBER 5

Stormy wind fulfilling His word (Psalm 148:8).

Stormy winds come not without mercy and blessing. There is music in the blast if we listen aright. Is there no music *in the heart of sorrow* that the Lord of all has chosen for His own? Are you not nearer to the Master, have you not grown in faith, in patience, in prayerfulness, in thankful hope, since the time the storm winds first sighed across your life?

It is no small matter to grow nearer to God; it is worth all the tempest your soul has known. The heart of the Lord was yearning over you, and could not be satisfied till His winds had driven your soul entirely into the refuge and protection of His love.

Do not tremble because of the winds of the future; your Lord will be living and loving tomorrow, even as He lives and loves today; and no storm waits in your path but shall leave behind another record that your Heavenly Father is stronger than the tempest, nearer than the grief.

We are traveling home to that beauteous shore where the chill winds never sweep, the hurricane makes no moan; yet, amid the rest of the painless Homeland, shall we not love the Lord a thousandfold more for every storm of earth in which He drew near to us, saying, "Fear not," and held us by the hand, and tenderly bore us through the hour that seemed the darkest? We shall glorify Him then that He has been to us, again and again, a covert from the blast; but let us not *wait* to glorify Him till the blast is over. Even now let us give thanks that all the winds of life—the rough ones as well as those that blow from the south—are of His appointing. Whose every purpose is for our eternal gain.

Set your thoughts, not on the storm, but on the Love that rules the storm; then the winds of trouble shall no longer seem as sad and restless voices, but as an AEolian harp attuned to peace, to hope, to everlasting victory.   *In Rainbow Weather.*

And I know not any trouble; for I have the tempest's King
To change my winter's fury to the gladness of His spring.

Blessed is the man who, when the tempest has spent its fury, recognizes his Father's voice in the undertone.

NOVEMBER 6 ——————————————————

But the gift of God is eternal life through Jesus Christ our Lord (Rom. 6:23).

The life of a loved one does not end. It simply goes on. Its work is done here only to take up its work in the other room. We are not summer birds that live but a brief day. Even Nature teaches us this: the rotation of the trees in the woods; the succession of the seasons; the leaf that falls in the autumn lives again in the new leaf of the spring. There is no end. It becomes easier to believe this when the other shore begins to be peopled by our loved ones. We can never feel for others until we have felt ourselves; we know not how to extend sympathy until it has been meted out to us. Life looks different after the light of a life dear to us has gone on. But *on, not out, it has gone;* and surely, if sometimes slowly, the truth comes home to us and enters our lives.

The physical presence may leave us, but the spiritual takes its place, strengthening, reviving, heartening, and uplifting. Those who leave us are never far off: they are real and near to us. And ofttimes when the heart is saddest, the load heaviest, and the trial greatest, it is they who stretch out their hands to us and give us fresh courage, so strong and buoyant that we wonder whence it came. It is only that with our eyes we can see not, and with our ears we can hear not. One only needs to lose a loved one to know this truth; to learn it so deeply and truly that no "-ism" or cult or creed can shake the belief. It is then that clarity of vision comes; when the eye sees clearly, and the mind and heart and soul unite in but one final truth—that we go on.

The western gates close only to let the eastern gates open.

CONSOLATION

Not Dead—oh no, but borne beyond the shadows
   Into the full clear light;
For ever done with mist and cloud and tempest
   Where all is calm and bright.

Not even sleeping—called to glad awakening
   In Heaven's cloudless day:
Not still and moveless—stepped from earth's rough places
   To walk the King's highway.

Not silent—just passed out of earthly hearing
   To sing Heaven's sweet new song;
Not lonely—dearly loved and dearly loving
   Amid the white-robed throng.

But not forgetful—keeping fond remembrance
   Of dear ones left awhile;
And looking gladly to the bright reunion
   With hand-clasp and with smile.

Oh no, not dead, but past all fear of dying,
   And with all suffering o'er;

Say not that I am dead when JESUS calls me
   To live for evermore.   *Anon.*

NOVEMBER 7 _____

*Therefore are they before the throne of God, and serve Him day and night
in his temple (Rev. 7:15).*

We do not know what are the occupations of heaven; but this
we know—those who have gone there are "satisfied"; for
we cannot conceive of those who were so busy here about their
Master's work being satisifed in idleness. Hence we believe that
there, as here, He finds work for them to do—work congenial,
satisfying—and, freed from the limitation of the earthly body, they
can pursue it joyously, "without weariness and without rest."

Do you think God will take the tools out of the workman's
hands just when he has learned to use them properly, or that He
will discharge His servants just when they are best able to serve
Him?

> So short the time—so much to leave undone,
>   Frets my impatient heart.
> Hush, for with God is time. Though I've begun,
>   To end is not my part.
>
> Perfect, or broken, is not mine to say;
>   I can but do my best
> Until the Master bids: "Leave work today
>   For new work and for rest."
>
> Test He will give, and labour He will give
>   In that day as in this;
> For life is both, and on through death we love
>   And love, and nothing miss.

NOVEMBER 8 _____

Leaning upon (the arm) of her beloved (Song of Sol. 8:5).

Bereaved mourner! Perhaps He who has taken your dear one
from the loves and affections of earth, wishes the more, and
the better, to raise your love to Himself. He points you to your

withered and blighted flower, and tests you with the challenge—
"Lovest thou ME *more* than these?" Seek, as one of the results of
your trial, to make Him increasingly the focus of your being—the
Centre in the circumference of your present sorrow. Earthly
"presences" are gone. But thus would the unchanging God speak
to you saying "My presence shall go with thee and I will give thee
rest." He would take you now, as Christ did His disciples, from the
Valley of trial up to the Mount of get these glimpses and pledges of
reunion—assurances that when those, like Moses and Elias on the
heights of Hermon, have departed, you are left with better than
the best of earthly friends: "They saw no man save *Jesus only!*"

> Gently loosens He thy hold
> Of the treasured FORMER things—
> Loves and joys that were of old,
> Shapes to which the spirit clings,
> And alone, above He stands,
> Stretching forth beseeching Hands.   *Teerstegan.*

NOVEMBER 9

He hath prepared for them a city (Heb. 11:16).

Go on, dear brethren. Many of you are nearer Home than you
think. A step more, and you shall rest. Many of you, though
far away yet, are under a safe convoy. Press forward: let nothing
discourage you. You are far from the host that waits for you. It
cannot be long before your sorrows shall end, and your eternal
joys begin. Then, be patient. Trust God, follow Him. Is the storm
fierce? Yet it is almost past, and the time of the singing of birds is at
hand. Look up, look away, a little! Forget the things which sound
in your ears from day to day, and bring yourself into that glorious
atmosphere in which you shall *see* that which is not to be seen by
the natural eye, that which is beyond reach, that you may have a
foretaste of that rest which remaineth for the people of God. The
glorious future is almost yours.

HOMEWARD

> The day dies slowly in the western sky;
>   The sunset splendor fades, and wan and cold
> The far peaks wait the sunrise; cheerily

The goatherd calls his wanderers to their fold.
My weary soul, that fain would cease to roam,
    Take comfort: evening bringeth all things home.

Homeward, the swift-winged sea-gun takes its flight;
    The ebbing tide breaks softly on the sand;
The sunlit boats draw shoreward for the night;
    The shadows deepen over sea and land;
Be still, my soul, thine hour shall also come:
    Behold, one evening God shall lead thee Home.

NOVEMBER 10

The memory of the just is blessed (Proverbs 10:7).

At the time of the first snow-fall, I heard a pear-tree in my garden sighing to itself as it shuddered in the November wind, and saying, "To what end is summer, if it must go away so soon? Why have I basked in the blessed sunshine, and drunk the evening dews, if now I am to be left by them both to the bitterness of this wintry desolation?" And it writhed and moaned in the agony of the storm.

An ancient apple-tree near by replied, "You have forgotten that you have helped beautify the garden with the luxuriance of your foliage; that you have sweetened the air with the odor of your blossoms; that you have gladdened the household by the lusciousness of your fruits; that children have played under your shade; and, more than all, that you have grown, and that you still retain the gift of the summer in full six inches of length of bough, by which amount you are nearer the sky, stronger to bear the storm, readier to meet the coming of another spring, and fitter to enter on its new career with advantage."

Then said I, "My dear ones are gone. Yes: but the influence of the summer of their lives is left upon me. My heart is larger and warmer, and more open, because of rejoicing in their light, and resting under their shadow, and I am better fitted for the coming spring of immortality, where the sun shall never go down."

Who would wish back the saints upon our rough
Wearisome road?
Wish back a breathless soul
Just at the goal?

318

My soul, praise God
For all dear souls which have enough.   *Christina Rosetti.*

NOVEMBER 11

Take therefore no thought for the morrow (Matt. 6:34).

L eave, says Christ, that morrow with Me. Take no thought, no needless, over-anxious thought about it. That morrow under My hand, will reveal itself. Instead of trying vainly in this "hurricane eclipse" to forecast the dusty, travel stained roads of life—"Commit thy way unto the Lord."

The morrow may doubtless to you, be all perplexity. Like a group of desert travelers of a future age—like the Magi, you may seem suddenly to have lost your guiding star. But, *Jehovah-Jireh (the Lord will provide).*

Seek to rise above these unworthy morbid forebodings. It is the nature of faith—the *triumph* of faith, to overcome difficulties, to feel assured that in due time the gloomiest cloud wil be braided with silver linings.

The disciples at the scene of Transfiguration at first "feared to enter *the cloud."* Ere long when they passed through its enfoldings, the bloom and mystery were dispelled. "They looked unto *Him* and were lightened," for "His face did shine as the Sun." That glimpse of transfigured glory prepared them for the great impending suffering in Gethsemane and Calvary. They were braced under the shadow of the cloud for the fiery trials that were so soon to try them.

Enter on your veiled future in a similar spirit.

> Benighted on a lone and dreary wild,
> Perplexed, exhausted, helpless, in despair,
> I cast me down, and thought to perish there.
> When through the gloom a Face appeared and smiled;
> And a sweet Voice said, "Courage! rise, My child!
> And I will guide thee safely by the way."
>
> As to night-watchers comes the morning ray,
> So came that voice to me; and on that Face
> I seemed a loving tenderness to trace,
> That soothed and cheered me as, forlorn, I lay;
> I felt as feels the child whose throbbing grief

A mother's love assuages in its source;
And asking strength of Him who gave relief,
I straightway rose, and onward held my course.

W. L. Alexander.

NOVEMBER 12

The thick darkness where God was (Ex. 20:21).

God has still His hidden secrets, hidden from the wise and prudent. Do not fear them; be content to accept things that you cannot understand; wait patiently. Presently He will reveal to you the treasures of darkness, the riches of the glory of the mystery. Mystery is only the veil of God's face. Do not be afraid to enter the cloud that is settling down on your life. God is in it. The other side is radiant with His glory.

"Think it not strange concerning the fiery trail which is to try you, as though some strange thing happened unto you; but rejoice, inasmuch as ye are partakers of Christ's sufferings."

When you seem loneliest and most forsaken, God is nigh. He is in the dark cloud. Plunge into the blackness of its darkness without flinching; under the shrouding curtain of His pavilion you will find God awaiting you. *Selected.*

For one thing only, Lord, dear Lord, I plead—
　Lead me aright.
Though strength should falter, and though heart
　　should bleed,
　Through peace to light.
I do not ask my cross to understand,
　My way to see—
Better in darkness just to feel Thy hand,
　And follow Thee.

HEART-HUSHINGS

Oh, ask in faith! Against the ill thou dreadest,
　Comes white-robed Peace, sweet angel of God's will;
Folding her wings beside thee as thou pleadest,
　Whispering as God's own word to thee, "Be still!"

"Be still!" how fearfully soever blended
　Thy day with dark, like twilight's flickering bars;

For God will make thy deepest midnight splendid,
    With all His countless wealth of glittering stars.   *Swan.*

NOVEMBER 13 ———————————————————————

Father, I will that they also, whom Thou hast given Me, be with me where I am: that they may behold My glory (John 17:24).

A ll our dear relations that died in Christ are triumphantly singing hallelujahs in the highest heavens. While we are fighting, sighing, and sobbing here below, they are with blessed Jesus above, according to His prayer for them, seeing His glory and participating in it.   *John Bunyan.*

WAITING YONDER

They are not dead, those loved ones who have passed
    Beyond our vision for a little while,
They have but reached the Light while we still grope
    In darkness where we cannot see them smile.

But smile they do, and love us, and do not
    Forget, nor ever go so far away
But that their hands still clasp our hands and hold
    Us safe from falling when we fain would stray.

They are not dead. Theirs is the fuller life,
    Theirs is the victory, the joy, the gain;
For us is still the waiting and the strife,
    For us the loneliness, for us the pain.

Then let us gird us once again with hope,
    And give them smile for smile the while we wait;
And loving, serving, when Our Father calls,
    We'll go to find our dear ones wait us at the gate.
                                        H. A. C.

And when I see the sunset gates unbar,
    Shall I not see Thee waiting stand?
And white against the evening star,
    The welcome of Thy beckoning hand.

321

If the clouds be full of rain, they empty themselves upon the earth (Eccl. 11:3).

The clouds are black; they lower; they shut out the sunlight; they obscure the landscape. The timid one looks up and says, "Alas, how black they are, and how they gather fold on fold! What a dark, gloomy day!" What makes them black? They are full, and hence light cannot pierce them; and if they be full, what then? Why, then it will rain, and every little plant and every tiny leaf and rootlet of that plant will suck up moisture, and begin to laugh for joy, and the hot earth will be refreshed. Now, Christian, perhaps your circumstances are not as you would like to arrange them. Losses come very closely upon one another. Friend after friend forsakes you. Sickness treads upon the heel of sickness. The Angel of Death enters your home. You are bereaved and desolate. The clouds are very black, and may they not be black for the very same reason as are the clouds above you—because they are full?

Can you not affirm your spiritual experience—certainly I can of my own—that the pelting showers and fiercer storms have been most soul-enriching?

Why are you called to suffer more than others? Perhaps, if you take it rightly, because God has for you some nobler work or some higher place assigned.

AFTER THE STORM

All night, in the pauses of sleep, I heard
    The moan of the snow-wind and the sea,
Like the wail of Thy sorrowing children, O God!
    Who cry unto Thee.

But in beauty and silence the morning broke,
    O'erflowing creation the glad light streamed;
And earth stood shining and white as the souls
    Of the blessed redeemed.

O glorious marvel in darkness wrought!
    With smiles of promise the blue sky bent,
As if to whisper to all who mourned—
    Love's hidden intent.   *Harriet McEwen Kimball.*

His kingdom ruleth over all (Psalm 103:19).

My soul! try to see God in everything, and everything in God! Lose thine own will in His. Each providence has a voice, if we would only hear it. It is a fingerpost in the journey, pointing us to "the *right* way," that we may go to the "city of habitation"!

Often what a mystic volume Providence is!—its every page full of dark hieroglypics, to which earth can furnish no key. But faith falls back on the assurance that "the Judge of all earth" *must* do right—the Father of all His people *cannot* do wrong.

To the common observer, the stars in the nightly heavens are all confused masses pursuing devious and erratic courses. But to the astronomer each has its allotted and prescribed pathway, and all are preserving inviolate one universal law of harmony and order. It is faith's loftiest prerogative, patiently to wait till that day of disclosures, when page by page the mystic book will be unravelled, and when the believer himself will endorse *every* page with, "It *is* well!"

O blessed day, when the long sealed book of mystery shall be unfolded, when the "fountains of the great deep shall be broken up," the channels of the waters seen, and *all* discovered to be one vast revelation of unerring wisdom and ineffable love! Here we are often baffled at the Lord's dispensations: we cannot fathom His ways; but soon the "mystery of God will be finished"; the enigmatical "seals," with all their inner meanings opened. When that "morning without clouds" shall break, each soul will be like an angel standing in the sun—there will be no shadow; all will be perfect day!

> Still we study, always failing!
>   God can read it, we must wait;
> Wait, until He teach the mystery,
> Then the wisdom-woven history
>   Faith shall read and love translate.
>
> Leaflets now unpaged and scattered
>   Time's great library receives;
> When Eternity shall bind them,
> Golden volumes we shall find them
>   God's light falling on the leaves.

Lord, increase our faith (Luke 17:5).

There is many a crisis in life when we need a faith like the
martyr's to support us. There are hours in life like martyr-
dom—as full of bitter anguish, as full of utter earthly desolation—
in which life itself loses its value, and we ask to die—in whose
dread struggle and agony, life might drop from us and not be
minded.

Oh, then must our cry, like that of Jesus, go up to the pitying
heavens for help, and nothing but the infinite and immortal can
help us. Then, when the world is sinking beneath us, must we seek
the everlasting arms to bear us up—to bear us up to heaven. Thus
was it with our great Example, and so must it be with us. "In Him
was life"; the life of self-renunciation, the life of love, the life of
spiritual and all-conquering faith; and that life is the light of men.

Oh, blessed light! come to our darkness; for our soul is dark, our
way is dark, for want of thee; come to our darkness and turn it into
day; and let it shine brighter and brighter, till it mingles with the
light of the all-perfect and everlasting day!　　　　　*Selected.*

WAIT

Oh! wait, impatient heart!
As Winter waits; her song-birds fled,
And every nestling blossom dead.
Beyond the purple seas they sing;
They only sleep. Sweet patience keep,
And wait, as Winter waits for Spring.

LIFT THINE EYES

O troubled soul of mine! lift up thine eyes
Unto the mountains, mighty and serene.
Full strangely checkered hath their fortune been;
And they have suffered veriest agonies.
And ofttimes still the tyrant tempest lies
Heavy upon them; with the thunder they
Do wrestle. Yet of fear and of dismay
Nothing they know, still rising to the skies.
With many a thousand battles are they scarred;
The floods have broken on each helmless head;
Yet for all this their beauty is not marred.

Nor in their hearts are they discomforted.
Still they endure, whatever whirlwinds roll
Around—still glorious they endure, my soul!

John W. Hales: Hindscarth Cairn.

NOVEMBER 17

Fear thou not for I am with thee (Isa. 41:10).

In a sketch of his boyhood the Rev. John McNeill, a Scotch minister and evangelist, tells this story of an experience with his father.

"I remember one Saturday night, it was nearly midnight, when I started to tramp six or seven miles through the lonely glen to get home. The road had a bad name. This particular night was very black, and two miles outside our little village the road gets blacker than ever. I was just entering the dark defile, when about one hundred yards ahead, in the densest of the darkness, there suddenly rang out a great, strong, cheery voice: 'Is that you, Johnny?'

"It was my father—the bravest, strongest man I ever knew. Many a time since, when things have been getting very black and gloomy about me, I have heard a voice greater than any earthly parent cry: 'Fear not; for I am with thee.' And lo! *God's foot is rising and falling on the road before us as we tread the journey of life. Let us not forget that.*"

> He walks with me when the blinding heat
>   Falls ever across the way,
> And I know the sound of His friendly feet
>   Wherever I chance to stray—
> It does not matter: in rain or shine,
>   His hand is always clasped close in mine.
>
> He talks with me when silence brings
>   Its harvest of peace and rest;
> He whispers until my tired heart sings
>   As I lean on His waiting breast.   *Will O. Muse.*

He saith to the sick of the palsy, Arise, and take up thy bed, and go thy way into thine house (Mark 2:11).

Lord, I have heard men say, "Go bury thy sorrow." Yet methinks the peace which Thou givest is deeper than that. It is not forgetfulness of my cross that I most require: it is glorified remembrance. I want my cross not to be buried, but to be lifted, upraised into the sunlight. The world can say, "Bury thy sorrow," but not, "Take up thy bed." Thou canst show me, not merely the burial of my cross, but is resurrection into newness of life.

E'EN THOUGH IT BE A CROSS THAT RAISETH ME

"It is by my fetters that I can fly; it is by my sorrows that I can soar; it is by reverses that I can run; it is by my tears that I can travel; it is by my cross that I can climb into the heart of humanity. Let me magnify my cross, O Lord!"   *George Matheson.*

God would have you to be "radiant in the thick of it."

And whosoever liveth and believeth in me shall never die (John 11:26).

How it would widen out all our thoughts, conceptions, hopes and plans if the walls that divide life here and hereafter were broken down and our eyes could see our own existence in perspective, stretching away into eternity, as real, as personal, as fraught with interest beyond the grave as on this side of it! How it would lift up, dignify, ennoble, inspire, awaken and deepen all our life if we could but hold the truth of personal immortality in our consciousness all the while as vividly and as really as we hold tomorrow!

The grave would not then be the end of anything save of mortality, weights and infirmities which belong to this earthly state. It would break up no plans. It would cut off nothing. If we see life only as a narrow stage bounded by the curtain that falls at death, ending there forever, how poor and little and limited does existence appear!

But how different if we see life with the veil torn away! The future is as much in our vision and as real as the little present. We may begin works here which shall require ten thousand years to complete. There is no hurry, for we shall have all eternity in which to work. We may scatter seeds which we know shall not come to havest for long ages. We may cherish hopes and aspirations whose goals lie far away in the life to come. We may endure sacrifices, hardships and toils which cannot bring any recompense or reward in this world. knowing that in the long yearless future we shall find glorious return.

For the Christian, the realization of the truth of immortality takes away the bitterness of earthly defeat. There are lives that are cut off here before any of their powers are developed. Dreams of greatness or of beauty fill the vision of loving friends. Then suddenly they are stricken down in the dim dawn or the early morning. The bud had not time to open out its beauties in the short summer of earthly existence. It is borne away still folding up in its close-shut calyxes all its germs and possibilities of power, loveliness and life. Sorrow weeps bitterly over the hopes that seem blighted and cuts its symbols of incompleteness upon the marble; and yet with the warmth of immortality pressing up against the gates, what matters it that the bud did not open here and unfold its beauties this side the grave? There will be time enough in heaven's long summer for every life to put out all its loveliness and glory.

No life is incomplete because it is cut off too soon to ripen, in an earthly home, into majesty of form and glory of fruitage; for death does not come to the Christian as a destroyer. It dims no splendor. It only takes out of life whatever is dull, earthly and opaque, and leaves it pure, brilliant, glorious.

The translation of a Christian life from earth to heaven is but the removal of a tender plant from a cold northern garden, where it is stunted and dying, into a tropical field, where it puts out most luxuriant growths and covers itself with splendor.

With immortality glowing before us, our brief years on earth should be marked by earnestness, reverence, love and faithfulness. Soon we shall break out of our narrow circle and traverse the boundless fields that we see now in the far-away and momentary glimpse. But it will be a blessed thing if we can get into our hearts even here something of the personal consciousness of our immortality, with its limitless possessions and possibilities, and feel something in our souls of the power of an endless life.

Then . . . face to face (1 Cor. 13:12).

AUF WIEDERSEHEN
(Till we meet again)

We walk along life's rugged road together
    Such a little way.
We face the sunshine or the stormy weather
    So brief a day.
Then paths diverge, from sorrow so appalling
    We shrink with pain,
Yet, parted far and farther, still keep calling,
    "Auf Wiedersehen."

Despair not! See, through tear dimmed eyes, before us
    Such a little way.
Lies God's dear garden, and His sun shines o'er us
    A long, long day.
There all paths end, long-parted loved ones, meeting,
    Clasp hands again.
The past, the pain forgot in rapturous greeting—
    "Auf Wiedersehen."   *Susie E. Abbey.*

Eternity together is just beyond.

Said I not unto thee, that, if thou wouldest believe, thou shouldest see the glory of God? (John 11:40).

Mary and Martha could not understand what their Lord was doing. Both of them said to Him, *"Lord, if thou hadst been here, my brother had not died."* Back of it all, we seem to read their thought: "Lord, we do not understand *why* you have stayed away so long. We do not understand *how* you could let death come to the man whom you loved. We do not understand how you could let sorrow and suffering ravage our lives when your presence might have stayed it all. *Why* did you not come? It is too late now, for already he has been dead four days!"

And to it all Jesus had but one great truth. "You may not understand; but I tell you if you *believe,* you will *see.* "

Abraham could not understand *why* God should ask the

sacrifice of the boy; but he trusted. And he *saw* the glory of God in his restoration to his love. Moses could not understand *why* God should keep him forty years in the wilderness, but he trusted; and he *saw* when God called him to lead forth Israel from bondage.

And so, perhaps, in your life. You say, "I do not understand why God let my dear one be taken. I do not understand my affliction has been permitted to smite me. I do not understand the devious paths by which the Lord is leading me. I do not understand why plans and purposes that seemed good to my eyes should be baffled. I do not understand why blessings I so much need are so long delayed.

Friend, you do not *have* to understand all God's ways with you. God does not *expect* you to understand them. You do not *expect* your child to understand, only believe. Some day you will *see* the glory of God in the things which you do not understand.

J. H. McConkey.

I will believe, though all around be darkness,
  Believe to see the rainbow after rain;
Believe that light will surely follow darkness,
  And frozen earth will yield her flowers again;
I must believe, He hears my faintest call—
  For Jesus lives and reigns, and God is over all.

MAY GOD DENY YOU PEACE BUT GIVE YOU GLORY.
Don Miguel De Unanumo
in "The Tragic Sense of Life."

NOVEMBER 22 _____

And the city had no need of the sun, neither of the moon, to shine in it: for the glory of God did lighten it, and the Lamb is the light thereof (Rev. 21:23).

IN HEAVEN

No shadows There! No evening twilight creepeth;
No midnight dark its mantle deep doth spread;
No silver star from through the darkness peepeth;
There is NO NIGHT where dwell the blessed dead.

There is no night! No night of crushing sorrow;
No night of pain for anguished hearts to bear;

No need to hope for some bright dawning morrow—
For with the blessed dead is no night There.

There is no night of sadness and of weeping;
No night of tossing on some couch of pain;
For—to the blessed dead, in Jesus' keeping,
These things of time and sense come not again.

There is no night of things unknown, uncertain;
Things which now try the heart to make it strong:
There is no night—there is the veiling curtain—
Just light; and bliss; and joy; and endless song!

J. Danson Smith.

NOVEMBER 23

And when they looked, they saw that the stone was rolled away: for it was very great. . . . He is risen; He is not here (Mark 16:4, 6).

THE OPEN DOOR

There is a narrow darkened pathway, with room for only one, which leads to a door opening into a wonderful realm of light. The Father is there in the shadows, and as we cross the threshold He gathers us close to His breast and all the weariness is gone.

This little journey is what we call Death. Some of us shrink from it frightened. How foolish! All our lives we have striven for closer communion with that wonderful Friend . . . and this little journey that we take is just the culmination of all that striving—It is *going home* to God to stay, to always be in perfect communion with Him, to never more falter or fail. Surely the One whom we have trusted so sincerely through this life, will brighten the darkness of those few last steps! That kindly light will lead us on to fuller life in His great Home.

At this doorway into that Other Room we stand in aching loneliness—for the door opens for only one of us at a time, and some of us are left behind a little while to carry on His work and grow a little braver ere we enter into rest. But *why* should we be grieving? Into that wonderful land our loved ones go—where they are safe forever.

Let us wave them a cheery good-bye, glad that they at last have found the secret of His presence. Perhaps we do feel lonely—but oh, there in the shadows I see a kneeling figure—Christ, who knew the greatest loneliness of all, the dearth of any human friends in the hour of greatest need. That wonderful heart of love, having known the utmost loneliness, will never leave us lonely. More and more His tenderness creeps in, showing us the perfect friendship—and telling us to lean upon Him when our feet are wearied and our hearts are faint.

Death is a ministering angel—it is a radiant thing, for it takes us *Home* at last.

When we see His face, shall we be afraid?   *Mary L. O'Hara.*

DEATH IS A DOOR

Death is only an old door
  Set in a garden wall.
On gentle hinges it gives, at dusk,
  When the thrushes call.

Along the lintel are green leaves,
  Beyond, the light lies still.
Very willing and weary feet
  Go over that sill.

There is nothing to trouble any heart,
  Nothing to hurt at all.
Death is only a quiet door
  In an old wall.   *Nancy Byrd Turner.*

Christ has made death but a narrow, star-lit strip between the companionship of yesterday and the re-union of tomorrow.

NOVEMBER 24 _____

And there was no more sea (Rev. 21:1).

CROSSING THE BAR

Sunset and evening star,
  And one clear call for me!
And may there be no moaning of the bar
  When I put out to sea.

Twilight and evening bell,
  And after that the dark!

And may there be no sadness of farewell
   When I embark.

For though from out our bourne of time and place
   The flood may bear me far,
I hope to meet my Pilot face to face
   When I have crossed the bar.   *Alfred Tennyson.*

For we are putting out to sea; a voyage and a haven! Enoch
Arden, when he lay dying, of a sudden called, "A sail! A sail!" and
Enoch Arden was right. A sail, to bear him to his babe, a ringlet of
whose hair he had worn upon his breast for many years, and
thought to bear it to his grave; a sail, to carry him to where the
Christ who had strengthened him and helped him in his heroic
unselfishness would meet him and welcome him; "A sail; a sail! to
where beyond these voices there is peace."

NOVEMBER 25 ─────────────────────────────

*Enter into His gates with thanksgiving, and into His courts with praise
(Psalm 100:4).*

Like a rare jewel in a tarnished setting, Thanksgiving Day gleams
   out brightly from its dull environment of somber skies and
frost-swept earth, the gladdest and the saddest day of the entire
twelve months. Another year, with its blessings and its burdens,
has slipped backward from our grasp, and, with hands and hearts
full of varied experiences, we gather once more for the annual
festival. In some faces only peace and content and quiet joy are
visible. God has been good to you, and your happy hearts
overflow with gratitude as you grasp the cup which is pressed
down and running over. Across other faces is thrown the shadow
of a great grief, and you murmur rebelliously through blinding
tears, "How can I be thankful? The day is a mockery!" Dear one,
in the midst of your bitter sorrow, do not forget that it is those
whom He loves that the Lord chastens.
   To many this holiday is one of the sacred "anniversaries of the
heart," of which no word can be spoken except to the One to
whom all secrets are open. There are others whose living trouble is
well-nigh greater than they can bear—to whom the sweep of the
death angel's wings would be rapture. And for those on beds of

weariness and pain; those widowed and fatherless, keeping poverty at bay; those fiercely assailed by temptation; those whose lives are hard and bare and unlovely—what can this day of praise bring? Shall not we whom goodness and mercy have followed, we who have much, share generously with the less fortunate, the less blessed, and make our lives one long Thanks-giving, Thanks-doing and Thanks-living Day?

THANKSGIVING DAY, AND THOU AWAY?

I mind me how in years gone by
 Across the wide, foam-crested sea
 Some pressing duty called for thee,
And though we wept to say "Good-bye,"
 And lonely were the hours, yet we
 Looked to the future hopefully;
And even our Thanksgiving cheer
 Thine absence did not wholly mar;
 Our hearts' love sped to thee afar,
And soon we hoped to greet thee near.

Ne'er to return, thou'rt now away—
How can it be Thanksgiving Day?
 Thanksgiving Day, and thou away?
Yet stay! Methinks, love, now I see.
 When the Pacific heaving tide
Its billows tossed 'twixt thee and me,
 What dangers might thy path betide
I knew not; yet faith gave me peace,
And all my anxious care surcease.
But now I know no grief can come,
Or danger, to that blissful home,
 Where thou at Heaven's Thanksgiving feast
 Dost find thyself a welcome quest.
 Till I shall share that joy and rest
Where thou art blessed, although away,
In faith I'll keep Thanksgiving Day. *Meta E. B. Thorne.*

NOVEMBER 26 _____

His understanding is infinite (Psalm 147:5).

How baffling often are God's dispensations! The more we attempt to fathom their mystery, the more we are driven to rest in the best earthly solution—"Thy judgments are very deep."

Beloved, are the dealings of thy God at present wearing a mysterious aspect to thee? Art thou about to enter some dark cloud, and exclaiming, "Verily Thou art a God that hidest Thyself"? Dost thou "fear to enter the cloud"? Take courage! It will be with thee as with the disciples; unexpected glimpses of heavenly glory—unlooked for tokens of the Saviour's presence and love await thee!

If thy Lord lead thee into the cloud, follow Him. If He "constrain thee to get into the ship," obey Him. The cloud will burst in blessing; the ship will conduct thee (may it be over a stormy sea) to quiet haven at last! It is only the surface of the ocean that is rough. All beneath is a deep calm, and every threatening wave is a "need-be"!

Under the blessed persuasion, that a day of disclosures is at hand, when, "in His light, I shall see light," I will trust the wisdom I cannot trace, and repeat, each night, as the shadows of earth's ignorance vanish before the breaking of an eternal day—

"I will trust."

> I find no answer, often, when beset
> With questions fierce and subtle on my way,
> And often have but strength to faintly pray.
>   But I can trust.

The God of Israel, the Saviour, is sometimes a God that hideth Himself, but never a God that absenteth Himself; sometimes in the dark, but never at a distance. *Matthew Henry.*

NOVEMBER 27 ———————————————————

Peace I leave with you, My peace I give unto you: not as the world giveth give I unto you (John 14:27).

We have but to go on trusting in Him, meeting each day's duties as best we can, taking up the daily burden and stumbling along with it over the steep road, and we shall come out into the place of peace. *Battles of Peace.*

Cast thou thy burden on the Lord!
What then? Will He bear it while I go free?
Nay, weary soul, not thus doth read the Word;
He will sustain—not it—not it—but thee!

THROUGH THE VALLEY AT SUNRISE

On either side the mountains lift their towering summits
high!
Alas, their step and rugged cliffs our human strength defy!
But down between there winds a path that leads at last to
home,
Where, sheltered from the piercing winds, the tender ones
may roam.

On either side, on either side, the woods in darkness lie,
And close the tree-tops overlean to hide the bending sky;
But creeping through the quiet shade the timid sunbeams
come
To tell of day that dawns afar, to light the pathway home.

On either side, on either side, shut in, we may not see
How near the tide that rolls beyond, our eager hearts
may be:
But, as we listen, through the hush we catch the sound
once more—
The music of the restless waves that beat upon the shore.

Beneath our feet, beneath our feet, how rugged lies
the way!
Footsore and weak we wander on, and weary grows
the day;
But through the opening vista how calm the blue hills lie,
Beneath whose shadows we shall sleep in comfort
by-and-by.   *Author Unknown.*

NOVEMBER 28

Wherefore . . . brethren, give diligence to make your calling and election sure . . . for so an entrance shall be ministered unto you abundantly into the everlasting kingdom of our Lord and Saviour, Jesus Christ (2 Peter 1:10, 11).

Now I saw in my dream, that these two men went in at the Gate; and lo, as they entered, they were transfigured and they had raiment put on them that shone like gold. There was also that met them with harps and crowns, and gave them to them; the harp to praise withal, and the crowns in token of honour. Then I heard in my dream that all the bells in the City rang for joy: and that it was said unto them, *Enter ye into the joy of the Lord.* I also heard the men themselves, that they sang with a loud voice, saying, *"Blessing Honour, Glory and Power, be to Him that sitteth upon the Throne, and to the Lamb forever and ever!"*

Now just as the Gates were opened to let in the men, I looked in after them; and behold, the City shone like the Sun, the streets were paved with gold, and in them walked many men, with crowns on their heads, palms in their hands, and golden harps to sing praises withal.

There were also of them that had wings, and they answered one another without intermission, saying, *Holy, Holy, Holy, is the Lord.* And after that, they shut up the gates: which when I had seen, I wished myself among them.   *Pilgrim's Progress.*

THE CITY BEAUTIFUL

Sometimes when the day is ended
    And its round of duties done,
I watch at the western windows
    The gleam of the setting sun.
When my heart has been unquiet
    And its longings unbeguiled
By the day's vexatious trials
    And cannot be reconciled,
I look on the slope of the mountains
    And o'er the restless sea,
And I think of the beautiful city
    That lieth not far from me.

And my spirit is hushed in a moment
    As the twilight falls tender and sweet;
And I cross in fancy the river,
    And kneel at the Master's feet.
And I rest in the shade that there falleth
    From the trees that with healing are rife—
That shadow the banks of the river—
    The river of water of life.

And some time, when the day is ended,
    And the duties He gave me are done,
I shall watch at life's western windows

The gleam of the setting sun.
I shall fall asleep in the twilight
  As I never have slept before,
To dream of the beautiful city,
  Till I waken to sleep no more.
There will fall on my restless spirit
  A hush, oh, so wondrously sweet,
And I shall cross over the river
  To rest at the Master's feet.   *Boston Globe.*

NOVEMBER 29

The heaven was black with clouds (1 Kings 18:45).

But there were blessings in the black—blessings in the heavens
black with clouds. For a long, long time—over three years in
Ahab's reign—there had been no rain. But after the rain the
brooks broke their silence, the rivers were no longer dumb, the
trees clapped their hands for joy, the fields and meadows rejoiced,
nature spread her carpets of green and hung her curtains of green.
Flocks and herds were saved from death. Just so in life—our lives
are black with sorrow and defeats and trials and bereavements.
But there are many spiritual blessings in the black in only we have
eyes to see, if only we have ears to hear, if only we have hands to
receive.

Black shadows will fall on your road. Do not be afraid of them.
Remember that when God lays on the black, He is preparing for
the gold, without which life misses its perfect beauty. "When He
hath tried me I shall come forth as gold (Job 23:10).

Where did you get your roses child?
  "I made them in this little room."
Your window happy with the the dawn?
  "No, sir; in fearful gloom."

What gave your roses color then?
  "My blood, sir, as I bent my head."
Your cheek is cold and lifeless now?
  "No, sir; that's my heart that bled."

One white rose in the basket child?
  "Yes, sir, it crowns the whole,"

337

What is it, fragile, soft and white?
  "I think it is my soul."   *Whirlwinds of God.*

The beauty came in the dark. The beauty came with bleeding!
And so also came the blessing. Treasures of darkness. Deep things
discovered out of the darkness.

Rose purple and a silvery gray
Is that cloud, the cloud which looked so black.
Evening brightens all today,
Looking back.

NOVEMBER 30

Within the veil (Heb. 6:19).

My friend has long since gone into the light; but his presence—
loved and familiar—walks noiseless by my side, his guiding
hand in mine.   *Helen Keller.*

Veiled from our sight, withheld from our embraces.
Wrapped in God's silence which we dare not break.
Yet in our dreams we see the well-loved faces,
And feel their presence near when we awake.
Closer perchance than those who walk beside us,
Who greet us face to face, and hand to hand;
Given, perchance, a power to shield and guide us—
Our unseen guardians from the Unknown land.

INSEPARABLE

'Twixt you and me, beloved friend
Death's hung a mystic screen,
Through which they say no human eye
Hath ever, ever seen.
And yet I hear your loving voice
In every wind that blows;
I see your eyes in morning skies,
Your face in every rose.
And when at twilight time I walk
Within our garden fair,
I'm not alone—ah, no, beloved—
I know your spirit's there.
I feel your kiss upon my cheek,
The pressure of your hand,

But only those who've loved as we,
These things can understand.   *Alice Whitson Norton.*

DECEMBER 1

And I saw a new heaven and a new earth: for the first heaven and the first earth were passed away; and there was no more sea (Rev. 21:1).

LAST THINGS

In December I think of the last things. May they be the best things in my chequered and changeful history.

A world without evil in it: let that be one. I find much that is good in the world of the present . . . but it is marred by man's foolishness and stained by man's transgressions. Yes, but I see a *new heaven and a new earth,* and they are to be my home.

A life without sorrow in it: let that await me too. Life is a glorious possession even now, if it is life ransomed, obedient, dowered with power and peace. But there are many griefs haunting it. "The skies themselves look low and positive": they seem "far off from God's celestial crystals." Ah, but the shadowless life is being kept for me. *He shall wipe away every tear from their eyes.*

A heart without sin in it: let that, also, be my heritage. No more temptation; no more wandering; no more sighing because of the iniquity that abounds; no more disappointment because the growth is so slow. I shall be faultless before the Throne. I shall be shut in with my Lord from tempestuous winds and raging sea. *There shall in no wise enter into it anything unclean.*

A city without a temple in it: let that be the portion in store for me. The church is good, but it is only the copy of a better thing. Here the communion is broken; there it is immediate, uninterrupted, face to face. I shall see Jesus. I shall walk with Him in white. My hands will touch His Hand. My feet will keep step with His. *The Lord God Almighty and the Lamb are the Temple of it.*

When my December reaches the end of its thirty-first day, may the New Sun rise, bringing the New Year!   *Dr. Alexander Smellie.*

> There's no last time in Heaven! The angels pour
> A still new song, though chanted evermore!
> There's no night following on their daylight hours,
> No fading-time for amaranthine bowers;

No change, no death, no harp that lies unstrung,
No vacant place those shadowed hills among.

DECEMBER 2 ───────────────────────────

*Then cometh Jesus with them unto a place called Gethsemane (oil press)
(Matt. 26:36).*

THE LONELY OLIVE MILL

There's a peaceful vale in a sunny land,
  Where the hills keep guard around;
And the soft breeze stirs the olive trees
  And the grass that clothes the ground;
And in the hush and the solitude
  Where even the birds are still,
There stands, untended and alone,
  An ancient olive-mill.

Through the long, bright day the mill-wheel turns
  And the fruit is crushed by the stone;
And drips in silence the fragrant oil,
  In silence and alone;
But somewhere, out in the circling hills—
  Unseen, unheard, unknown—
The Master of the olive-mill
  Is mindful of His own.

So many hours the wheel must turn,
  And stone on stone must grind;
And then He will come to His olive-mill
  His meed of oil to find,
He knows how heavy the weight must be,
  How long to let it lie,
Ere He can gather the precious oil
  And throw the refuse by.

O child of God! Are you lying crushed
  'Neath trial, pain or woe?
No eye to pity, no ear to hear,
  No voice to whisper low?
Alone in your Gethsemane,
  Christ watches with you there;
He will not suffer one ounce of weight
  More than your strength can bear.

340

He chasteneth but to purity,
  He crusheth but to raise;
In love He worketh His blessed will
  To His glory's endless praise;
In our affliction afflicted still,
  He leaveth us not alone;
He will not forget, He will not forsake,
  He is mindful of His own.   *Annie Johnson Flint.*

DECEMBER 3 ────────────────────────────

In everything ye are enriched by Him (1 Cor. 1:5).

O Mother! my heart breaks with your heart when your cradle is empty. But shall I call back the child? Nay; sooner pluck a star out of heaven then call back that child to this wintry blast.

Your child is in a spring-land. It is a summer-world. It is with God. You have given it back to Him who lent it to you.

Now, the giving back is very hard. But you can not give back to God all that you received with your child. You can not give back to God those springs of new and deeper affection which were awakened by the coming of this little one. You can not give back to God the experiences which you have had in dwelling with your darling. You can not give back to God the hours which, when you look upon them now, seem like one golden chain of linked happiness.

You are better, you are riper, you are richer, even in this hour of bereavement, than you were. God gave, and He has not taken away except in outward form. He holds, He keeps, He watches, He loves. You shall have again that which you have given back to Him only outwardly.

Meanwhile the key is in your hand, and it is not a black iron key: it is a golden key of faith, of hope and of love. This little child has taught you to follow it. There will not be a sunrise or a sunset when you will not in imagination go through the gate of heaven after it. There is no door so fast that a mother's love and a father's love will not open it, and follow a beloved child. And so, by its ministration, this child will guide you a thousand times into a realization of the great spirit-land, and into a faith of the invisible, which will make you as much larger as it makes you less dependent on the body, and more rich in the fruitage of the spirit.

The Lord gave, and the Lord hath taken away; blessed by the name of the Lord (Job 1:21).

Therefore let your grief be such that your consolation shall be more; for ye have not lost them, but sent them before you, that they may be kept forever blessed.   *Luther.*

THE LOVED AND LOST

"The loved and lost!" Why do we call them lost?—
    Because we miss them from our onward road?
God's unseen angel o'er our pathway crossed,
Looked on us all, and loving them the most,
    Straightway relieved them from life's weary load.

They are not lost; they are within the door
    That shuts out loss, and every hurtful thing,
With angels bright, and loved ones gone before,
In their Redeemer's presence evermore,
    And God Himself their Lord, and Judge and King.

And this we call a "loss"! Oh selfish sorrow
    Of selfish hearts! O we of little faith!
Let us look round, some argument to borrow
Why we in patience should await the morrow
    That surely must succeed this night of death.

Aye, look upon this dreary desert path,
    The thorns and thistles whereso'er we turn;
What trials and what tears, what wrongs and wrath,
What struggles and what strife the journey hath!
    They have escaped from these; and lo! we mourn.

A poor wayfarer, leading by the hand
    A little child, has halted by the well
To wash from off her feet the clinging sand,
And tell the tired boy of that bright land
    Where, this long journey past, they longed to dwell.

When lo! the Lord, who many mansions had,
    Drew near and looked upon the suffering twain,
Then pitying spake, "Give Me the little lad;
In strength renewed, and glorious beauty clad,
    I'll bring him with Me when I come again."

Did she make answer selfishly and wrong—
     "Nay, but the woes I feel he too must share"?
No! rather, bursting into grateful song,
She went her way rejoicing, and made strong
     To struggle on, since he was freed from care.

We will do likewise; death hath made no breach
     In love and sympathy, in hope and trust;
No outward sign or sound our ears can reach,
But there's an inward, spiritual speech,
     That greets us still, though mortal tongues be dust.

It bids us do the work that they laid down—
     Take up the song where they broke off the strain;
So journeying till we reach the heavenly town,
Where are laid up our treasures and our crown,
     And our lost loved ones will be found again.   *Selected.*

DECEMBER 5

Abide with us (Luke 24:29).

Abide with us, Thou Christ of God! Abide with us! Life is all too serious for us to manage in our own strength. The stress and toil of daily life would hide Thee from our gaze. The cares and troubles of this world would occupy the hearts designed for Thee. Come, Saviour Divine, into our dull, clouded lives, and make them bright with Thine own immediate Presence, and thus transform us in the world. Come, we pray Thee, and abide with us!

And how abide with us? Come first into our hearts as Saviour; as the Lamb slain from the foundation of the world, the Lamb of God which taketh away the sin of the world. If any of us have never really known Thee, have never felt the magic of Thy Presence, Oh, may such hear the gracious summons: "Behold I stand . . . and knock."

Constrain us to make that first living contact with Thyself which shall transfer the burden of sin, of life, of service, from us to Thee. Oh, come, abide with us!

And then abide with us always. Once having come, never depart. Come in, oh, come, Thou Heavenly Guest: and yet not Guest, but Master. May all our hearts be bared to Thee; all wills be

bowed to Thine. Take control of our lives; place the government
on Thy shoulder.   *Northcote Deck.*

DECEMBER 6 ─────────────────────────────

Trust in Him at all times . . . God is a refuge for us (Psalm 62:8).

Where there is light on the song, there is no need for darkness
on the way. If I had never gone into darkened rooms where
the soul stands at the parting of the worlds; or grasped the hands
of strong men when all they had toiled for was gone—nothing left
but honor; or ministered to men mangled on the battle-field; and
heard, in all those places where darkness was on the way,
melodies—*melodies* that I never heard among the common
places of prosperity—I could not be so sure as I am, that God
often darkens the way that the way may grow clear and entire in
the soul.   *Robert Collyer.*

TRUST

Though the rain may fall and the wind is blowing,
  And cold and chill is the wintry blast,
Though the cloudy sky is still cloudier growing,
  And the dead leaves tell that summer has passed.
My face I hold to the stormy heaven,
  My heart is as calm as the summer sea,
Glad to receive what God has given,
    Whate'er it be.

When I feel the cold I can say, "He sends it,"
  And His wind blows blessing I surely know,
For I've never a want but that He attends it,
  And my heart beats warm though the winds may blow.
The soft sweet summer was warm and glowing;
  Bright were the blossoms on every bough;
I trusted Him when the roses were blowing—
    I trust Him now.

Small were my faith should it weakly falter,
  Now that the roses have ceased to grow;
Frail were the trust that now should alter,
  Doubting His love when storm clouds blow.
If I trust Him once, I must trust Him ever,
  And his way is best, though I stand or fall,

Through wind and storm, He will leave me never—
    He sends it all.

Why should my heart be faint and fearing?
    Mighty He rules above the storm;
Even the wintry blast is cheering,
    Showing his power to keep me warm.
Never a care on my heart is pressing,
    Never a fear can disturb my breast,
Everything that He sends is blessing,
    For He knows best.   *Song of a Bird in a Winter Storm.*

DECEMBER 7 ─────────────────────

Ye have done it unto Me (Matt. 25:40).

There is no anodyne for heart-sorrow like ministry to others. If your life is woven with the dark shades of sorrow, do not sit down to deplore in solitude your hapless lot, but arise to seek out those who are more sorrowful than you are, bearing them balm for their wounds and love for their heart-breaks.   *F. B. Meyer.*

Forget thyself; console the sadness near thee;
    Thine own shall then depart,
And songs of joy, like heavenly birds, shall cheer thee
    And dwell within thy heart.

THE POWER OF LITTLE THINGS

The memory of a kindly word
For long gone by,
The fragrance of a fading flower
Sent lovingly,
The gleaming of a sudden smile
Or sudden tear,
The warm pressure of the hand,
The tone of cheer.
The note that only bears a verse
From God's own Word:—
Such tiny things we hardly count
As ministry,
The givers deeming they have shown
Scant sympathy;
But when the heart is overwrought,
Oh, who can tell

The power of such tiny things
To make it well!   *Francis Ridley Havergal.*

DECEMBER 8 ────────────────────────

I will not leave you comfortless: I will come to you (John 14:18).

Your life and mine has its lonely aspect. It was said of Jesus "Of the people there was none with Him, His own forsook Him and fled." There is about Jesus a poignant solitariness, and He passed through it in order that He might understand what it is to be lonely, and to become the Companion of the solitary, that none of us should walk alone.   *Rev. John McBeath.*

ALONE

My pathway is desolate—all joy has fled,
I look on the past and the future as dead.
The things that were linked with the promise of God
Seem buried—still deeper than under the sod.
My friends have forsaken—my loved ones have gone,
And I stand in the midst of these things—all alone.
I lift up my face and I lift up my eye,
And I see but a deep, unrelenting, dark sky.
I look at the earth and its beauty I see;
But it seems as if flow'rs bloomed for all but for me.
I gaze to the left and I gaze to the right,
The scenes that once thrilled by their beauteous sight
Are clouded and covered. The words that I hear
Fall heavy and meaningless on my dull ear;
The song that once soared with a joyous refrain,
With a broken wing falls, and a dull note of pain;
The thoughts that were kindled from torches within
Are like the dead ashes—or something akin,
Has earth lost its fragrance—has heav'n lost its light,
That nothing is beauteous—and nothing is bright?
Or, is it that shadows have entered my soul
With a darkness that deepens, and waters that roll?
Can there be a sorrow that others have borne,
Now breaking my heart—making night of my morn?
Alone in this sorrow—alone, in this grief—
'Tis that breaks the spirit and blocks all relief.
Alone, midst the many—alone, when alone
With a loneness so deep that forbids e'en a moan.

YET ... NOT ALONE.

"Alone, yet . . . not alone" What are these words I hear
That rise and fall in some new way upon my dulled ear?
"Alone, yet . . . not alone." The phrase familiar seems.
Did I once read it long ago, or hear it in my dreams?
"Alone, yet . . . not alone." Stronger and fuller free,
These words re-echo in my heart and even speak to me!
"My child, thy Father's here; say not thou art alone.
He said that He would ne'er forsake and never leave
    His own.
Look farther than the clouds of that relentless sky,
And thou shalt meet Thy Father's gaze to guide thee with
    His eye;
On earth's fresh beauty look—canst thou not see His face,
And in each flower and each fern His providences trace?
E'en in the water's roll and in the bitter wind,
Canst thou not hear His undertone and some sweet
    solace find?
The thoughts that flamed within, the song and every word
That filled thy heart with love untold and melody
    unheard—
Thou say'st these things are gone, that they're forever lost;
This is not so; they are but taken, and—at such a
    little cost.
Instead of thoughts of earth, the "mind of Christ" He gives,
And for the song that soars and falls, the Song and Word
    that lives.
The love which thou didst grasp—the friends on whom
    thou leaned
Filled many places in thy heart, and thou wast from Me
    weaned.
The many things are gone—and heavy is the rod;
'Tis that the many should be one, and that one—
    only God.
Let Him fulfill His word, in His eternal way.
And when thou seest the path grow dark upon His
    promise stay.
Count not, as men do count, thy sorrow as thy loss;
For thou shalt find the brightest crown hung on the
    heaviest cross.
Thus every loss is gain and healing in each dart;
For thine Almighty, loving God dwells "in a broken heart."

Selected.

Why sayest thou . . . my way is hid from the Lord? (Isa. 40:27).

S trong, impassioned as are these words, how truthfully they interpret the thoughts of many a sorrowing heart! Yes, many a *Christian* heart. Disguise it as we may, in the depths of profound grief, and despite all accepted dogmas and creeds, such reflections *will* obtrude themselves.

"Has not God forgotten me?" I adore Him and cling to Him as my Heavenly Father—it is the assurance I shall be the last to surrender. But why this terrible trial? Where are any footsteps of His love. Life is bereft of its beauty and brightness, my prayers are apparently unheard. Surely He is leaving me to cry unsuccoured in the lonely desert—"My soul thirsteth for Thee, in a dry and weary land, where no water is."

These, sorrowing one, in your seasons of despondency—it may be even now—are the tones of your muffled harp.

Christ could Himself enter into the mystery—shall I say, the *terribleness* of apparently unheard and unsuccoured prayer. Read the Psalm so unquestionably His own; the psalm of the Eloi-cry, "My God, My God, why hast Thou forsaken Me?"

What is His solace and balm-word in that hour of seeming desolation? He rests contented with the assurance, "But Thou art Holy" (Psalm 22:3).

Think, in the midst of your crisis-hours with their silences of grief, how He traversed this, as well as other solitudes—how He drank this, as well as other sorrow-brooks by the way (Psalm 110:7). Under the shade of these moonlit olives, the Master is giving utterance to importunate pleadings.

He will not surrender His confidence in God—in His heavenly Father's righteousness, faithfulness and truth. At last, light breaks through the darkness; and ere the Psalm of Agony closes, He can tell of joyful experiences, imparting help and hope and courage to all His people in their hours of misgiving—"Thou hast heard Me from the horns of the unicorns . . . They shall praise the Lord that seek Him. Your heart shall live forever" (Psalm 22:21, 26).

Take courage from the example and experience of the Great Sufferer. Plead the promise of this same praying Saviour, whose heart vibrates and throbs on the throne to the woes of humanity.

The great lesson He would teach His children is, "Be patient."

Let faith rise above the obscuration of sight and sense. This was the philosophy of affliction manifested in the case of the smitten patriarch of Uz. "Behold we count them happy which *endure.* " The mysterious dealings came at last to be vindicated; and in anticipation he sang the song of victory on his bed of ashes. "For I know that my Redeemer liveth!"

God's "silences," rightly understood, have deep meanings, if not in most cases triumphant issues, and alluring at all events, to higher hopes, even though the way lead through shadow and darkness.

Soldier of God! Hope on; trust on; fight on; pray on. Feel the calm assurance that "the prayer of faith shall save," and that, too, despite thwarted purposes and apparently unanswered requests.

Dr. Macduff.

DECEMBER 10

Permit the children to be coming unto Me, be not hindering them, for of such as these is the kingdom of God. And folding them in His arms, He was blessing them, having laid His hands upon them (Mark 10:14-16, Rotherham translation).

> "Who plucked that flower?"
> cried the gardener, as he walked through the garden.
> His fellow-servant answered,
> "THE MASTER!"
> And the gardener held his peace.
> *Inscription in an old English churchyard.*

GOD'S GARDEN

God's garden had need of a little flower,
It had grown for a time here below,
But in tender love He took it above,
In more favorable clime to grow.

It might have been marred had He left it below,
Although we had tended with care,
Had tilled and watered and hedged about,
Watching each petal fair.

There with His smile for sunshine,
It will grow to perfection of bloom

No withering blight or destructive storm
To crush out its sweet perfume.

Perhaps sometimes, in the quiet hours,
We shall notice its sweet perfume
Steel softly down from the heavenly place,
'Till it seems to fill the room.

Then the earthly spot will seem less bare,
As we think of the time to come,
When we shall enter the garden fair,
And find our transplanted bloom.

THE LORD GIVETH

God lent him to me for my very own,
Let me become his father, me alone!
Gave him to me not for an hour—for years!
('Tis gratefulness gleams in my eyes, not tears.)
No joy that fathers know but it was mine,
And fathering that laddie strong and fine.

Time after time I said: "'Tis but a dream;
I shall wake to find things only seem
Grand as they are." Yet still he lingered on
Till year on sweeter year had come and gone.
My heart is filled forever with a song,
Because God let me have my lad so long.

He was my own until I fully knew
And never could forget how deep and true
A father's love for his own son may be.
It drew me nearer God Himself; for He
Has loved His Son. (These are but grateful tears—
That he was with me all those happy years!)

Strickland Gillilan.

DECEMBER 11 ⎯⎯⎯⎯⎯⎯⎯⎯⎯⎯⎯⎯⎯⎯⎯⎯⎯⎯⎯

And He bearing His cross went forth (John 19:17).

Every true cross-bearer learns to carry his cross as if it were an
ornament rather than a burden, and finds after a time that it
carries him. It gives more strength to him than he gives to it. Yet

how many persons there are who scarcely attempt to carry the cross! It is thrown on them, and they sink down under it.

Shall grief be forever a tyrant? Shall sorrow stand forever domineering over men? I marvel that there is not more glorifying over the cross. I marvel that there are not more songs of victory sung. *Selected.*

BALANCE

I fear no more the coming years—
    What they may bring.
   Days will be sunless, nights bereft of stars;
Mayhap the brightest blossoms of Spring
    Shall first be bound with Winter's icy bars.
But still beyond the cloud is always light,
The stars are in the sky all night,
And deepest snows are they which hide the bright
    Green heart of Spring.

Not all of life is dreamed away
    In Summer skies;
   Time holds a loss, a loneliness for me;
But Hope is strong, and Faith dare not be weak,
    And love abides—the greatest of the three.
Enough if sweet tomorrow will repay
The disappointment of today,
Light follows dark; sun, rain; seas ebb away
    Again to rise.

And if the rugged road of life
    Doth wind around
   The mountain side, where heavy clouds hang low;
And, as I climb, the pilgrim staff be changed
    Into a cross, still onward would I go!
The peaks of only highest mountains rise
Above the clouds to bluest skies,
And round the heaviest cross is hung the prize,
    The brightest crown. *Amy Seville Wolff.*

May we trust in Thy wise choice of rough and smooth, of time and tide, of sun and shower. Give us all that we need to enable us to fight the good fight and finish our course with joy.

This sickness is . . . for the glory of God, that the Son of God might be glorified thereby (John 11:4).

There is no place, no occasion where God can be more glorified than on a couch of pain, or where more real spiritual strength is imparted. Remember this, you who are now undergoing the desert experience, wandering through the wilderness "in a solitary way."

How many in that peculiar school of suffering have "graduated with honors." They came out of "great tribulation." Tribulation— the grain-sifter, the threshing-flail, as the root-word imports, winnowing the husk from the seed. And this tribulation "worketh" not *impatience* but *"patience. "*

It was the SMITTEN rock of the desert that yielded the refreshing waters.

Your own feelings, perhaps, may be that with you there can be no such stream; that pent up in that couch of suffering, life is useless—effort for good is denied.

You are like the wounded bird with broken wing struggling in the furrow; envying those around you in their capacity of flight and soaring. Perhaps, though reluctant to own it, you may be among the faithful toilers who have broken down by reason of your very fidelity to duty. The bow was overstrained, and the bowstring has snapped; the harp-chord was overstrained, and the music has ceased.

This is the history of many an arrested ministry at home or in the Mission-field. The life of excessive consecration has only paid its martyrs penalties.

Many a sick-bed sufferer reminds one of the Maréchal Niel rose that flowers so luxuriantly as often to bloom itself to death. By the very profusion of goodness the root becomes weakened, the overloaded blossom exhausts the mortal energy.

But, be still; God has work for you to do, when the wings are clipped and the eye is filmed. If activities are impossible, not so the exercise of the passive virtues.

While you may be bewailing curtained opportunities and baffled purposes, you can in other ways "glorify Him in the fires." You may see in your shattered body only the house in ruins, while in His sight and under His loving discipline, you may in truth be noiselessly rearing an angel-haunted temple.

Yours is a shadowed couch; but it is in "the shadow of His hand" He hath "hid you." You may be able to say nothing and to do nothing; but you can remember, in your very helplessness, Milton's noble line: *They also serve who only stand and WAIT.*

> And they, who, like the gentle wind, uplift
> The petals of the dew-wet flowers, and drift
>   Their perfume on the air,
> Alike may serve Him, each with their own gift,
>   Making their lives a prayer.

DECEMBER 13

I shall go to him (2 Samuel 12:23).

BEATING ME HOME

> Through the shady lane, ere the sun has set,
>   We strolled together, my boy and I;
> Far above our heads, where the treetops met
> And the blue sky shone through a lacy net,
>   The birds were singing a lullaby.
>
> And the small boy chattered, as small boys can
>   Of all that he meant to do and be;
> How he'd grow and grow to a great big man—
> And the short arms stretched to their utmost span—
>   And work his hardest, and all for me.
>
> At the end of the lane he stayed his feet,
>   With wistful eyes on the way that led
> From the sleepy calm of the village street
> To the city's noise and the city's heat:
>   "Oh, why do we never go there?" he said.
>
> So I answered again the old demand,
>   The road was dusty and hard and long;
> And I gathered closer the little hand,
> For I fain would keep him in childhood's land,
>   Untouched by sorrow and pain and wrong.
>
> Then, his quest forgotten in eager play,
>   He turned to the home land, cool and green,

He loosed my hand as he sped away
And I heard him calling me, clear and gay,
    When swaying branches had dropped between.

Now his words are echoing o'er and o'er,
    Through my empty heart and the empty air:—
"Mother, dear, I'm beating you home once more
I'll go ahead and open the door,
    Just follow me slow and you'll find me there."

Oh, the Home he has reached is safe and sweet,
    And slow my walk through a long, long lane
As I follow the prints of his flying feet,
And list for his laughter mine ears to greet,
    Follow and listen, and not in vain.

I have done forever with all my fears;
    No care shall sadden his joyous song,
And his eyes shall never be dimmed by tears,
For the child heart beats through the endless years
    Untouched by sorrow and pain and wrong.

And I know, though the silence hurts me sore
    And still to my longing his voice is dumb,
He has only "beaten me home" once more,
HE HAS "GONE AHEAD TO OPEN THE DOOR,"
    And there he's waiting for me to come.

                        Annie Johnson Flint.

DECEMBER 14

Comfort ye, comfort ye my people (Isa. 40:1).

EMPTY LIVES

My life is empty now," said a widowed mother whose only son had been laid to rest. "I have nothing to do now."

She sat in her luxurious home, her hands in her lap, grieving and mourning. She would not even read books of consolation, which were offered to her. She could think of nothing but her loss, of how empty her life was. She refused her friends' invitations to go out into the world again. It only reminded her more bitterly of what others had and what she had lost, she told them. So she sat day after day, grieving over her loss, engulfed in a darkness which no ray of light could penetrate.

"My life is empty now," said another widowed mother, when her only daughter married and moved to a distant city. "There is no reason for me to keep up the home longer. There is nothing for me to do. I will travel and try to forget my loneliness."

She traveled from one land to another, but found nothing with which to fill her empty life. On the trains, on the steamers, she gave herself up to memories of the past. She brooded, sorrowed, pitied herself, and she found no solace in all her journeyings. Her life was "empty."

"My life is empty now," said still another mother, who had been bereft and was lonely and alone, "but I must fill it." Instead of sitting at home brooding, or traveling far in search of diversion, she threw herself into every outside, broadening good work which she could find. She was active in church societies, ever ready to do what was needed, always on the alert as to how she could help, comfort and cheer someone more sad, more lonely, more needy than herself. Every minute of her day she filled with helpful, absorbing works. She visited the sick and the sorrowing; sewed and made garments for the needy; taught in the Sunday School, and won many young hearts for the Master. Her life was full, rich and *happy.* She had loved her dear ones as truly as those other women who could find no consolation; but she accepted God's will, and filled the precious, fleeting moments with work for the Master.

No life is ever so empty that God cannot fill it, if we seek His guidance.

NEW VISION

I walked in sunlit streets,
And looked with wondering sympathy
Through casements, into darkened rooms,
At death.
I tapped the knocker of a door or two,
And gave such awkward pity as I knew,
And, still uncomprehending, journeyed on.
Between my heart and theirs a gulf was set—
The gulf that lies twixt midnight and the dawn.

At last I, too, sat lonely in the dusk
Of shuttered windows.
My ears, too,
Learned the sad, futile self-reproach

Of constant listening for steps they knew—
For steps forever gone.

Time passed. I walked in sunlit streets once more,
And looked through casements as I had before.
But now I asked no entrance. At a door
I paused, and with no signal, stepped inside,
Softly as one who had the right to go.
Silently, side by side, we kept the slow
Grim vigil for the dead.
Still wordlessly, I left. Yet in that hour
Heart spoke to heart of things beyond the power of
    language to express.
What need of words? The parching lips
Of both our souls had tasted sorrow's bread.

Lucille Stearns.

DECEMBER 15

What I do thou knowest not now; but thou shalt know hereafter (John 13:7).

IT JUST HAS TO BE

A man was once asked why he believed that life persisted after the change which we call death. He answered, "It just has to be, to finish things."

This seems like a pretty good reason, when you think about it. A boy does not spend his days in making an airplane, and then, when he has the parts properly adjusted, throw it on the trash pile. No; he wants to see it take off and fly, out in the open. A man does not install an expensive radio in his home, and let it stand silent day and night; he tunes in and listens to the wonderful things that are always "on the air." Then is it reasonable to think God does otherwise with us?

"We'll catch the broken thread again, and finish what we here began."

It just has to be!

Not now, but in the coming years,
    It may be in the Better Land,
We'll read the meaning of our tears,
    And there, sometime, we'll understand.

We'll catch the broken thread again,
　And finish what we here began;
Heaven will the mysteries explain,
　And then, ah then, we'll understand.

We'll know why clouds instead of sun
　Were over many a cherished plan;
Why song has ceased, when scarce begun;
　'Tis there, sometime, we'll understand.

God knows the way, He holds the key,
　He guides us with unerring Hand;
Sometimes with tearless eyes we'll see;
　Yes, there, up there, we'll understand.

Then trust in God through all thy days;
　Fear not, for He doth hold thy hand;
Though dark the way, still sing and praise;—
　Sometime, sometime, we'll understand.

James McGranahan.

DECEMBER 16

Absent from the body . . . present with the Lord (2 Cor. 5:8).

SINCE YESTERDAY

Where has she gone since Yesterday,
　And left us lonely here?
Tonight she seems so far away
　Who yester-eve was near;
No map of ours on sea or land
　That journeying may trace,
We only know she's reached her Home,
　And seen her Father's face.

And, oh, she knows since Yesterday,
　And she'll be learning fast;
The mists of Earth are cleared away,
　The mysteries are past;
The sun of truth in radiance glows
　All shadowless and bright,
Undimmed by any cloud of Earth,
　Undarkened by its night.

And she has grown since Yesterday,
    And she'll be growing still;
The bonds of Time and Sense and Space
    That irked the eager will
Were dropped like shackles from the soul
    In that first upward flight,
The weary body frets no more
    The spirit, freed and light.

O dear, familiar Yesterday!
    O sad and strange Today!
Yet who would call the glad soul back
    To rouse the resting clay?
Or who could wish that she might share
    Our Morrow's toil and strife,
Who, loosed from Death and all its pains,
    Has entered into Life?   *Annie Johnson Flint.*

Life's sunsetting here is the sunrising there.

DECEMBER 17 ⎯⎯⎯⎯⎯⎯⎯⎯⎯⎯⎯⎯⎯⎯⎯⎯⎯

Through many tribulations we must enter the kingdom of God (Acts 14:22).

The sweetest joys of life are the fruits of sorrow. Human nature seems to need suffering to fit it for being a blessing to the world. If you would pour something beyond commonplace consolation into a broken and bleeding heart, you must be content to pay the price of a costly education—like your Master, you must suffer.

The crushing of a thousand petals, Lord,
Distills one drop of essence from a flower—
Crush me, O God, if through it my song makes
Some tired heart walk with beauty for an hour.

If under the bruising pestles I give voice
To the high white rapture of a faint perfume—
And, catching it, one weary of paved ways
Turns back a lost path where wood violets bloom;

If I can bring the quick relief of tears
To dry eyes dulled with bitterness for long—
Gather the fragrant petals of my life—

And crush them, Lord—then help me sing the song.
Grace Noll Crowell.

There are no great souls without great sorrows.

DECEMBER 18 _____

I have seen his ways, and will heal him; I will lead him also, and restore comforts unto him and to his mourners (Isa. 57:18).

It is indeed no small part of trial, especially after a lacerating bereavement, when the tendrils of the heart are wrenched from creature props, to face the world again; to encounter the old engagements; to toil through the old imperious mechanical drudgeries and grapple with the conventional commonplaces of life. But anything better than becoming a prey to morbid feelings and querulous inaction.

There is a Divine panacea in work.

Weep, if thou wilt, but weep not all too long,
Or weep and work, for work will lead to song.

Elijah was miserable away from former activities, as he sat moping under his desert-juniper, or crouched within the cave of Sinai. "Go, return on thy way to the wilderness," was God's bracing missive and antidote; and his crushed spirit revived. The solitudes of Horeb were left; the moodiness of the lonely life was exorcised in the resumption of the ministries of Jezreel and Carmel.

Do not expect a sudden or miraculous illumination. The Great Physician bids you wait His time. "I will (leaving the period indefinite) heal him, and restore to him comforts." They are strangely unskilled in trial—the sanctities of bereavement—who would expect and exact the suddenness of an unnatural submission, and harshly forbid the heart a season of sorrow.

Are you tempted at times to travel onwards with drooping head and faltering step? Let the watchword of the primitive believers in their hours of "suffering affliction" be heard: *Sursum Corda* ("To heaven with your hearts"). Let your response, like theirs, be: "We have raised them to the Lord!"

We shall see Him as He is (1 John 3:2).

Here? Oh, no, not here, for "here, we see through a glass darkly, but *then* face to face." What a joy it is to us to just see the face of someone whom we love. How we cherish their photographs when they are absent from us. They write us letters and how we long to receive them, but when the doors open, and we see the loved one's face, what an exquisite and thrilling satisfaction is ours! The Word tells us that it will be just so in Heaven, when "*we shall see Him as He is.*"

Our Saviour did not have a handsome Face, probably, as men count beauty. Somewhat too old and careworn; with His visage "so marred"; looking nearly fifty when He was only thirty-three; not beauty there, that men, as men, should desire Him.

Yet in that somewhat unlovely face the eye of faith beholds "the light of the glory of God." For the lack of loveliness is due to that self-sacrifice which is the highest manifestation of the Divine, as it is His transcendant characteristic. Those lines were carved by the suffering born of sympathy with sorrow and with sinners.

And yet, in spite of its furrows and its pallor, what a face to contemplate would be that of Jesus of Nazareth! What tenderness, what power, what purity, what steadfastness, what nobility of soul, would those sacred, yet human lineaments display! Who could look at that countenance and remain unilluminated, unsanctified by the vision?

What, then, will it be to see the glorified face of our Risen Lord! Can we wonder that, when the full flame of the Divine effulgence shall burst upon us, it shall transform us into its own ethereal beauty, and that we shall be like Him because we shall "see Him as He is"?   *Anon.*

VISION!

I SAW GOD'S FACE!
Its radiance bared my spirit's direst need,
Disclosed unholiness and narrow creed;
Then all the hoardings in my earthly store,
Appeared as faded toys and worthless—for
I SAW GOD'S FACE!

I SAW GOD'S FACE!

And like the drooping blossoms kissed with dew,
My soul revived, my courage rose anew;
Setting my face toward the sun once more,
I grasped the plough so long neglected—for
  I SAW GOD'S FACE!   *Catherine Baird.*

DECEMBER 20

Neither shall there be any more pain; for the former things are passed away (Rev. 21:4).

Mark that weary disciple, who had a long and sorrowing experience. The hour of redemption at length arrives; the submerging waters are passed, and in an instant the celestial glory stands all revealed. As the darkness settles heavily here, the light opens transportingly there, and the body begins to sing, the spirit begins to hear, and even join in those heavenly melodies.

Cullen whispered in his last moments: "I wish I had the power of writing or speaking, for then I would describe to you how pleasant a thing it is to die."

I DID NOT WEEP

I did not weep to see him dead, because upon his face
  I saw a smile of glory spread a touch of heavenly
    grace
And tho' my form he could not see, I fancied that he knew
  That I was there, and spoke to me the way he used
    to do.
I fancied that I heard him say, who battled long with pain,
  "A miracle occurred today, and I am well again!
I did not cough last night and wake from fever's restless
  sleep,
  To wait to see the morning break and hear the wagons
    creep,
And I am well and I am strong and glad am I today,
  The burden I have borne so long has now been put
    away."
And standing in that darkened place, the smile of long
  ago,
  Which God had left upon his face, told me 'twas
    better so.   *Edgar Guest.*

And I have but to hark to hear thy song;
    Be still to feel thy presence, cheer and grace;
And in my dreams I see thy shining face.
    Angel of God, to bid me still "BE STRONG."

DECEMBER 21

Stay firm and let thine heart take courage (Psalm 27:14—Osterwald).

When you stand in a belfry, you are stunned with the sound of bells immediately above you; but at a distance you discover that they are ringing in mellow beauty. In the pressure of the hour, when you seemed to be overwhelmed by the waves of sorrow, you cannot discern God's purpose; but wait; when an interval of time and space has passed, you will detect the music of God's purpose.

WAIT

If but one message I may leave behind,
One single words of courage for my kind,
It would be this—Oh, brother, sister, friend,
Whatever life may bring—what God may send,
No matter whether clouds lift soon or late—
Take heart and wait.

Despair may tangle darkly at your feet,
Your faith be dimmed, and hope, once cool and sweet,
Be lost—but suddenly, above a hill,
A heavenly lamp set on a heavenly sill
Will shine for you and point the way to go.
How well I know!

For I have waited through the dark, and I
Have seen a star rise in the blackest sky,
Repeatedly—it has not failed me yet.
And I have learned God never will forget
To light His lamp. If we but wait for it,
It will be lit.   *Grace Noll Crowell.*

DECEMBER 22

(D. L. Moody's "Coronation Day," 1899.)

362

With long life will I satisfy him (Psalm 91:16).

We are all the time coming to the end of things here—the end of the week, the end of the month, the end of the year. It is end, end, end all the time. But, thank God, He is going to satisfy us with long life, endless life, with no end to it!

Once the great evangelist, Moody, said in his buoyant way: "Some day you will read in the papers that D. L. Moody, of East Northfield, is dead. Don't you believe a word of it. At that moment I shall be more alive than I am now; I shall have gone up higher—that is all;—out of this old clay tenement into a house that is immortal, a body that death cannot touch, that sin cannot taint, a body fashioned like unto His glorious body."

That is the way to meet present-day skepticism concerning immortality. When agnostics and infidels deny that blessed truth, "don't you believe a word of it." I have heard even Christians say, "Oh, I wish I could be sure of life after death!" Sure—when our Lord rose from the dead? When He said that we are to rise even as He? When He declared that He was the resurrection and the life? To doubt the immortality of the soul is to doubt Jesus Christ.

Let us get Moody's common sense, the staunchness of his faith. Let us learn to say, "Don't you believe a word of it!"

Shortly before his departure he was heard saying: "Earth is receding and Heaven is opening." Waking up at intervals during his last hours on earth, he said: "This is my triumph; this is my Coronation day!"

Then his face lit up and he said, in a voice of joyful rapture, "Dwight! Irene! I see the children's faces," referring to two little grandchildren God had taken. And again to his son: "No, this is no dream, Will. It is beautiful. There is no valley here. If this is death it is sweet. God is calling me." Soon after this he passed into the presence of the Lord.

> Weep not, my friends! rather rejoice with me.
> I shall not feel the pain, but shall be gone,
> And you will have another friend in Heaven.
> Then start not at the creaking of the door
> Through which I pass. I see what lies beyond it.

There shall be no more death, neither sorrow, nor crying: . . . for the former things are passed away (Rev. 21:4).

A long the streets of the Celestial City the rumbling wheels of the hearse shall never be heard. The many mansions on either side of its great thoroughfares are sunlit homes in which tears and sorrow are unknown. We are going there some day!

> No shadows yonder! All light and song!
> Each day I wonder and say, "How long
> Shall time me sunder from that dear throng?"
>
> No weeping yonder! All fled away!
> While here I wander each weary day
> And sigh as I ponder my long, long stay.
>
> No partings yonder! Time and space never
> Again shall sunder, hearts cannot sever,
> Dearer and fonder hands clasp forever.
>
> None wanting yonder! Bought by the Lamb,
> All gathered under the evergreen palm,
> Loud as night's thunder ascends the glad psalm.

The storms of the pilgrimage are there hushed to silence; fierce tempests cease to blow; all is blessed sunshine, calm and sweet repose, there in the Land of Beulah! *Pilgrim's Progress.*

Ye . . . shall leave me alone: and yet I am not alone, because the Father is with me (John 16:32).

CENTURIES AGO

> It is the calm and silent night!
>   A thousand bells ring out, and throw
> Their joyous peals abroad, and smite
>   The darkness, charmed and holy now!
> The night that erst no name had worn,
>   To it a happy name is given!
> For in that stable lay, new-born,
>   The peaceful Prince of earth and heaven—

> In the solemn midnight,
>   Centuries ago!

If we are sitting in peace and joy, our hearts filled with sweet Christmas thoughts, we should remember those whose homes will be dark and sad tomorrow. Perhaps we can do little to give them comfort; but we can pray for them, and thus call down blessing upon them.

A PRAYER FOR CHRISTMAS EVE

O Lord, there sit apart in lonely places,
    On this, the gladdest night of all the year,
Some stricken ones with sad and weary faces,
    To whom the thought of Christmas brings no cheer.
For these, O Father, our petition hear,
And send the pitying Christ-child very near.

Lord, some sit by lonely hearthstones, sobbing,
    Who feel this night all earthly love denied,
Who hear but dirges in the loud bells' throbbing
    For loved ones lost who blessed last Christmastide;—
For these, O Father, our petition hear,
And send the loving Christ-child very near.   *Selected.*

Ah, human comfort! None but God is great enough for loneliness!

ON CHRISTMAS EVE

You think of the dead on Christmas eve,
    Whenever the dead are sleeping,
And we, from the land where we may not grieve,
    Look tenderly down on your weeping.

You think us far, we are very near
    To you and the earth, though parted
We sing tonight to console and cheer
    The hearts of the broken-hearted.

The earth watches over the lifeless clay
    Of each of its countless sleepers;
And the sleepless spirits that passed away
    Watch over all earth's weepers.

We shall meet again in a brighter land,
    Where farewell is never spoken;

We shall clasp each other hand in hand,
　　And the clasp shall not be broken.

We shall meet again in a bright, calm clime,
　　Where we'll never know a sadness;
And our lives shall be filled, like a Christmas chime,
　　With rapture and with gladness.

Its snows shall pass from our graves away,
　　And you from the earth remember,
And the flowers of a bright, eternal May
　　Shall follow earth's December.

When you think of us, think not of the tomb
　　Where you laid us down in sorrow;
But look aloft, and beyond earth's gloom,
　　And wait for the great tomorrow.

DECEMBER 25

When they saw the star, they rejoiced with exceeding great joy (Matt. 2:10).

To many ears Christmas bells are set to a minor key. Their note is melancholy. They awaken painful memories. Since last year's happy reunion, desolation has come. Death has claimed our treasures. . . . A hundred things just as this time remind us of our loss, and open again the wounds of our sorrow. These are Christmas shadows. But let us not dwell in bitterness upon our losses. . . . Be patient. Be trustful. Dry those scalding tears. Look up! Look up! Drive out the lengthening shadows. There is an earth side and there is a heaven side. "The things which are seen are temporal, but the things which are not seen are eternal." Make this Christmas time forever memorable, because on that day you place thought, will, affection, and life upon the heaven side.

J. F. Berry, D.D.

How good it is for those who are bereaved and sorrowful that our Christian festivals point forward and upward as well as backward; that the eternal joy to which we are drawing ever nearer is linked to the earthly joy which has passed away.

Mrs. Charles.

366

Let us do as the Christ did: Give ourselves for others; deny ourselves that those who need may have a share in the good which has been given to us. Thus by giving we shall first know the joy of having, and we shall truly join in the chorus that sounded over Bethlehem on the first Christmas morning. Our deeds of help will have more music in them than cathedral chimes in the tower, or cathedral carols in the choir, and from humble homes and happy hearts will sound the antiphon of the angels' song. Bring holly and mistletoe, hemlock and cedar; festoon the walls with vines of smilax, soft and green and tender; scatter flowers; light tapers on Christmas trees; put greens on Christian graves; fill house and street and earth and heaven with shouts of exultation!

Bishop Vincent.

My latch is on the string tonight,
    For stranger, kith or kin;
I would not bar a single door
    Where Christ may enter in.

DECEMBER 26

He shall cover thee with His feathers (Psalm 91:4).

WHEN SHADOWS FALL

When shadows fall, dear, and lonesome seems the way,
Thy faltering steps must daily, hourly go:
Remember God is leading to the cloudless day,
    Where shadows never fall.

When shadows fall, dear, and disappointments press
With heavy weight upon thine aching heart—
God help thee in those hours of bitterness,
    As shadows fall.

When shadows fall, dear, and cast a nameless dread
O'er burdened heart, of what the years may bring,
Remember how the Lord on countless ways hath led,
    Love shadowing all.

When shadows fall, dear, and childhood's rosy dreams
Of what the future years might hold in store
Have flown, and nothing but the "might have been"
        remains,
    And shadows fall:

Look on beyond those shadows to the golden west,
Which tells us of the land where dreams come true;
Look up and say, "God knoweth what is best",
    Though shadows fall.

When shadows fall, dear, and mysteries deep and dim
Perplex thy soul, till faith is well-nigh gone;
Remember, what is dark to thee is light to Him,
    Above, no shadows fall.

When shadows fall, dear—and fall they surely will,
So long as sun, and moon, and stars, shine on—
Then whisper softly to thyself, "Oh, heart, be still!"
    God shadows all.   *Phyllis King.*

"And under (the shadow) of His wings shalt thou trust" (Psalm 91:4).

DECEMBER 27

Wherefore seeing we also are compassed about with so great a cloud of witnesses . . . let us run with patience the race that is set before us (Heb. 12:1).

YOURS AND MINE

Where bide they all?—
Dear friends of yesterday, last year, and long ago
Who walked with us when life was all aglow,
    And rainbows spanned the gloom.
    Not far away we know—
    They're only gone, we trow,
    Into the next room.

How sweet and strange!
We hear their tender voices as in olden days,
While we drift backward into sunny bays
    With lilies all abloom—
    In murmurs low they say:
    "Love lights the mystic way
    Into the next room."

Years wear apace.
Days dark, with heavy mist now deep'ning into rain,
Close down upon us, and we view with pain
    The spectral shadows loom—

A mournful gleam! and lo,
We too lift latch and go
Into the next room.   *Etta M. Gardner.*

Strive to be one of those—so few—who walk the earth with ever-present consciousness—all mornings, middays, star-times—that the unknown which men call Heaven is "close behind the visible scene of things."

DECEMBER 28 _____

Many shall some from the east and from the west and the north and the south and sit down with Abraham and Isaac and Jacob in the kingdom of heaven (Matt. 8:11).

The reunion of the saints will not be limited to the little circle that makes the family here. We belong to a bigger family than the one we live with in the flesh, like elder children born and out in the world before the younger children appear, the poets, prophets, painters, and martyrs preceded us. We never saw them in the flesh. Never heard their voices, but they will be with us in the great family reunion in the Father's house.

Can you imagine yourself in the great throng that will crowd the Father's house, hearing the blessed Saviour saying, "We will now hear Paul on the story of his conversion"? And later, "We will now listen to Judson on his work in Burmah"? Can you catch the thrill that will vibrate when Luther, Wycliffe, Carey, Moody, Wesley, rise to speak?

Like every family reunion, there shall be One, however, whose personality shall be dominant. What would the gathering of all the saints amount to if He would not be there who went to prepare the place? It would be a palace without a hearth. It would be a tree without foliage. It would be a sky without sun.

We all want to see the loved ones with whom we walked dusty miles. We all want to see the immortals who went on before us. But far above and beyond all cravings is the desire to see our Lord and Master.

We have seen Him in the sacred page. We have seen Him on the artist's canvas. We have seen Him in the light of faith. But we want to see Him as He is.

We have often heard Him in the multitude. But we want to

know Him as the family of Bethany knew Him. We want to hear Him as the group of Emmaus heard Him. Free from all the restraints of mortality and time, we want to grasp the nail-pierced hand, hear the love-filled voice of our Saviour in His Heavenly Home.

The joy of fellowship with our Saviour will not obliterate the joy of fellowship with each other, but it will subordinate it as the enjoyment of a soul-stirring sermon or chorus subordinates minor relations. Through eternity we shall be together in our Father's house, each real enough to each other, yet entranced by his Lord.

Whirlwinds of God.

"And so shall WE"—WE—the members of families who have lived, and loved, and prayed, and rejoiced together—WE, regathered in *bundles* by the Angel-reapers—"WE shall ever be with the Lord (I Thess. 4:17).

> The stars come nightly to the sky;
> The tidal wave unto the sea;
> Nor time nor space, nor deep nor high,
> Can keep my own away from me.   *John Burroughs.*

DECEMBER 29

At evening time it shall be light (Zech. 14:7).

IN THE EVENING

> All day the wind had howled along the leas;
> All day the wind had swept across the plain;
> All day on rustling grass and waving trees
> Had fallen the "useful trouble of the rain";
> All day, beneath the low-hung dreary sky,
> The dripping earth had cowered sullenly.
>
> At last the wind has sobbed itself to rest;
> At last to weary calmness sank the storm;
> A crimson line gleamed sudden in the west,
> Where golden flecks rose wavering into form;
> A hushed revival heralded the night,
> And with evening time awoke the light.
>
> The rosy color flushed the long gray waves;
> The rosy color tinged the mountains brown;

And where the old church watched the village graves,
　　Wooed to a passing blush the yew-trees' frown.
Bird, beast, and flower relenting Nature knew
And one pale star rose shimmering in the blue.

So, to a life long crushed in heavy grief,
　　So, to a path long darkened by despair,
The slow, sad hours bring touches of relief,
　　Whispers of hope, and strength of trustful prayer.
"Tarry His leisure,"—God of love and might—
And with the evening time there will be light!"

All the Year Round.

DECEMBER 30

Surely goodness and mercy shall follow me all the days of my life (Psalm 23:6).

A ll the days. What days may not come? *Spring days,* when all the world shall be full of glad young life—frolicking in the fields; caroling in the skies; bursting into leaf and flower at our feet. *Summer days,* in which the year shall have reached its glorious prime, with golden light and long drawn-out evening and balmy nights. *Autumn days,* when the fields shall be filled with sheaves of corn, while busy hands tear from orchard boughs and trailing vines the rich produce of the year. *Winter days,* in which the foot shall tread down the crackling leaves that carpet the forest glade; days of mists and rain and somber light, when we gather round the bier of the departed glory of the year, and lay it to the dust.

We sometimes stand, as it were, on the brow of an overhanging hill, peering wonderingly into the valley at our feet, and asking what kind of days lie there, enveloped in the impenetrable mists, which only part as we advance. What lies in the course of the years? Will the days be *golden,* lit by heaven's warm sunny glow? Will they be *red-letter,* because stained with the blood of suffering and sacrifice? Will they be *drab,* attired in sombre tints, dark and sad? Birthdays; death-days; marriage-days—anniversaries of a dead past, which refuse to be forgotten.

There will never come a day throughout all the future in which we shall not have the two guardian angels, *Goodness and Mercy,* who have been commissioned to attend the believer during all the days of his earthly pilgrimage.

Fearful and fainting hearts, dreading the dark way alone, take heart; gird yourself with new courage; lift up the hands which hang down, and confirm the feeble knees! God knows just how many days of life remain; He knows their needs, their temptations, their sorrows; and He pledges Himself that the day shall never come which shall be unblessed with His goodness and mercy, and that He Himself, will be with us all the days, "even unto the end of the age." *Selected.*

> "He leadeth me!"
> I shall not take one needless step through all,
>   In wind, or heat, or cold;
> And all day long He sees the peaceful end,
>   Through trials manifold;
> Up the fair hill-side, like some sweet surprise,
>   Waiteth the quiet Fold.
>
> Rest comes at length; though life be dark and dreary,
> The day must dawn, and darksome night be past:
>
> Angels, sing on! your faithful watches keeping;
> Sing us sweet fragments of the song above;
> Till morning's joy shall end the night of weeping,
> And life's long shadows break in cloudless love.   *Faber.*

DECEMBER 31

Lo, I am with you all the appointed days (Matt. 28:20—Variorum Version).

The winding road! The winding road of life. It has been a winding road! Had God foretold the surprises of it, we should never have believed Him. Ever the landscape changed. Onward, ever onward, sometimes footsore and weary, and sometimes strangely refreshed! There we saw the mountain flushed with the dawn's rare glory, and there at that other turning, the plain lay 'neath our gaze all somber with shade and suggesting fear.

At that other wind in the road Sorrow stood, ah, that is the year when she went away; at that other corner she said, "I shall return soon," soon, well, a thousand years are sometimes a day, and God help us all, sometimes a day is a millennium in duration.

Round that turn—so well remembered—Duty met us with a

challenge in which a Crown lay hidden. And one day a stern voice called to sacrifice; but that was only God's gauntlet with a gift in it! Round the other corner we met Joy with his hands full of flowers and fruits. What a day that was! It was Springtide you remember and we can recall the look, the thrill that said, "At last, at long last!"

Still the Road winds. It ever winds. And no man knoweth what lies round the corner over the hill, or in the morning's palm, but we walk it, the dear old winding Road o'er which so many have gone, down which so many are coming. We walk it resolutely with the swinging stride that suggests Eternity; or we walk it limpingly as the heroic One limped up the skull-shaped Hill; but we keep on walking.

There is another wind in the Road just before us. What waits for us around that clump of bushes Dear, sighing or song, storm or singing birds, gray or golden weather? Ah, well, we do not know, and yet we do know! You are on the Way and He is on the Way. And somewhere we shall meet. There can be no doubt of that in either mind or heart. Thy sky-vault for the star, the ocean for the wave, Heaven for the Angel, and God for our souls   *Dr. Hinson.*

THE LONG LAST MILE

Carry me over the long last mile,
    Man of Nazareth, Christ for me!
Weary I wait by Death's dark stile,
In the wild and the waste, where the winds blow free,
And the shades and sorrows come out of my past,
    Look keen through my heart,
    And will not depart,
Now that my poor world has come to its last!

Lord, is it long that my spirit must wait?
    Man of Nazareth, Christ for me!
Deep is the stream, and the night is late,
And grief blinds my soul that I cannot see,
    Speak to me out of the silences, Lord,
      That my spirit may know
      As forward I go,
Thy pierced hands are lifting me over the ford!
              L. Maclean Watt—From "The Tryst".

When my heart beats too quickly I think of Thee,
And the leisure of Thy long eternity.

FAREWELL, OLD YEAR

Farewell, old year, we walk no more together,
  I catch the sweetness of thy latest sigh;
And crowned with yellow brake and withered heather,
  I see thee stand beneath this cloudy sky.

Here in the dim light of a gray December,
  We part in smiles, and yet we met in tears;
Watching thy chilly dawn, I well remember,
  I thought thee saddest born of all the years.

I knew not then what precious gifts were hidden
  Under the mists that veiled thy path from sight;
I knew not then that joy would come unbidden,
  To make thy closing hours divinely bright.

I only saw the dreary clouds unbroken,
  I stumbled on in weariness and blindness—
And in the winter gloom I found no token
  To tell me that the sun would shine again.

O dear old year, I wronged a Father's kindness,
  I would not trust Him with my load of care;
I stumbled on in weariness and blindness—
  And lo! He blessed me with an answered prayer!

Goodbye, kind year; we walk no more together,
  But here in quiet happiness we part;
And from thy wreath of faded fern and heather
  I take some sprays and wear them on my heart.

And now, year of our Lord, go up to God! Slip out, little broken bit of Time, into the circle of Eternity! As dew-drop slides into the shining Sea, so drop you Old Year into the Timeless Deep!

One more year of days has been sown by us in the Furrow of Time and the harvest is sure to come. Snatches of song and words of cheer we fling out on the air, and those echoes will roll from soul to soul forever. And the Cross stays! And Christ has larger grown!   *Dr. W. B. Hinson.*

WE ARE JOURNEYING . . . (Num. 10:29).

TOWARD THE SUN-RISING . . . (Num. 21:11).

LOOKING FOR . . . THE GLORIOUS APPEARING . . . (Titus 2:13).

A MORNING WITHOUT CLOUDS . . . (2 Samuel 23:4).

SUNRISE TOMORROW

ACKNOWLEDGMENTS

The compiler takes pleasure in acknowledging the kindness of authors and publishers who so generously have granted permission to use extracts from their copyrighted publications.

Among those are B. McCall Bourbour, Edinburgh, for the poems by J. Danson Smith; Doubleday, Doran and Co. for an excerpt from "Singing in the Rain," by Anne Shannon Monroe; The Silver Publishing Co. for extracts from the writings of James McConkey; Thomas Y. Crowell & Co. for quotations from "The Book of Comfort," by J. R. Miller; W. B. Conkey Co. for a quotation from "A Heap o' Livin'" by Edgar A. Guest; The Sunday School Board of the Southern Convention, Nashville, for excerpts from their publications; The Evengelical Publishers, Toronto, for the poems by Annie Johnson Flint; Frederick A. Stokes Co. for poems; The George Matthew Adams Service, New York, for the poems by Edgar A. Guest; also to the Good-Housekeeping Magazine for the use of poems.

I have used many quotations that have been a blessing to me, of some of which I do not know the authorship. So far as knowledge has permitted I have given due recognition. I trust I have not trespassed upon the rights of others. Indulgence is begged, if failure was made to reach any other author or holder of copyrighted selections. If such has been done a correction will be made in the next edition.